Saints
for Every
Occasion

Saints
for Every
Occasion

101 of Heaven's Most Powerful Patrons

Thomas J. Craughwell

STAMPLEY

Scripture quotations are taken from
The Catholic Edition of the Revised Standard Version of the Bible,
copyright 1965, 1966 by the Division of Christian Education of the National
Council of the Churches of Christ in the United States
of America. Used by permission. All rights reserved.

Attention: Schools, Parishes and Organizations
Stampley offers special pricing to schools, parishes and organizations
when purchasing in quantity for fund raisers, textbooks or other purposes.
For more information on quantity pricing, write to us at:
C.D. Stampley Enterprises, Inc.
Attention: Special Sales
P.O. Box 33172
Charlotte, N.C. 28233
or call us toll-free at 1-800-280-6631.

Library of Congress Cataloging-in-Publication Data

Craughwell, Thomas J., 1956-
  Saints for every occasion : 101 of heaven's most powerful patrons /
Thomas J. Craughwell.
      p. cm.
  Includes bibliographical references and index.
  ISBN 1-58087-059-7
  1. Christian patron saints–Biography. I. Title.
  BX4656.5 .C73 2001
  282'.092'2–dc21

                              2001006248

*In memory
of my great-grandmother,
Mary Schabhuettl
and my grandparents,
Caroline and Thomas Scheck.*

ACKNOWLEDGEMENTS

My first word of thanks goes to my editor Rick Rotondi who took the seed of an idea and turned it into a book.

Thanks also to my friends Deborah VanderBilt, PhD, and Rev. Joseph Ponessa, SSD, for translating thorny Latin texts that were giving me migraines; Rev. Msgr. Richard Soseman, JCL, for his insights into matters relating to canon law and the regulations of the Congregation for the Causes of Saints; Teri Mostad, MD, for her diagnosis of St. Lydwina; and John Hardacre, curator of Winchester Cathedral, for patiently answering my questions regarding St. Swithun.

I am grateful to Roger McCaffrey for permitting me to use here portions of articles I wrote for his magazines.

Finally, my thanks to my friend Jim Charlton, a prince among agents. May the saints preserve him!

Contents

INTRODUCTION   xi

PREFACE   xv

Friends of the Family: Saints for the Home   1

For Expectant Mothers	5
For Single Mothers	10
For In-law Problems	15
For Healing Family Rifts	19
For Those Divorced or Divorcing	22
When Children Disappoint	27
When Stressed by Household Chores	31
When Stressed by Entertaining	34

Teachers and Guides: Saints for Students   37

A Role Model for Students	41
For Help in Learning	44
For Those Struggling With Science	51
To Understand the Bible	55
To Make the Best Use of Time	60

Models of Faith: Saints for the Christian Life   69

For First Communicants	73
For Help Making a Good Confession	75
For Altar Servers	81
For a Good Retreat	84
When Mocked for Christian Living	90
For Lapsed Catholics	94
For Deacons	102

For Cloistered Nuns   105
For Parish Priests   107
When Hurt by the Church   114

Heavenly Mentors: Saints for the Workplace   127

For Advertisers   131
For Members of the Armed Services   133
For Astronauts   135
For Booksellers   137
For Chefs   140
For Farmers   142
For Financial Professionals   144
For Firefighters   145
For Florists   147
For Funeral Directors   153
For Hairdressers   155
For Highway Construction Workers   157
For Lawyers   160
For Nurses   166
For Physicians   170
For Police Officers   172
For Postal Workers   175
For Psychiatrists   176
For Teachers   178
For Writers   181

Joy in the Lord: Saints to Play With   185

For Archers   189
For Actors and Drama Students   192
For Fishermen   193
For Horseback Riders   198
For Hunters   204
For Mountain and Rock Climbers   206
For Musicians and Singers   208
For Painters   212

For Skaters   214

For Swimmers   217

For All Lovers of Sport   219

Thirsting for Justice: Saints for Social Action   223

For the Homeless   227

For Immigrants   229

To Save the Environment   233

To Save the Whales   239

To End Abortion   242

To Prevent Child Abuse   247

To Prevent Sexual Abuse   249

For Racial Justice   251

For Political Prisoners   256

For the Peaceful Transition of Power   262

A Healing Touch: Saints for Good Health   265

For Headaches   269

For Toothaches   270

For Stomach Ailments   272

For Throat Ailments   273

For Arthritis and Rheumatism   275

For Eye Trouble   278

For Cancer   280

For Breast Cancer   282

For AIDS Sufferers   284

For the Mentally Ill   293

To Protect and Guide: Saints to Keep you Safe   295

For Safe Travel   299

For Safeguard Against Thieves   303

To Avoid or End Drought   305

Against Lightning   308

Against Earthquakes   314

Against Volcanic Eruptions   315

Against Snakebite 317

Against Temptations of the Devil 326

Comforters and Consolers: Saints for Various Needs 331

For the Lovelorn 335

For the Infertile 337

To Overcome Religious Doubts 339

For Confidence in Divine Mercy 341

For Those Suffering Discrimination 344

For the Falsely Accused 347

For Prisoners 351

For Impossible Cases 353

For the Dying 355

Followers of the Little Way: Saints for Children 357

For Children 361

For Adopted Children 364

For Youth 366

For Preventing Nightmares 372

To Find Lost Objects 375

For Wholesome Television 380

For Wholesome Web Surfing 386

For Good Friendships 389

Epilogue: Queen of All Saints 393

In Every Necessity 395

CALENDAR OF SAINTS' FEASTS 399

SOURCES 403

SUBJECT INDEX 409

Introduction

Prayer to the saints is a powerful thing. No matter what problem or difficulty you struggle with right now, no matter what challenges you face, chances are that at least one of the patrons in *Saints for Every Occasion* has been a source of heavenly help for someone just like you. Our hope is that you will approach with confidence the saints featured in these pages. Prayer to the saints works.

This is not simply a matter of religious faith. Scientists testify to hundreds of inexplicable cures and healings of seriously ill men and women who have sought the help of a saint. Today the Church will not canonize, or confer sainthood on, anyone without evidence of at least one such miraculous cure. Scientific accounts of such healings make for fascinating reading.

Consider, for example, a cure wrought by the recently canonized St. Faustina Kowalska (recommended here in *Saints for Every Occasion* as a special patron of those seeking confidence in God's mercy). In 1995, American priest Father Ron Pytel's severely damaged heart was suddenly and inexplicably restored to full health after he and some friends prayed to Faustina and venerated, or honored, one of her relics.

Another miraculous cure is attributed to the intercession of the saintly friar Padre Pio (proposed here for help in making a good confession). Medical doctors confess they cannot explain the sudden and complete recovery of Matteo Pio, an Italian boy who, stricken with meningitis, was in a coma near death. Matteo

says that he awoke from his coma after dreaming of being visited by Padre Pio.

Padre Pio is not the only holy person said to have brought
healing while visiting the sick in their dreams. The Church is
currently investigating a Palestinian girl who was found free of
cancer after Mother Teresa appeared in her dreams and said,
"Child, you are cured."

Medical miracles that baffle science may be the most powerful signs of how saints are present in our lives. But saints are
ready and willing to help us in subtler ways, too. Saints can help
us obtain the grace that will mend a marriage, or lead a wayward
son or daughter back to God. Saints can help us find our keys
when they are lost, help us find work when we are unemployed,
and help us find the strength and skill to perform our jobs well.

Saints also protect us. Residents of Naples credit the intercession of their patron, St. Januarius, with stopping threatening
eruptions of Mount Vesuvius. St. Michael the Archangel has been
viewed since Biblical times as a powerful protector of God's People;
he is credited with saving the Israelites from a besieging Assyrian
army (2 Kings 19:35), and is also said to have saved a Lombard
army from its enemies in 663.

The greatest protector of the Christian faithful is the
Queen of All Saints, Mary. Mary is "the woman" spoken of in
Genesis 3:15 who crushes the head of the serpent. By remaining
absolutely untouched by sin her entire life, and by making possible through her *fiat* the birth of Christ and thus the Redemption
of the world, she has vanquished the devil in a manner greater
than any other saint. At times of fierce trial the faithful have
turned to Mary, asking her assistance through rosaries and prayers—often with dramatic results.

The Church honors Mary for obtaining victory in the Battle of Lepanto in 1571, in which a Christian navy defeated a massive
Turkish armada and halted Moslem expansion in Europe. More

recently, many see Mary's hand in the collapse of the Soviet Union. This peaceful ending to the Cold War was achieved after the Pope and most bishops solemnly consecrated, or entrusted, the entire world to Mary's motherly care in 1984.

Prayer to the saints works. But this must not be understood in a magical way. Every grace or blessing the saints win for us comes not from themselves, but from Christ, the source of every grace and blessing. When we pray to the saints, we are not worshipping them. We are honoring them as fellow believers who are especially close to the Lord. We are asking them to intercede with the Lord on our behalf, just as we might ask friends, family, or colleagues to keep us in their prayers.

Prayer to the saints is not a substitute for developing a prayer relationship directly with God. Learning to love and worship God directly, "in spirit and truth" (John 4:23) is the chief reason why we were created—the saints themselves tell us this is so. But one might suggest that part of developing a relationship with God is learning to love what He loves and honor what He honors. In the Bible we see Jesus honoring some of His followers in a special way. It is in imitation of this practice that many Christians honor the saints.

The Gospels record several incidents where the Lord publicly praises one of His followers, and calls upon the rest of His disciples to take notice of that follower's extraordinary faith or goodness. For example, Jesus praises the honesty of the soon-to-be apostle Nathanael (John 1:47), and invites others to behold it; He marvels at the faith of a centurion, and points it out to the multitude following Him (Luke 7:9); He defends the woman who anoints Him with expensive oil, calls her actions "a beautiful thing" and promises that "wherever this gospel is preached in the whole world, what she has done will be told in memory of her." (Matthew 26:6ff).

Such passages may suggest the Lord wants His followers

who display exceptional virtue to be noticed and remembered. He wants to cultivate our desire to imitate them. This is what the Church hopes to accomplish in erecting the "cult" of the saints. By regularly setting before us examples of Christian holiness in the prayers and feast days of our liturgical life, the Church hopes that we will make the holiness of the saints our own.

The Bible gives one example in which the early Christians approached a special follower of the Lord for help, and were not disappointed. The *Acts of the Apostles* recounts how the very first Christians brought their sick out into the streets of Jerusalem, hoping they would be healed as the shadow of St. Peter passed over them as he walked by (Acts 5:15-16). According to *Acts*, all the sick who approached Peter in this way were healed.

Nearly two thousand years have passed since St. Peter's shadow healed the sick on those Jerusalem streets. Yet he is still a source of healing, help, and strength to the faithful who call upon him, as are the hundred other saints in this book. Our hope is that by meeting the saints profiled in *Saints for Every Occasion*, you may benefit from the help and healing these saints are so eager to give. We have but to ask, and the saints will intercede for us to be blessed with every blessing Heaven has to offer, including the greatest blessing of all—to become saints ourselves. Prayer to the saints is a powerful thing!

The Editors

November 1, 2001
Feast of All Saints

Preface

Sixteen-year-old Augustine was in despair. After only one year away at school his parents had called him home. Patricius and Monica had managed to scrape together enough money for Augustine's first year, but now it was apparent that the cost of keeping him in the academy at Madaura was beyond their means.

For help Patricius turned to Romanianus, the wealthiest and most important man in the district, and Patricius' patron. Romanianus graciously offered to subsidize Augustine's entire education—not at some backwater like Madaura but at Carthage, the greatest city in Roman Africa.

This episode from the life of St. Augustine is typical of the patron-client relationships that existed throughout the Roman world. It is also an earthly model of the relationship the faithful have with patron saints.

In the early centuries of the Church a Christian would have described as his patron any saint who answered his prayers. A classic example from that period is St. Paulinus of Nola's (c.354-431) devotion to the martyr St. Felix of Nola (died 287). Felix, as described by Paulinus, was an intimate friend, a heavenly protector, an "eternal patron." In return for the favors Felix granted him, Paulinus constructed an elaborate shrine around St. Felix's tomb and wrote poetry in his honor.

Today, anyone who prays to a favorite saint first thing in the morning, carries a medal of the saint or lights a candle before the saint's image, is operating under the same impulse that inspired Paulinus—a desire to show esteem for a kind benefactor who can assist us on earth and will plead with God to be merciful at the judgment seat of Heaven.

The narrower, specialized concept of patron saints also has its roots in the early Church. Well-to-do Christians who buried the body of a martyr in their own family tomb regarded the saint as uniquely their own. In 304 an aristocratic Christian matron named Asclepia built a mausoleum large enough to accommodate tombs for her family and the tomb of the martyr St. Anastasius. Even if Asclepia granted her fellow Christians access to St. Anastasius' tomb, she and her family would still have considered the martyr their private patron saint.

Today very few families personally possess the complete relics of a saint, but many cities and towns do, and like the Lady Asclepia the residents of these places expect the saint to show them a little favoritism. St. Agatha, St. Januarius (San Gennaro), and St. Spiridon are honored throughout the Christian world, but their cults are especially intense in Catania, Naples, and Corfu where their relics are enshrined.

At the heart of the cult of patron saints is what academics might call a principle of affinity. We pray to saints whom we resemble in some way, or who during their lives experienced the same difficulties we experience. Doctors venerate Ss. Cosmas and Damian who were doctors. During both World War I and World War II French Catholics prayed to St. Joan of Arc to save France as she had saved it during the Hundred Years War. Native Americans invoke Blessed Kateri Tekakwitha because she was a member of the Mohawk tribe. People who are divorced or divorcing pray to St. Helen, who was cast off by her husband after 20 years of marriage.

In the case of many patron saints this principle of affinity operates in reverse. St. Sebastian is the patron saint of archers, not because he was an archer himself but because he was the archers' target. St. Christina the Astonishing, the patron of psychiatrists, did not practice psychiatry but probably could have used a little psychiatric help. And in spite of the nasty fall she took on the ice that left her a life-long invalid, St. Lydwina is the patron of ice skaters.

This is not a comprehensive book on patron saints. The Patron Saints Index website at catholic-forum.com lists nearly 2900 saints who are patrons of places, professions, ailments, even animals. Writing the story of each patron saint would be the labor of a lifetime; thus I have selected 101 saints whose particular areas of patronage are especially relevant today and address widespread needs.

Of course some saints will always be relevant. As long as house keys are misplaced St. Anthony will never lack clients. Other saints might be described as "cutting edge," having been adopted by users of new technologies. In this category we find St. Isidore of Seville, whom Catholic web surfers and dot.com workers have made the patron of the internet. In still other cases the patronage of various saints has evolved. St. Margaret of Cortona, once venerated as "a second Magdalene," has become the patron of single mothers; St. Aloysius Gonzaga, for many years esteemed as a model of chastity, is venerated today as the patron of AIDS sufferers and AIDS caregivers; and St. Peter Claver, whom Pope Leo XIII named patron of the African missions, is more likely to be invoked today as the patron of racial justice.

A saint who acquires a new area of patronage does not relinquish old areas of expertise. St. Joseph, for example, is the patron of the dying, of Mexico, of the missions in China, and of the Universal Church. He is also a bulwark against Communism, the guardian of families, and is invoked by people who want to sell their house or buy a new one.

Many patron saints are problem solvers. In order to emphasize this point the patronage of some of the saints in this book has been given a little "twist." St. Valentine, the patron of lovers, is recommended here as an intercessor for the lovelorn. St. Dismas, the patron of thieves, is proposed as the saint to protect you from being robbed.

The purpose of this book is to educate readers about the saints, to encourage devotion to them, and to tell a few good stories. The English mystic Dame Julian of Norwich (c.1342-c.1423) once described one of her favorite saints as "a kind neighbor." Heaven is full of such "kind neighbors," who are able, even eager, to help us in our various needs. My wish for all who read this book is that you may make the acquaintance of a few of these "neighbors" now—and one day deepen the friendship in Heaven.

Friends of the Family:
Saints for the Home

SAINT ZITA

Friends of the Family:
Saints for the Home

When St. Margaret of Cortona was canonized in 1728 she was held up to the faithful as "a second Magdalene," a woman who turned away from her sinful life and spent the rest of her days in prayer and penance. That single mothers might have a patron saint was unthinkable at the time.

Nor would it have occurred to the pilgrims at the tomb of St. Elizabeth of Hungary to ask her help with problematic in-laws. They sought out St. Elizabeth because in her life she had cared for the sick and the dying, and they hoped that through her intercession they would be healed of their illnesses.

But the cult of the saints is not a rigid thing. History shows us that the reasons why the faithful turn to certain saints change from place to place and from age to age. When divorce was rare, a patron saint for divorcing couples was unnecessary. Today, when so marry marriages end in divorce, the divorced and the divorcing have as their patron St. Helen, whose husband terminated their marriage so he could marry a Roman princess.

St. Matilda is a classic example of how devotion to a saint has evolved over the centuries. At the beginning of her cult she

3

was considered the special patron of her descendants, the guardian of the Ottonian dynasty she and her husband, Henry the Fowler, had started in Germany. Once the royal line of the Ottonians had died out, Matilda's patronage was expanded. Throughout the Middle Ages, when selflessness was not a common trait among the upper classes, the Church held up St. Matilda as a model for all female rulers. Queens and empresses are rare today, but parents with disappointing children are common. So devotion to St. Matilda has shifted once again.

Among the saints presented in this chapter, only St. Gerard Majella has remained consistent. Since his death he has been the favored intercessor for expectant mothers. Certainly the Redemptorists have fostered this devotion to their greatest wonder-working saint, but there is another reason why St. Gerard's "specialty" has not changed: in spite of advances in medical science, the anxiety of pregnancy and childbirth remains universal. And the many miracles in the delivery room attributed to St. Gerard's intercession only strengthen devotion to him under this title.

For Expectant Mothers
St. Gerard Majella (1726-1755) Feast day: October 16

*The first expectant mothers who invoked St. Gerard Majella did
so at a time when many mothers and infants did not survive
childbirth. Although most pregnancies these days end happily,
expectant mothers still invoke St. Gerard to protect them
and safeguard the life within their wombs.*

Gerard Majella was born in Mura Lucano, a town fifty
miles south of Naples. While still a little boy he showed signs of
piety, so much so that he was granted permission to receive Holy
Communion every other day, a rare privilege for the time. His
mother said her son "was born for Heaven."

Gerard was twelve when his father died. His mother apprenticed Gerard to a tailor in town so he could help support the
family. The tailor was mean-spirited and irreligious. He mocked
Gerard for giving one third of his pay to charity and spending
time praying before the Blessed Sacrament. But the tailor's foreman was worse—he beat Gerard on any pretext.

After four years Gerard's apprenticeship ended. Although he
was qualified to go into business for himself, he took a job as a servant to the bishop of Lacedogna. The man was a notorious tyrant
who cursed and abused his household staff. Most servants left after
a few days, but Gerard stayed for three years, until the bishop died.
Gerard believed that by enduring the anger and abuse of others
patiently he was cultivating the virtue of humility.

With the bishop's death, Gerard did at last open his own
tailor shop. He was nineteen years old. He worked at his trade

5

for the next seven years. Gerard's ambition, however, was to enter a religious order.

He applied for admittance to the Capuchins, but the friars rejected him because his health was so poor. Then, in 1749, when Gerard was 23, a group of priests from the recently established Redemptorist Congregation arrived in Mura Lucano to preach a mission. Gerard was deeply impressed by the eloquence and devotion of these priests. He asked the mission team if he could join the Redemptorists as a lay brother. Just as the Capuchins had done before, the Redemptorists expressed concern about Gerard's health and refused his request.

Gerard would not give up. He pestered the fathers so relentlessly that when the Redemptorists were leaving at the end of the mission, a priest suggested to Gerard's mother that she lock her son in his room so they could depart without causing a scene.

In fact Gerard did chase after the Redemptorists. He pleaded persistently to join them until at last one of the priests, Father Paul Cafaro, sent Gerard to the Redemptorist house at Deliceto. Father Cafaro sent a note to the master of novices there that the new recruit was "useless." But he left the final decision of what should be done with Gerard to the superiors at Deliceto.

In the novitiate Gerard worked so hard and advanced in holiness so quickly that St. Alphonsus de Liguori, the founder of the Redemptorists, intervened and granted him permission to take his vows as a lay brother early.

The three years of Gerard's religious life were extraordinary. St. Alphonsus and his fellow Redemptorists found that the frail tailor from Mura Lucano was a miracle worker. At least twenty cases are recorded of Gerard bringing sinners to repentance by revealing to them secret sins they had been unwilling to confess to a priest. We have testimony from eyewitnesses who swear they saw Gerard levitate while he was deep in prayer. A poor family said that by Gerard's prayer their meager supply of wheat lasted for

months, tiding them over until the next harvest. Fishermen asserted that during a storm Gerard walked across the waves to lead
their boat to safety. A mother and father credited Gerard with
restoring life to their son after the boy had fallen from a cliff.

Today Gerard is most often invoked by pregnant women.
Two stories tell how Gerard became the patron of expectant mothers. On one occasion he visited a woman who was in danger of
dying in childbirth. She begged Gerard to help her. With his prayers the woman and the baby came through the delivery safely.

Another time Gerard was leaving the home of his friends,
the Pirofalo family, when one of the young daughters of the
house called after him; he had dropped his handkerchief. "Keep
it," Gerard said. "Someday you'll find it useful." A few years later,
after Gerard had died, that same young woman was in labor. The
delivery was going badly and the midwives feared the young
mother and the unborn infant would die. Recalling what Gerard
had said to her years before, the young woman asked for his
handkerchief, pressed it to her stomach, and prayed to Gerard to
fulfill his promise and help her. At once the danger passed and
the woman delivered a strong, healthy child.

The darkest time in Gerard's life came in 1754. A young
woman in Lacedogna named Neria Caggiano wanted to enter
the convent of San Salvatore but did not have the necessary
dowry. Gerard admired the nuns of San Salvatore and had recommended them to other young women with vocations to the
religious life. When Neria asked for his help Gerard was happy to
oblige. He solicited contributions from his friends until he had
collected enough for Neria's dowry.

Neria entered San Salvatore but she stayed barely three
weeks. She had no vocation, but she could not bring herself to admit this to her family and friends. Instead, she said she had left
because the nuns were irredeemably wicked. Many of Neria's
friends had a hard time believing her. The nuns were friends of

Brother Gerard. A man so saintly would not have anything to do with religious hypocrites.

Neria realized that the only way to make her story credible was to slander Gerard. She went to her confessor, Father Benigno Bonaventura, and told him that Gerard was guilty of the seduction of Nicoletta Capucci. The Capuccis were devoted supporters of the Redemptorists and close friends of Gerard and his superior, St. Alphonsus. Gerard was a frequent guest in their home. Under his influence, two of the Capucci daughters had entered the convent of San Salvatore. If Neria's story were true Gerard was a monster.

Father Bonaventura commanded Neria to write a letter to St. Alphonsus detailing her accusation. Then he received her permission to send a letter of his own to Alphonsus asserting that he felt that Neria's accusations were true.

The two letters were a devastating blow to Alphonsus. Gerard was the pride of his order. How could a young man of such apparent holiness, a man said to work miracles, have corrupted a young girl?

Alphonsus sent Father Andrew Villani, a most trusted colleague, to investigate the charges. Father Villani met with Neria and Father Bonaventura. Both asserted that everything they had written about Gerard was true.

Alphonsus had no choice but to confront Gerard. He summoned him and read the two letters aloud. He waited to hear what Gerard would say, but the young lay brother said nothing at all. Under the circumstances Gerard's silence was highly suspicious. Alphonsus would have been within his rights to expel Gerard from the Redemptorists, yet he held back. Instead, he sequestered Gerard from all contact with the outside world and forbade him to receive Holy Communion.

Why did Gerard keep silent? For two reasons, both of which were hard to accept in his own day and are even harder to understand in our own. To foster the virtue of humility, the Redemptorist Rule charged its members to keep silent if blamed for something they had not done. Gerard was taking this precept to an extreme which was never intended, but he genuinely believed that by not defending himself and permitting people to think the worst of him he was rooting out pride.

Gerard's second reason was his desire to imitate Christ. Jesus had stood silent before Pontius Pilate and not answered the false accusations made against him. Gerard would do the same.

Apparently many people found it hard to believe that Gerard would have an affair. Some of his brother Redemptorists, convinced of his innocence, urged Gerard to go to Alphonsus and ask permission to receive Communion once again. Gerard refused. "We must die under the winepress of God's Will," he said.

Months went by without Gerard ever breaking his silence. Then Alphonsus received another letter from Neria. She was gravely ill and believed she was about to die. Afraid to go before God with calumny on her soul, Neria admitted that everything she had said about Gerard was a lie. We can only imagine Alphonsus' relief and joy as he read this letter.

He summoned Gerard and told him that his reputation had been cleared. Then Alphonsus asked why he had not defended himself against Neria's false accusations. "How could I, Father?" Gerard replied. "The Rule says I may never make excuses but must bear in silence whatever penances the superior imposes."

In October 1755, Gerard's health, which had always been precarious, finally failed him. He suffered a mortal attack of tuberculosis accompanied by violent hemorrhages. On the night of October 15-16, Gerard Majella was "born into Heaven" at last, arriving safely and triumphantly after much suffering—as do so many of the newborns for whom his protection is invoked.

For Single Mothers

St. Margaret of Cortona (1247-1297) Feast day: February 22

St. Margaret of Cortona, originally hailed as "a second Mary Magdalene," is invoked today as the patron of single mothers. Her lover refused to marry her, even after she bore him a son. After her lover was murdered Margaret's father would not take her in. She became a nurse to support herself and her son.

Margaret was a beautiful child whose parents spoiled and indulged her. She grew up self-centered and headstrong, accustomed to getting her way. At age seven Margaret experienced the first real sorrow of her life. Her mother died and her father remarried. Almost from the moment they met, Margaret and her stepmother detested each other.

In order to escape the unpleasantness at home Margaret spent more and more of her time outside the house. In the village and the surrounding countryside she found the attention she craved. Adults thought she was precocious and charming. Boys her age and a little older were especially attracted to the pretty girl.

Margaret was twelve or thirteen when she met Arsenio, the fifteen-year-old son of a petty nobleman from the region of Montepulciano. When Arsenio showed an interest in her, Margaret responded. Although his rank made it impossible for Arsenio to marry a peasant girl like Margaret, he could take her as his mistress. Margaret consented and moved into Arsenio's house. It was an arrangement that gave her almost everything she wanted— affection, privilege, luxuries, and freedom from the drudgery of peasant life and the constant scolding of her stepmother.

Soon Margaret gave birth to a son. (Her biographers never say what she named the child.) She hoped the baby would strengthen her claim on Arsenio, but Arsenio showed no sign that he wanted Margaret as anything other than his lover. And so Margaret continued as Arsenio's mistress for nine years.

One day Arsenio went on a routine errand to one of his outlying estates. Margaret became anxious when Arsenio did not return as expected. The next day Arsenio's dog appeared alone at the house and ran to Margaret's room. Whining and agitated, the animal walked in circles around Margaret, then grabbed her gown in its teeth and began to pull. Apprehensive and agitated herself, Margaret followed where the dog led.

In the woods not far from the house the dog stopped at a pile of dead wood and began to paw at the branches. Frightened, perhaps even a little frantic, Margaret cleared away the dead tree limbs. Under the wood, lying in a shallow trench, she found the murdered, decaying corpse of Arsenio.

The horror of death and decay was a common theme in sermons in Margaret's day. No doubt she had heard at least one preacher describe in grisly detail what a few days of lying in the grave did to even the fairest, strongest, and most pampered body. But what she could once have dismissed as a preacher's cliché was now staring her in the face. And this was no nameless corpse, but the body of the man she loved.

At first Margaret grieved only for her loss of Arsenio. Then as her conscience began to trouble her, she grieved at the thought of what might have become of Arsenio's immortal soul—and what might become of her own soul if death should come to her suddenly.

Filled with remorse, Margaret took her son and returned to her father's house. Sobbing, she knelt at his feet and begged her father to forgive her. Like the father in the parable of the Prodigal Son, Margaret's father welcomed her home. Her stepmother did not want Margaret and her son in the house, but there was nothing she could do about it for the moment. She waited, certain that in time Margaret would give her a good reason to throw her out. And Margaret did play into her stepmother's hands, although not in a way anyone would have predicted.

Margaret was in the middle of a violent conversion experience. Where once she had been proud, now she looked for imaginative ways to humiliate herself. She abandoned the fine clothes Arsenio had given her and put on the rough clothes of a penitent. When she went to church she wore a noose around her neck. After Mass she knelt at the church door so none of her old neighbors could help but see her shame.

Margaret's father did not like these public exhibitions, but he endured them, believing they couldn't last long. For Margaret, however, this was only the beginning. One day in the village church she walked to the front of the congregation and recited all the sins she had committed during the past nine years. This was more repentance than Margaret's father could tolerate. He threw his daughter and her son out of his house.

On the road with her little boy, Margaret wondered what she should do next. She could go back to Montepulciano where she still had friends and where she could enjoy, up to a point, the kind of comfortable life she had known with Arsenio. It was a powerful temptation, particularly for one like Margaret who had always sought pleasure. But she was too far along now in her conversion. So she turned her back on her father's village and her lover's castle and headed for Cortona where the Franciscan fathers had a reputation for their kindness to repentant sinners.

The Franciscans listened sympathetically to Margaret's story. Two priests, Giunta Bevegnati and John da Castiglione, became her spiritual directors. She asked to be accepted as a member of the Franciscan Third Order, which would have enabled her to take the vows of a nun without having to live in a convent. The friars said it was too soon for her to be talking about a religious vocation. They placed her on three years probation and sent Margaret and her son to live with two devout and charitable women, Marinana and Raneria Moscari, who worked with the friars and quite often opened their home to penitent women.

No sooner had she settled in at the Moscari house than Margaret began a routine of rigorous penances. She slept on the floor and lived on a starvation diet. Her penances left her looking haggard but still beautiful, so she beat her face until it was cut and bruised. Father Giunta and Father John tried to restrain her, but Margaret believed that the only way to atone for her sins was to punish her body.

When Father Giunta learned that Margaret planned to go back to Montepulciano and have a woman lead her by a rope through the streets proclaiming her sins, the good man lost his patience and commanded Margaret to give up these public melodramas. Margaret abandoned her plan to humiliate herself in Montepulciano but continued her mortifications. In spite of all her prayers and acts of penance, sexual temptations troubled Margaret all of her life. She once told Father Giunta, "Do not ask me to come to terms with this body of mine because I cannot afford it. Between me and my body there will be a struggle until death."

At the end of three years Margaret was admitted to the Third Order of St. Francis. About the same time she sent her son to a school in Arezzo. Eventually he became a Franciscan.

During her probation Margaret supported herself and her son by nursing the sick and the dying. Now she decided to open a hospital for the poor in Cortona. She founded two organizations, one for women, the other for men. The women would operate the hospital and the men would work to support it. Uguccio Casali, one of the Cortona town councilors, supported Margaret's plan and persuaded his fellow councilors to fund the hospital.

Unfortunately, Margaret's bad reputation never entirely left her. Scandalmongers whispered that Margaret was having an affair with her confessor, Father Giunta. Erring on the side of caution, Father Giunta's superiors transferred him to the order's monastery in Siena. Seven years later, when the rumors had faded away, the Franciscans let Father Giunta return.

After her conversion Margaret had become especially devoted to the Poor Souls in Purgatory, perhaps because she was still uncertain about what might become of her soul after death. As she lay dying, she had a vision of a crowd coming from Heaven to fetch her. These were the souls Margaret had ransomed from Purgatory by her penances and prayers.

For In-law Problems

St. Elizabeth of Hungary (1207-1231) Feast day: November 17

People who experience in-law trouble invoke St. Elizabeth of Hungary. Her in-laws tried to prevent her marriage, mocked her piety, and drove her away after her husband's death.

Elizabeth was only four years old when her parents, Andrew II and Gertrude, the king and queen of Hungary, arranged for her to marry a young German prince, Ludwig, the eleven-year-old heir of the Landgrave of Thuringia. After the betrothal Elizabeth was taken from her home to grow up with her future husband and his family in Wartburg Castle.

Not everyone at Wartburg welcomed her. An uneasy peace existed between Hungary and Germany, and many German nobles did not want their prince allied with a Hungarian princess. As the years passed and the date for Elizabeth's marriage drew near, the anti-Hungarian faction became more shrill in its demands that the betrothal be broken off. But Ludwig refused to give Elizabeth up; the young couple were in love. In 1221, fourteen-year-old Elizabeth and twenty-one-year-old Ludwig were married.

Elizabeth and Ludwig were happy together, although some of Elizabeth's acts of devotion and charity put a strain on their marriage. Ludwig's mother, Sophia, a religious woman herself, often lost patience with Elizabeth's spontaneous gestures of piety. Once while the family was walking in procession to Mass on the Feast of the Assumption, Elizabeth threw off her gold and pearl crown and prostrated herself in front of a crucifix. "What's wrong? Is your crown too heavy?" Sophia asked. "Get up! You look like

15

a tired old mule bent over like that."

Ludwig's sister, Agnes, also found fault with Elizabeth. She was offended by Elizabeth's meekness. "You might as well be a housemaid," Agnes told her.

On at least two occasions even Ludwig thought Elizabeth had gone too far. Once when Elizabeth was carrying bread in the folds of her gown to give to the hungry Ludwig confronted her, annoyed that she was abandoning her royal dignity by ministering directly to the poor. Ludwig demanded that Elizabeth show him what she had hidden in her robes. When Elizabeth opened her gown, out spilled roses.

On another occasion a member of the court told Ludwig that Elizabeth had brought a dying leper into the castle and was nursing him in their own bed. In a rage Ludwig hurried to his room and yanked off the blankets. There, indeed, was a leper stretched out in his bed, but God softened Ludwig's heart so that he saw in the dying man the image of Jesus Crucified.

In 1227 Ludwig decided to join Emperor Frederick II on a crusade to the Holy Land. The prospect of being separated from Ludwig made Elizabeth sick with grief. They had two children already—a 5-year-old son Hermann and a three-year-old daughter Sophia—and Elizabeth was pregnant with their third child.

Ludwig never got to Palestine. On September 11 he died in an epidemic that was raging in the Italian port of Otranto. Word of his death reached Wartburg in October, on the very day Elizabeth gave birth to a baby girl. She was still recovering from the birth when her mother-in-law came into the room to tell her that Ludwig was gone. In her exhaustion Elizabeth did not understand what Sophia was saying. She thought Ludwig had been taken prisoner. When at last she understood that he was dead, she cried, "The world is dead to me, and all its joys!" For days Elizabeth was unable to control her grief. Servants encountered her in the corridors, leaning against the wall, sobbing.

Now that Ludwig was dead, the faction in court that had always resented Elizabeth made its move. Her brother-in-law, Henry, had been named regent until Elizabeth and Ludwig's son came of age. He told Elizabeth there was no place for her any longer in Wartburg. To her credit, Sophia protested this cruel expulsion, and followed Elizabeth, weeping, to the door of the castle. But Henry was determined to be rid of his sister-in-law at last. In the middle of winter, Elizabeth, three-year-old Sophia, the infant Gertrude, and two loyal ladies-in-waiting named Irmgard and Isentrud were driven out of the castle.

At first they had no place to go. For fear of Henry, no one in the town would give them shelter. The refugees spent their first night in an unheated shed. Then Elizabeth's aunt, Matilda, the Abbess of Kitzingen, heard of her niece's trouble and invited her to come live at the convent.

During the next few months Elizabeth considered her options. Her uncle, the bishop of Bamberg, was eager to help her find another husband, but Elizabeth and Ludwig had promised each other never to remarry. During Lent Elizabeth made her decision. She left her children in the care of Abbess Matilda. On Good Friday 1228, Elizabeth and her two ladies-in-waiting took vows as Franciscan sisters of the Third Order.

At Marburg Elizabeth built a hospital. There she and her companions dedicated themselves to nursing the sick and the dying. Elizabeth took as her spiritual director Conrad of Marburg, a zealous, ascetical Franciscan priest. It was a poor choice. Elizabeth was spontaneous and generous; Conrad was rigorous and severe. He felt it his duty to bring Elizabeth to a life of strict self-denial. He sent away Elizabeth's two companions and replaced them with two stern, bad-tempered women who reported Elizabeth's most insignificant faults to Conrad. He was known to slap Elizabeth across the face and even to beat her with a thick wooden staff. She bore all of this because Ludwig had once mentioned that he believed Conrad to be a truly holy man.

Nonetheless, Elizabeth realized that she and Conrad were not suited to each other. To a friend she once compared herself to tall grass and Conrad to a raging stream. "The stream overflows its banks and crushes the grass," she said. "But the water recedes and the grass springs back up again."

Late in 1231, when she was only 24 years old, Elizabeth's health began to fail. On the evening of November 17 she died. Local people who came to pray at her tomb in the hospital chapel reported that many miracles were being wrought through Elizabeth's intercession. Conrad, to his credit, took the lead in gathering material for her canonization, but he did not live to see it.

Conrad had accused a nobleman, Count Henry of Sayn, of heresy. Henry was cleared of the charge, but Conrad would not accept the verdict. He was on his way to Rome to argue for Henry's condemnation when he was ambushed along the road and murdered, most likely by Henry's friends.

Elizabeth's in-laws built a beautiful church in Marburg and enshrined her relics before the high altar. Her tomb was a goal of pilgrims until 1539, when Elizabeth's descendant, Landgrave Philip, became a Lutheran. He ordered the shrine dismantled and consigned St. Elizabeth's remains to an unmarked grave. To this day, no one knows where her relics are buried.

For Healing Family Rifts

St. Elizabeth of Portugal (1271-1336) Feast day: July 4

Squabbling families pray to St. Elizabeth of Portugal, who tried to reconcile her husband and her son and restore peace when other members of her family waged war on one another.

Many parents name their child after a favorite saint or after a beloved relative. Elizabeth of Portugal was named for both. When King Pedro III of Aragon and Queen Constanza brought their infant daughter to the baptismal font, they gave her the name of her great-aunt, St. Elizabeth of Hungary, who had been canonized 36 years earlier.

Elizabeth grew up in her family's palace in Saragossa and received a typical education for the time. She was schooled in reading, writing and embroidery. She also studied Latin, music and poetry. Someone, perhaps one of her servants, showed Elizabeth the rudiments of the healing arts. And of course she was also encouraged to be pious. All of this was intended merely as a veneer, a social polish necessary for any princess who hoped someday to marry a king.

Elizabeth's wedding day came in 1283 when she was only twelve years old. Her groom was Dinis, the twenty-year-old king of Portugal. Today such a match is shocking, but child brides were commonplace in the Middle Ages. Among royal families every marriage was a political alliance. The sooner the alliance was sealed at the altar, the better.

Seven years passed before Elizabeth gave birth to her first child, Constanza. The following year, 1291, she and Dinis had a son whom they named Alfonso.

We should not be surprised that it took Elizabeth and Dinis so long to start a family. A twenty-year-old man is not likely to show much interest in a twelve-year-old girl. Besides, Dinis was far from lonely. He had a string of mistresses. By the time he died, Dinis had fathered seven (some sources say nine) illegitimate children, all of whom he acknowledged. In fact, he brought them to the palace and commanded Elizabeth to bring them up.

Yet Dinis was not an ogre. He tried to be a good king. He improved the code of law in Portugal, founded the country's first university at Coimbra, and collaborated with his wife in building churches and religious houses. Some historians have looked on Dinis' reign as a golden age for medieval Portugal.

Whatever historians may think of Dinis, his family had a different view, born out of his callous disregard for their feelings. Surrounded by his father's illegitimate children, Prince Alfonso grew up angry and resentful. When Dinis showed too much attention to one of his illegitimate sons Prince Alfonso lost control. Fearing that he would lose his right to the throne, the prince plotted to murder his half-brother, depose his father, and seize the crown. The plot failed, and it took all of Elizabeth's persuasive powers to keep Dinis from punishing the prince.

By interceding for Alfonso, however, Elizabeth aroused Dinis' suspicion and paranoia. He became convinced that Elizabeth was in league with the prince to do away with him. Dinis sent his wife away from the court and kept her under house arrest in a distant castle in Alenquer. Several nobles were so outraged by Elizabeth's unjust exile they went to Alenquer and offered to raise an army to free her. Elizabeth declined the nobles' offer, and delivered a mild rebuke at the same time. "My primary obligation," she said, "and the obligation of all vassals, is to obey the commands of the king, our lord."

Elizabeth never managed to dispel the animosity between

Dinis and Alfonso. Four times she intervened to reconcile her embittered son with his father. On two other occasions she stepped in to stop wars raging between other members of her family.

Elizabeth and Dinis eventually reconciled. Indeed, Elizabeth nursed the king in his final illness, never losing the heroic patience that was the dominant feature of her character. When Dinis knew he was dying, he asked to see his illegitimate children. Elizabeth herself brought them to the king. After he said good-bye to the children he probably loved best, he summoned his heir, Alfonso, to his bedside and charged him, "Look after your mother and my lady, the queen, for she remains alone. Stand by her, as is your duty....Think that having given you life, and for the many tears you have cost her, she is twice your mother."

Dinis I died in 1325 at the age of 63. We do not know if he ever begged Elizabeth's forgiveness for all the pain he had caused her. We do know that when Dinis' will was read, it was found that he had made Elizabeth his executor. If he could not show his trust and esteem for Elizabeth in life, at least Dinis displayed it after death.

Following Dinis' funeral, Elizabeth took off her finery and began to wear the rough habit of a Franciscan sister. She moved into a small house beside the convent of the Poor Clares at Coimbra. There she built a hospital dedicated to her aunt, St. Elizabeth of Hungary. The widowed queen worked in the wards everyday, often caring for the most repulsive cases herself.

Queen Elizabeth died on July 4, 1336. Her last words were a prayer to the Blessed Virgin: "From the foe shield us; in the hour of death take us."

For Those Divorced or Divorcing

St. Helen (249-329) Feast day: August 18

Husbands and wives whose marriages have come apart have as their patron St. Helen. After more than 20 years of marriage, Helen's husband divorced her to make a politically advantageous match with a young woman who was a member of Rome's Imperial Family.

A medieval legend claims that St. Helen was a British princess, the daughter of King Cole, the "merry old soul" of the nursery rhyme. Nothing could be further from the truth. Helen was born in the town of Drepanum in northern Turkey, at the opposite end of the social spectrum—her father and mother were innkeepers. It was while she was working at her parents' inn that Helen met a Roman soldier named Constantius Chlorus. He was a rough, powerfully built, pale-skinned man whose origins were as humble as Helen's: Constantius' father was a goatherd, his mother was the daughter of a freed slave. But Constantius was a man of ambition who saw in the military a way to rise above his low birth. It's likely that he was already an officer when he met Helen.

The couple married in 270. Two years later they were in Serbia at Constantius' new post in the town of Nish. There on February 27, 272 Helen gave birth to a son, Constantine.

We have no documents to tell us what happened to the family between the year of Constantine's birth and 288, the year Constantius was appointed governor of Dalmatia. At some point during that interval Constantius had won the confidence of the co-emperors, Diocletian and Maximian. Imperial patronage dic-

22

tated that Constantius was poised for great things; whether Helen would be included in these great things was another matter.

The Roman Empire had grown so vast and the troubles besetting it so complex that it was more than one man could manage. Emperor Diocletian had addressed this administrative dilemma by naming Maximian, a successful general, his co-emperor. Under this arrangement Diocletian would set policy and rule in the East while Maximian would rule in the West. Furthermore, each emperor would be assisted by a caesar who would be granted authority over a handful of provinces.

In 292 Maximian selected Constantius to be his caesar and gave him the provinces of Gaul, Spain and Britain to administer. As a sign of special favor the emperor urged Constantius to divorce Helen and marry Flavia Maximiana Theodora, Maximian's step-daughter. Maximian and Diocletian also arranged for 20-year-old Constantine to be taken into the household of Diocletian's caesar, Galerius, where the young man would finish his military training by fighting Rome's enemies in Egypt.

These were heady days for Constantius and Constantine, but it must have been a wretched time for Helen. After 22 years of family life she found herself discarded by her husband and deprived of the company of her son.

We do not know where Helen settled after Constantius divorced her. Ancient historians rarely take much notice of cast-off wives. But there is reason to believe that Helen settled in Trier, in Germany, and this may be the place where she first became interested in Christianity. If so, Trier was a fortunate choice.

In 303 Diocletian and Maximian began an empire-wide persecution of Christians—the most violent the Church had ever known. Thousands died for the faith, including such martyrs as St. Agnes, St. George, and St. Lucy. Yet Christians in the provinces governed by Constantius Chlorus enjoyed relative peace.

Although we can never be sure why Constantius proved so

reluctant to persecute the Church, one tantalizing clue has come down to us. Constantius and Theodora had a daughter whom they named Anastasia, a name favored by Christians because it comes from the Greek word for resurrection. It is possible that Theodora, or Constantius, or both were secret Christians.

In 305, Diocletian and Maximian abdicated and passed the imperial crown to Constantius and Galerius. The following year Constantine, after 13 years in the East, joined his father on the Scottish border to put down a Pict uprising. Only a few weeks after their campaign, Constantius fell ill and died at York. The troops proclaimed Constantine emperor. But Constantine had powerful adversaries vying for control of the empire. He decided to establish his headquarters in Trier, consolidate his power, and visit his mother, Helen.

Constantine bided his time in Trier, waiting for the right moment to make a play for the whole empire. It was during those years that Helen was baptized at the age of 60. Constantine, however, remained a pagan.

Finally, in 312, Constantine marched on Rome. The day before a decisive battle with his rival Maxentius, the son of the old co-emperor Maximian, Constantine had a vision of a cross of light and the words "In this sign, conquer." While the vision was still fresh in his mind, Constantine called goldsmiths to his tent and ordered them to make a cross-shaped standard surmounted by the Greek monogram Chi-Rho, the first two letters in the name Christ. Led by the cross, Constantine's army went into battle against Maxentius' forces at the Milvian Bridge outside Rome. By the end of the day Maxentius was dead, his army scattered, and Constantine was victorious—just as the vision had promised.

Perhaps to console his mother for years of neglect, Emperor Constantine showered honors on Helen. He granted her the imperial title Augusta, renamed her birthplace Helenopolis, and had coins struck bearing her image. In Rome Constantine gave

Helen as her residence the Sessorian Palace, part of which survives today as the Basilica of Santa Croce in Gerusalemme.

The following year, 313, Constantine published the Edict of Milan, which guaranteed toleration to Christians throughout the Roman Empire. Overnight, bishops, priests and deacons who had been living in hiding became honored members of the young emperor's court. Inconspicuous house-churches began to be replaced by grand basilicas, with Constantine himself financing the construction of three basilicas in Rome: St. Peter on the Vatican Hill, St. Paul Outside the Walls, and St. John Lateran, the cathedral of Rome. Constantine himself became a catechumen (although he put off baptism until he was on his deathbed).

Yet Helen's family troubles were not over. As a young man Constantine had married a woman, Minervina, with whom he had a son, Crispus. Like his father, Constantine had put aside his first wife to make a politically advantageous marriage with a woman from the imperial family. Constantine's new wife, Fausta, gave birth to three sons in quick succession. It looked like the start of a dynasty, but none of Fausta's sons would be emperor unless Crispus was out of the picture. So Fausta whispered to Constantine that his eldest son was plotting against him. With a suddenness that stunned both Christian and pagan members of his court, the emperor ordered Crispus' arrest and execution.

Fausta's triumph was short lived. Crispus had not been dead long when Constantine began to suspect that Fausta had manipulated him into murdering his own son. Angry and remorseful, Constantine compounded his guilt by ordering the death of his wife. She was executed in her own bath, locked in an overheated steam room where she suffocated. One can only imagine how Helen felt about these two violent crimes committed by her son on members of his own family.

Soon after Fausta's execution, Helen announced her decision to make a pilgrimage to the Holy Land. Tradition says that she went to Palestine with the express purpose of uncovering the Cross and the Tomb of Christ. Some historians suggest that Helen's pilgrimage was actually to expiate Constantine's terrible crimes. Whatever her reason, once Helen arrived in Jerusalem she found that it would be more difficult than she imagined to venerate Calvary and the Holy Sepulchre; the site was covered by a temple to Venus built almost 200 years earlier by the Emperor Hadrian.

Helen ordered the temple torn down. It was during the dismantling that the tomb of Christ and three wooden crosses were uncovered. The story of how Helen knew which cross was Christ's has come down to us with minor variations. Some stories say that a dying old woman was placed upon each cross; other stories say that the crosses were applied to a sick boy, or to a blind child. But all versions agree that the cross which wrought a miraculous cure for the sufferer was recognized as the Cross of Our Lord.

On the site of her great discovery Helen built the Basilica of the Holy Sepulchre. Then she went to Bethlehem where she built another church over the cave where Christ had been born. Finally, she built a third basilica on the Mount of Olives from which Christ had ascended into Heaven. Constantine, who had financed Helen's building program, called the Ascension church 'the Eleona' in honor of his mother.

In 328 Helen, now 80 years old, returned to Rome. She brought with her large pieces of the cross and enshrined the relics in her palace's private chapel, where they can still be seen today. In 329 Helen died with her son Constantine at her side. The massive red porphyry sarcophagus in which Constantine buried his mother is on display in the Vatican Museum, and the relics of St. Helen are entombed in the Church of Santa Maria in Aracoeli, overlooking the Roman Forum.

When Children Disappoint
St. Matilda (c.895-968) Feast day: March 14

Parents who are bewildered by the actions of their own children will find a patron in St. Matilda. Her own sons publicly humiliated Matilda, deprived her of her independence, and even tried to kill one another.

*M*atilda's earliest biographers tell us she was descended from Widukind, the savage chief of the pagan Saxons and Charlemagne's most determined enemy, who surprised friend and foe alike when he suddenly asked to be baptized. Throughout Matilda's life, Saxony remained the frontier of the Christian world. To the north the Viking pirates invoked Odin and Thor as they set out to plunder the monasteries and Christian towns of Europe. To the east, the people of Hungary, Poland, and Lithuania still worshipped their grim forest gods. Even in Germany paganism had not entirely given way to Christianity.

Into this dark, rough, and bloody world Matilda was born in 895. Her father was Dietrich, duke of Westphalia. Her mother was Reinhild, a member of the royal family of Denmark.

While Matilda was still a little girl her parents sent her to the convent at Erfurt where her paternal grandmother, Maud, was abbess. In the quiet, orderly, prayerful life of the Benedictine cloister Matilda felt safe. In every crisis of her adult life she would retreat to a convent.

In 909 Matilda married Henry the Fowler, heir to the duchy of Saxony. (Her young husband had acquired his nickname because of his passion for hunting birds). Three years later

Matilda's father-in-law died and Henry became duke. Seven years after that the nobles and bishops of Germany elected Henry king. The election gave Henry and Matilda power, wealth, and the opportunity to found a royal dynasty. But the crown also brought Henry a world of trouble. Germany's borders were under constant assault from the Hungarians, the Danes, and the Bavarians. Henry's reign would be an endless series of wars.

At home, however, Henry and Matilda knew no strife. They loved and respected each other. Matilda had always been charitable; as queen of Germany she could be more generous than ever before. Her favorite charities were churches, monasteries and convents, but she also gave abundantly to the poor. Matilda's kindness even extended to criminals and prisoners from her husband's wars. Those she could not persuade Henry to release she comforted in their cells, bringing food, light and warm clothes. Henry never tried to limit Matilda's acts of charity. Rather, he attributed his victories to his wife's prayers and good works.

Matilda and Henry had five children: Otto, who would become emperor; Gerberga, who married Louis IV, king of France; Hedwig, who married Hugh, founder of France's Capet dynasty; Henry, (Matilda's favorite) the future Duke of Bavaria; and Bruno, who became the archbishop of Cologne and was canonized after his death.

In 936 Henry became ill and died. While the royal household was lamenting his death, Matilda went to the castle chapel and called for a priest to say Mass for her husband's soul. As the priest stood at the altar Matilda cut the jewels off her gown. After Mass she handed all the precious stones to the priest as a sign that from that day forward she renounced her rank and privileges and intended to follow a life dedicated to prayer and works of charity.

With the death of her husband Matilda's troubles began. Some of them she brought on herself. In 937, when the nobles and bishops of Germany assembled to elect a new king, Matilda lobbied for Henry. She argued that although Otto was the first-born, young Henry was the first son born to Henry the Fowler after he had been named king of Germany. Matilda's argument was flimsy, yet a handful of nobles indulged their queen and cast their vote for her favorite. Nonetheless, the overwhelming majority of the lords of the realm chose Otto.

Matilda was embarrassed to have her partiality publicly exposed and rejected. Henry, on the other hand, was angry and jealous. He allied himself with Louis IV, his brother-in-law, and led an army against his brother. Otto had no trouble defeating the rebels. Afterwards he compelled Henry to swear allegiance to him.

Now a strange thing happened. The brothers put aside their quarrels for a moment and joined forces against Matilda. They accused their mother of being irresponsible with her resources. To keep her from squandering any more of the treasure of the kingdom on religious houses and the poor, Otto and Henry confiscated everything Matilda had inherited from her late husband.

To lessen the pain of being persecuted by her own children, Matilda indulged in a little irony, saying how good it was to see her boys working in harmony at last. Then Matilda departed the court and went back home to Westphalia.

Matilda was not in exile long. Edith, Otto's wife, interceded for her mother-in-law until the king agreed to bring his mother back to court. As a sign of respect, Otto sent a large embassy of bishops and nobles to serve as his mother's escort. When she arrived, Otto begged Matilda to forgive him and returned to her all her previous wealth and property. Like a loving mother, Matilda forgave her son. Then she took up again the lavish works of charity which Otto found so irritating.

Henry was still making trouble, so Matilda went to Otto with a request. "Make your brother a ruler in his own right," she said. "Grant him the title of Duke of Bavaria." She hoped that once he had lands of his own to rule, Henry would give up trying to steal the crown from his older brother. Whether to humor his mother or to pacify his brother, Otto agreed.

And for twelve years Henry was quiet. Then in 953, Henry hatched a plot with Otto's son Ludolf, Otto's son-in-law Conrad, and Frederick, archbishop of Mainz, to assassinate Otto. This, the most ambitious and most wicked of all Henry's schemes, was no more successful than the others. Otto survived the conspiracy unharmed. Incredibly, he did not avenge himself against his brother.

In 955 Matilda sent a message to Henry to come see her. She had premonitions that he would not live much longer. She begged him to repent of a life marked by bloodshed and treachery and make a lasting peace with Otto. Henry refused, and as Matilda predicted, he died soon afterward.

Matilda's grief at the death of her most beloved and most wayward son was almost more than she could bear. To take her mind off her sorrow, she devoted herself to founding Benedictine convents and monasteries at Pohlde, Quedlinburg, and Nordhausen. Then Matilda had her husband's body exhumed and reburied in the monastery church of Quedlinburg.

As the years went by, Otto's relationship with his mother improved so much that when he went to Rome in 962 to be crowned Holy Roman Emperor by Pope John XII, he named her one of the regents authorized to rule Germany in his absence.

Finally, as her life was drawing to an end, Matilda retired to the convent; first to the one at Nordhausen, then, as death approached, to Quedlinburg, where her husband was buried.

Before dying, Matilda gave away what was left of her estate, including the shroud that had been prepared for her burial. Her grandson William, archbishop of Mainz, came to hear her last confession. Her granddaughter, Matilda, came to be with her in those final days. Matilda died in utter poverty, lying on the floor, her head covered with ashes, surrounded by priests, monks, and nuns praying for her soul.

When Stressed by Household Chores
St. Zita (1212-1272) Feast day: April 27

*Housework can be tedious. In St. Zita, however, we have
a model of someone who saw in ordinary, repetitive
tasks an opportunity to grow in holiness.*

Zita was born in the village of Montsegradi outside the
city of Lucca. Holiness was a family trait. One of Zita's sisters became a Cistercian nun, and her uncle Graziano lived as a hermit
and was regarded by the local people as a saint.

At age 12 Zita left home to work as a servant in the
household of the Fatinelli family in Lucca. The Fatinellis were
well-to-do silk merchants who lived in a fine house near the
Church of St. Frediano. There were other servants in the house,
of course, and within days of her arrival Zita knew that none of
them liked her. Her fellow servants took her piety for posturing,
her submissiveness for stupidity, her diligence for a mean-spirited way to make them look indolent.

One would think that Zita's employers would have been
thrilled to find a girl who was honest, religious, quiet, and hard-
working. This was not the case. Signora Fatinelli, who had a lifetime of experience with servants, suspected that Zita had to be up
to something dishonest. She treated Zita coldly, sometimes even
cruelly. And Signor Fatinelli, a man notorious for his short temper, was driven nearly mad when he could not discover what mis-
chief Zita was up to. Entirely convinced that in some secret way
this little servant girl was cheating him, Fatinelli often flew into a
rage just at the sight of her. Yet for some inexplicable reason the

Fatinellis never dismissed Zita from their service.

As the new girl, Zita was given all the dirtiest and most tedious household tasks. When the drudgery of her work became oppressive she would say a very short prayer and remind herself that she wasn't doing this unpleasant job to win praise from the Fatinellis but out of love for God.

Zita was sustained by prayer. She went to Mass daily at the Church of St. Frediano, and frequently during the work day she slipped away to pray. One story tells of the time Zita snatched a few minutes for prayer in her "chapel" in the attic, right after having put some bread in the oven to bake. Her prayers became so intense and the sweetness of being in conversation with God so delightful that Zita lost all track of time. When she finally came to her senses, she rushed back to the kitchen, certain that the bread must be burned. But instead of a kitchen filled with acrid smoke, she found beautiful, fragrant loaves laid out on the table. While Zita talked with God, angels watched over her baking.

With the passage of time the Fatinellis and Zita's fellow servants came to realize that she was not a hypocrite or a cheat but a genuine saint. The family made her mistress of the household and eventually governess of the Fatinelli children.

Her new authority revealed Zita's one flaw: her zeal for helping the poor often led her to give away property that belonged to someone else. She was a soft touch, and the beggars and the poor in and around Lucca knew it. She shared her own food with whoever came to the door, and when she had given away her portion, she dipped into the Fatinellis' pantry. During a famine an endless procession of hungry people came to Zita for help. She wound up giving away the Fatinellis' entire store of dried beans—the one thing the household was counting on to get through the crisis. This was too much for Signor Fatinelli. He indulged in one of his famous rages and dragged Zita into the storeroom to impress upon her what she had done. But when

Zita and Fatinelli arrived in the pantry, they found to their surprise that the stores of dried beans were undiminished.

One bitterly cold Christmas morning, as Zita was about to set out for Mass, Fatinelli stopped her and wrapped his fine fur mantle around her. But the merchant was savvy even when softhearted. "Remember! I want the coat back," Fatinelli told Zita. "It would be just like you to give it away."

Zita promised to return with the fur, and set off for church. At the church door she saw a poor man shivering in thin rags. She could never walk away from a beggar, so she took off the fur and gave it to the poor man. "This will keep you warm for now," she said. "But when I come out of church you must return the coat to me. It's not mine to give away."

After Mass Zita returned to the very spot where she had left the beggar. He was gone, and Signor Fatinelli's valuable mantle was gone with him. Zita did not know what was worse, the humiliation of having abused her master's kindness, or the sharp disappointment of having been played for a fool by someone she had tried to help.

One can imagine the scene back at the Fatinelli house when Zita returned without the fur. Yet the story does not end there. The day after Christmas, a stranger came to the Fatinellis' door with the fine coat, as good as new. The neighbors agreed among themselves that it was no beggar Zita had met outside the church but an angel come to test the compassion of Christians on Christmas morning. To this day, the portal where Zita met the beggar is known as the Angel Door.

So the years passed, with Zita exasperating Signor Fatinelli with her works of charity, only to be bailed out at the last moment by divine intervention.

Zita died peacefully on April 27, 1272, in the Fatinelli house. She was 60 years old, and had served and edified the family for 48 years.

When Stressed by Entertaining
St. Martha (1st century) Feast day: July 29

If any saint understands the strain of preparing the house for guests it is St. Martha. Entertaining family, friends and business associates can be stressful enough, but St. Martha had the task of preparing dinner for the Son of God.

St. John tells us: "Now Jesus loved Martha and her sister and Lazarus." Three times the gospels record that Our Lord was a guest in their home in Bethany, a village barely two miles from Jerusalem. Of the members of this family, we get the strongest picture of Martha. She is a practical, down-to-earth, outspoken woman.

The first time Martha appears in the New Testament she is rushing about preparing a meal and trying to make everything perfect for Jesus, who has come to the family's house for dinner. Mary is not helping her sister. Instead, she has sat down on the floor, at the Lord's feet, to hear every word Christ says. Martha finds the situation galling. Twenty centuries after the event, we can still hear the irritation in her voice when she appeals to Jesus, "Lord do you not care that my sister has left me to serve alone? Tell her then to help me." Our Lord answers, "Martha, Martha, you are anxious and troubled about many things; one thing is needful. Mary has chosen the good portion, which shall not be taken away from her." (Luke 10:40-41)

At the time, Martha may have found Jesus' reply irksome. But the next time we read of Martha in the gospels she has obviously discovered the one thing that is necessary—faith in Christ.

St. John tells us that when Lazarus fell ill, his sisters sent word to Jesus asking him to come. Jesus delayed going to Bethany for two days. By the time he reached the town Lazarus was dead and buried. As Jesus approaches the village Martha, once again, takes the active part, going out to meet him while Mary sits at home with the mourners. The first thing she says to Christ is both a declaration of faith and a rebuke: "Lord, if you had been here, my brother would not have died." But now that she has vented her grief, Martha makes an even more profound act of faith in Christ: "I know that whatever you ask from God, God will give you."

Jesus for his part prompts Martha to make an even more candid declaration that will demonstrate to her neighbors and all future generations that she has indeed embraced the best part. And Martha does not disappoint: "You are the Christ, the Son of God, he who is coming into the world."

The scene moves to Lazarus' tomb. Christ commands that the stone be taken away. Martha, ever practical, reminds the Lord that Lazarus has lain in the ground for four days—there is sure to be a foul stench. Jesus insists nonetheless. The tomb is opened, and Christ raises his friend Lazarus from the dead.

The last time we see Martha and Mary and Lazarus is the day before the first Palm Sunday. Once again Jesus is a guest at his friends' home. Lazarus is at the table with Christ and his apostles. St. John records that as usual "Martha served." Then Mary enters the room with a pound of expensive ointment. Without a word she pours it over Christ's feet, then wipes his feet with her hair. The gospel says "the house was filled with the fragrance of the ointment" (John 12:3), a beautiful image that can also be read as a metaphor for the faith of the family.

It is strange that we do not hear of Martha, Mary and Lazarus after the Resurrection. Tradition says that they traveled to southern France to preach the gospel. The town of Tarascon claims that Martha delivered the region from a terrible monster, the Tarasque, which was half lion, half fish, and larger than an ox. Another legend says that once while Martha was preaching, a teenage boy tried to swim across the river Rhone, the better to hear her. The current, however, was stronger than the young swimmer. He was carried downstream and drowned. When his family and friends brought the boy's body to Martha, she stretched out on the ground in the form of a cross and prayed earnestly to Christ, reminding him that he had raised her brother Lazarus from the dead. Then, addressing the Lord as "my dear guest," she begged him to restore life to this young man. Her prayer done, Martha stood up and took the boy's hand. Immediately, he came back to life.

Teachers and Guides:
Saints for Students

SAINT JEROME

Teachers and Guides:
Saints for Students

There is no shortage of wise and learned men and women in the calendar of the saints. If anything, students will find a bewildering array of likely patrons who can be invoked to assist them with schoolwork.

St. Brigid is one of the Church's many patrons for students. Brigid's cult has been spread far and wide by Irish teachers and scholars. A nun well-versed in Celtic wisdom and Christian doctrine, Brigid founded the first Christian schools in Ireland.

Those who think of themselves as "dumb in science" can turn to St. Albert the Great, a man of powerful intellect who discerned some of the basic principles of the universe by observation and experimentation.

In today's parlance we would say that St. Ambrose was a lifelong learner. He was a lawyer with no theological training when he was made bishop of Milan against his will. Ambrose found a tutor to instruct him in theology so he would not make a fool of himself in the pulpit, or lead his people into error.

St. Jerome reminds us that there is more to understanding the Bible than simply reading the text and drawing our own conclusions. While it is too much to expect everyone to follow Jerome's example and become fluent in Hebrew and Greek in order to read the sacred texts in their original languages, he still teaches us that one should seek out the help of well-informed teachers and sound commentaries as guides when studying the Scriptures.

Finally, for procrastinators and others who find it difficult to make the best use of their time, we offer St. Alphonsus de Liguori, one of the busiest saints the Church has ever produced. In his 91 years, he founded and governed the Redemptorist order, wrote nearly 100 books, gave parish missions throughout southern Italy, composed hymns (and taught congregations to sing them), and even painted holy pictures to adorn Redemptorist houses. Furthermore, for thirteen years he labored to reform the clergy and convert the people of one of the Italy's most troubled dioceses.

The one trait all the learned saints possess is the desire to put their knowledge to a useful, holy purpose. They were not like the foolish servant in the parable who buried his treasure in the ground. St. Jerome struggled to master Hebrew so millions of Catholics yet unborn could have a reliable edition of the Bible. St. Ambrose studied theology so he could teach the truths of the faith forcefully and confidently, and thereby lead souls out of error and back to God. Certainly St. Albert the Great studied the natural sciences to satisfy his desire to know how the world works, but also to appreciate the marvelous intelligent design of God's creation. As St. Thomas Aquinas says in the *Summa Theologica,* "A scrap of knowledge about sublime things is worth more than any amount about trivialities."

A Role Model for Students

St. Brigid (c.452-525) Feast day: February 1

Students enjoy a host of patron saints, but Irish schoolchildren have always had a preference for St. Brigid. A nun well-versed in Celtic wisdom and Christian doctrine, she founded the first Christian schools in Ireland.

Within the course of her life St. Brigid witnessed the twilight of the pagan Celtic world and the dawn of the Church in Ireland. Her feast day coincides with the old Celtic festival of Imbolc which marked the waning of winter and the coming of spring. She was named for the Celtic goddess of wisdom, but she devoted her life to the truths of the Catholic faith. Her family was steeped in the ancient ways of pagan Ireland but Brigid was brought up a Christian.

About the time St. Patrick died Dubthach, a chieftain in Leinster, bought a slave woman named Broicsech. He kept her as his concubine, and soon Broicsech became pregnant. When Dubthach's wife got wind of the situation she threatened to take her dowry and go home to her father if Dubthach did not take his mistress to some distant corner of Ireland and sell her. But Dubthach could not part with Broicsech and Dubthach's wife was not prepared to make good on her threat. So the threesome settled into an uneasy stalemate.

Sometime around the year 452 Broicsech gave birth to an infant girl. It is said that three angels robed as priests came down from Heaven, named the child Brigid, and baptized her. This is the first in an endless stream of miracles reported about Brigid's childhood. When her nurse longed for a drink of ale and there was none to be had, Brigid satisfied the woman's craving by changing water into delicious ale. On another occasion she was preparing five slabs of bacon for guests when a starving dog came to the kitchen door. Out of pity Brigid gave the animal one of the pieces of bacon. It wolfed down the meat but still looked hungry, so Brigid gave the dog a second piece. Yet when her father came into the kitchen to see if the meal was done, Brigid showed him a platter with five slabs of bacon ready to be served.

As a young woman Brigid decided to enter the religious life. With eight female companions she received the nun's veil from St. Mel, a bishop who was St. Patrick's nephew. The women founded a convent at Kildare beside a massive oak tree, sacred to the druids. On the convent grounds the nuns tended a perpetual flame, an old pagan Celtic custom that Brigid "baptized" by consecrating the fire to Christ the Light of the World.

Under Brigid's guidance Kildare became a center of Irish Christian civilization. She opened the first Christian schools in Ireland, one for women, the other for men. She also established a library and *scriptorium* where Christian books were copied. In the twelfth century Giraldus Cambrensis, a Welsh priest, visited Brigid's abbey. He wanted to see the most famous volume in the library's collection, the *Book of Kildare*, an illuminated manuscript which Giraldus said was so exquisite it must have been wrought by an angel. The Welshman's comment gave birth to the legend that the *Book of Kildare* was a collaborative effort between St. Brigid and an angel.

As abbess of Kildare Brigid's life was even richer in miracles than when she was a child. Her cows produced an entire lake of milk. From a single barrel Brigid produced enough ale to supply seventeen churches for the entire octave of Easter. A few drops of her blood gave the gift of speech to two mute women. By her prayers she healed lepers, madmen, and the blind. One of the most dramatic stories tells of a woman who falsely accused one of St. Patrick's disciples of fathering her child. To get to the truth of the matter Brigid made the sign of the cross over the newborn. At once the child spoke up and named his true father.

No details of Brigid's death have come down to us. We do know that her body was buried in the Kildare Cathedral and remained there until about 870, when her relics were moved north to Downpatrick to keep them safe from the Vikings. Although her shrine was destroyed in the 16th century by English agents of the Reformation, the Irish have carried St. Brigid's fame to the farthest corners of the world. "Though great be her honor here at present," St. Brigid's biographer wrote in the eighth century, "greater by far will it be when she shall arise like a shining lamp... at the great assembly of Doomsday."

For Help in Learning

St. Ambrose (c.340–397) Feast day: December 7

St. Ambrose is the patron saint of learning. All his life he pursued knowledge as ardently as others pursue wealth or fame. Like all wise people he was aware of his shortcomings; as bishop of Milan he hired a theology tutor to ensure he would never mistakenly teach his people false doctrine.

St. Ambrose's family had been Christian for several generations. It was a source of pride to him that among his ancestors was the virgin martyr St. Soteris, who had been tortured and beheaded at Rome about the year 304.

Ambrose, born in Trier in Germany, was the youngest of three children. His father—also named Ambrose—was prefect of Gaul. We don't know his mother's name. The family was not aristocratic, but members of the well-to-do administrative class that ran Rome's empire.

When Ambrose was fourteen his father died. His mother took the family back to Rome where Ambrose's education began in earnest. He studied the Latin classics, of course, but he also learned Greek, an accomplishment which eluded St. Augustine and many other bishops of the West. On this solid liberal arts foundation Ambrose moved on to study the law.

While still a novice lawyer Ambrose was called upon to argue a case before a judge named Anicius Probus. Impressed by the young lawyer's intelligence and eloquence, Probus became Ambrose's patron. He wrote to Emperor Valentinian recommending Ambrose for the post of prefect of the provinces of Liguria and Aemilia in northern Italy. His residence would be in Milan, a city which had been torn by religious strife for twenty years. The bishop, Auxentius, was an Arian, a member of the heretical sect which denied the divinity of Christ. To the outrage of the Catholics of Milan, the Arians were in possession of the city's main basilica.

Ambrose had not been long in Milan when Auxentius died. According to the custom of the time, the Christians of Milan—Catholics and Arians—met in the main basilica to elect a new bishop. Given the fierce rivalry between Catholics and Arians, the election promised to be tumultuous. In his role as prefect, Ambrose went to the basilica to address the crowds and to make sure the election was conducted fairly and peacefully. No sooner had he finished speaking than a voice cried out in the basilica, "Ambrose for bishop!" Others took up the cry, and soon "Ambrose for bishop!" echoed mightily from the basilica's walls.

Not only was Ambrose not a priest, he had not even been baptized—as was common in the early days of the Church when many people delayed baptism until they were on their deathbed. He felt unqualified for the sacred office and he was afraid the emperor would interpret his speech in the basilica as gross official misconduct, an attempt to use his position as prefect to campaign to become bishop.

Ambrose hurried out of the church and back to his post. The crowd followed. He ordered several of the noisiest people in the crowd arrested and punished for inciting a riot. Even this did not dissuade his supporters. Ambrose then made a series of pathetic gestures to dampen the crowd's enthusiasm. He claimed he was about to retire to become a full time philosopher. The crowd did not believe him. He invited prostitutes into his house to prove he was unworthy to be bishop. Out in the street the people shouted, "Your sin be upon our heads!" He waited until nightfall and tried to escape the city, but the people had posted their own guards at the city gates. They stopped Ambrose, escorted him back to his home, and kept him under house arrest. Meanwhile, the clergy and people of Milan sent a message to Emperor Valentinian declaring that there would not be peace in Milan unless Ambrose became their bishop. The emperor replied promptly: Ambrose must accept the election. And so Ambrose gave in.

Over the course of a week Ambrose was baptized, ordained a priest, and consecrated bishop. As a clear sign of the direction in which he would lead the Church in Milan, Ambrose insisted that no Arian clergy could officiate at these ceremonies.

As a lawyer and a governor Ambrose felt entirely at ease. As a bishop, however, he believed he was out of his depth. He began a period of intense study of theology, and set to work improving his Greek. He asked a learned priest, St. Simplician, to act as his tutor.

Every day Ambrose said Mass, offering it for the intentions of his people. He also established an open door policy. Anyone of any rank could see him at any time. Satyrus, Ambrose's older brother, moved to Milan and took over the tedious administrative affairs of the diocese so Ambrose could focus on pastoral and intellectual pursuits such as writing.

The first book Ambrose published was *De Virginibus,* in praise of a life of consecrated virginity. As a teenager Ambrose had seen his own sister, St. Marcellina, take a vow of perpetual virginity, receiving her veil from Pope Liberius himself. Throughout his life Ambrose seldom missed an opportunity to express his admiration for women who dedicated their lives to Christ in this way. In fact, St. Ambrose preached the glories of consecrated virginity so eloquently as bishop that many mothers—hoping for a good marriage in the family—refused to take their young daughters to church if Ambrose was scheduled to say the Mass.

We can see how far Ambrose progressed in his theological studies in a small book he wrote for the 25-year-old Emperor

Gratian. Ambrose produced a bold statement of orthodox belief that was also a stylistic masterpiece. Ambrose's comparisons of Arianism with monsters from classical mythology may strike modern readers as a little over the top, but the book won the admiration of the literati of Gratian's court. (Gratian, however, must have been less impressed by Ambrose's book—assuming he read it. The emperor never committed himself to either the Catholic faith or to Arianism. Three years later, he was killed in a military coup.)

The next emperor, Valentinian II, was openly sympathetic to the Arians. His mother, Justina, urged her son to order Ambrose to turn over to the Arians Milan's Portian Basilica. Ambrose refused. Justina then demanded the Church of the Holy Apostles for Arian worship. Again Ambrose refused. When Valentinian sent officers to occupy Holy Apostles, a Catholic mob seized an Arian priest and held him hostage.

Ambrose defused the situation by sending an embassy of priests and deacons to win the Arian priest's freedom. He never backed away from his refusal to turn over any church in his diocese to the Arians, but he also declined all invitations to come and say Mass in any of the disputed churches for fear of starting a riot.

In 386 Valentinian published a new law that forbade any person, under pain of death, from interfering with the transfer of Catholic churches to the Arians. Two days before Palm Sunday, a delegation from Valentinian asked Ambrose to permit the Arians to use his cathedral on the upcoming holy day. He refused. On Palm Sunday, imperial servants began to prepare the Portian Basilica for Arian services. When word reached Ambrose at the cathedral, part of his congregation hurried to the Basilica, occupied it, and refused to let Valentinian's official enter. Imperial troops surrounded the church, while ultimatums passed back and forth between the emperor's representatives and Ambrose. Even if the crisis compromised the emperor's authority

Ambrose was determined not to give in. "The emperor is in the Church," Ambrose said, "not over it." The stalemate lingered until Holy Thursday when Valentinian recalled the imperial troops to their barracks. No blood had been spilled, and no Milan church had been delivered into Arian hands.

Present in the cathedral during that tense Holy Week was St. Monica. For years she had wept and prayed that her brilliant son, Augustine, would repent of his sinful life, give up his Manichean heresy, and accept baptism. In the learned, eloquent, and courageous Ambrose she believed she had found the bishop who could at last convert her son.

In order to please his mother, Augustine began attending Ambrose's sermons. He was impressed by Ambrose's style, which blended the philosophy of Plato with the revelation of Sacred Scripture. Soon Ambrose was personally instructing Augustine in the Catholic faith. At the Mass of the Easter Vigil, the night of April 24-25, 387, Ambrose led Augustine into the baptistery of the cathedral. There Augustine removed his clothes and entered naked into the deep pool. Three times Ambrose immersed Augustine in the water, baptizing him in the name of the Father, and of the Son, and of the Holy Spirit. Of all the great things St. Ambrose accomplished for the Church, the conversion of St. Augustine is the most significant.

Valentinian II was deposed in 387 and the staunchly Catholic Theodosius I became emperor. When Ambrose and Theodosius locked horns, it was not over heresy, but over religious authority.

The first confrontation occurred in 388. In the town of Callinicum in what is now Iraq, a Christian mob, led by their bishop, had attacked and destroyed a synagogue. The imperial representative in the region wrote to Theodosius asking what he should do. To Theodosius, it was a simple case: punish the mob and make the bishop pay the cost of rebuilding the synagogue. Ambrose disagreed with the emperor's verdict.

He approached the case as if he were a lawyer arguing before a court. He offered precedents—no compensation had ever been paid for Christian churches destroyed by Jewish mobs during the reign of Julian the Apostate. He presented shrewd arguments—no Christian should be compelled to build a house of worship "where Christ is denied." And he warned Theodosius against setting a precedent which his successors might deplore.

Whether Ambrose's heart was really in these arguments we don't know. He may indeed have hated the Jews and found the idea of rebuilding a synagogue offensive. Or perhaps he felt like a lawyer stuck with a thoroughly unpleasant client—the rabble-rousing bishop of Callinicum. Whatever his feelings, Ambrose was determined to preserve the Church's independence, to keep the state from telling it what it must do.

In the end, Theodosius backed down. The Jews of Callinicum had to find the money to rebuild their synagogue themselves.

Most contemporary readers will feel more comfortable with Ambrose's second confrontation with Theodosius. In the summer of 390, Theodosius, in a fit of rage, unleashed his troops stationed in Thessalonika on the inhabitants of the city. A local uprising had resulted in the murder of one of Theodosius' generals, and Theodosius loosed his troops on the city in reprisal. Seven thousand men, women, and children were massacred in the space of only three hours.

Ambrose insisted that the only way the emperor could make restitution and be permitted once again to receive Holy Communion was to do public penance. At Sunday Mass in Ambrose's basilica, Theodosius stood before the congregation, stripped off all signs of his imperial office, confessed responsibility for the massacre, and tearfully begged the people to pray for him. Traditionally Theodosius' penance has been viewed as a complete victory for Ambrose. He had compelled a Roman emperor to humiliate himself before his subjects. One modern biographer of St. Ambrose, however, sees the event in a different light. Neil B. McLynn argues that Ambrose "turned the catastrophe (of the massacre) into a public relations triumph" for Theodosius. The emperor's dramatic gesture in the basilica won the admiration of his Christian subjects; he had confessed his guilt like any other sinner and his sin had been forgiven. Theodosius' public repentance was indeed so successful that no surviving contemporary source mentions the massacre without also telling of the emperor's penance.

In Lent 397 Ambrose fell ill. During Holy Week it became clear that he was dying. Bishops came from the surrounding dioceses to be with the holy man at the end. Ambrose's friend, Honoratus, bishop of Vecelli, gave him the Last Rites. His old tutor, St. Simplician, was at his side. Ambrose died on Good Friday. On Holy Saturday his body was carried to his basilica where the Mass of the Easter Vigil blended seamlessly into Ambrose's funeral Mass.

On Easter Sunday an enormous crowd followed the funeral procession to a basilica Ambrose had built outside the walls of Milan. There he was buried beside the martyrs St. Gervasius and St. Protasius, the two patron saints of Milan whose relics Ambrose himself had discovered.

For Those Struggling With Science
St. Albert the Great (c.1206–1280) Feast day: November 15

In 1931 Pope Pius XI declared St. Albert the Great a Doctor
of the Church. He also named Albert the patron of students of
the natural sciences. As a man with an active curiosity about the
workings of nature, Albert, the pope said, is an ideal patron
for a world "so full of hope in its scientific discoveries."

*V*ery few individuals enjoy during their lifetime the respect and acclaim which St. Albert knew. His colleagues and his
students referred to him as *Albertus Magnus* (Albert the Great)
and *doctor universalis* (the universal teacher).

Albert, the eldest son of Count von Bollstadt, was born at
Lauingen, on the Danube, not far from the city of Ulm. We know
little of Albert's childhood. Sometime before 1222 his family sent
him to the University of Padua for a liberal arts education.

In Padua Albert heard the Master General of the Dominicans, Blessed Jordan of Saxony, preach. Jordan was a dynamic
presence in the pulpit. It is said that by the force of his oratory
he brought one thousand new members into the Dominican order
over a period of fifteen years. Albert was one of those thousand.
In 1223, despite family objections, Albert joined the Dominicans.

After taking his vows, Albert taught theology at a series
of schools in Germany. Early in the 1240s he was assigned to
teach at the University of Paris, the greatest school in medieval
Europe. Albert arrived at a golden time. The theory that the works
of Aristotle could be reconciled with Christianity and even help
Christians better understand their faith had caused a sensation.

The bookshops of Paris were flooded with new works by Jewish, Moslem, and Greek scholars who debated the value and influence of Aristotle in every branch of human learning. Albert immersed himself in the new scholarship and in 1245 began writing a detailed explanation of Aristotle's teaching on the natural sciences.

Albert's book became an encyclopedia of human knowledge that included discussions of logic, rhetoric, mathematics, astronomy, economics, politics, ethics and metaphysics. Albert's book was distinctive because he did not simply repeat the conclusions of Aristotle; he challenged and corrected Aristotle's statements if they contradicted what Albert had observed through his own study of science.

While many teachers in 13th-century Europe were content to echo the conclusions of earlier authorities, Albert wanted to see and understand the workings of nature first hand. "The aim of natural science is not simply to accept the statements of others," he wrote, "but to investigate the causes that are at work in nature."

The whole world was Albert's laboratory. He wrote books on botany, astronomy, physics, mineralogy, and chemistry, and asserted that "experiment is the only safe guide" in scientific inquiry. In his book on geography he taught how latitude affects climate. In his book on zoology he disproved the colorful but wildly implausible fables about the animal kingdom that were current in his day, such as that beavers castrate themselves, and that barnacle geese are born from trees. Albert was the first man to accurately describe a Greenland whale—to get first-hand information about the creature he joined a whale hunt in Friesland.

About the time Albert began his encyclopedia, a new student arrived in Paris—Thomas Aquinas, a quiet, stout, young Italian Dominican who possessed the finest mind Albert would ever know. In 1248, when Albert's superiors sent him to Cologne to open a Dominican house of study, he took Thomas with him.

All his life Albert would be Thomas Aquinas' champion. After Thomas' death Stephen Tempier, bishop of Paris, and several theologians moved to proscribe Thomas' writings for being too heavily influenced by pagan philosophers. Albert journeyed to Paris to defend his friend's work. In spite of his best effort and his own impeccable reputation, the Paris theologians still condemned part of Aquinas' work.

The year after Thomas returned home to Italy, Albert was elected head of the Dominican order's German Province. It was an enormous administrative headache that required visiting every Dominican monastery and convent in Germany. In addition to his duties as Provincial, Albert was called upon during this time to come to Italy to defend the Dominican order before Church officials. The theologian William of St. Amour had just published an attack on the Dominicans and Franciscans, who together comprised a new form of religious life in the Church known as mendicant, or begging, orders. William asserted that the religious poverty of the mendicants was only a sham, and went so far as to accuse them of being in league with the Antichrist. But the mendicants had formidable champions in Albert (for the Dominicans) and St. Bonaventure (for the Franciscans). At the end of the hearing, Pope Alexander IV ruled in favor of the mendicant orders, and ordered William of St. Amour's book burned.

In 1260 Albert reluctantly accepted an appointment as bishop of Regensburg. The previous bishop had been so corrupt he was removed from office; and the pope himself described the priests of Regensburg as "sacrilegious" for their drunkenness, sexual misconduct, and greed. The local nobles were just as bad. Under the old bishop, priests and barons had caroused together in the bishop's residence. The clergy resisted Albert's attempts to restore religious discipline. The nobility resented Albert's poor style of living—he had sold off many of the lavish furnishings in the bishop's house, as well as his predecessor's stable of fine horses, and distributed the money to the poor.

Albert did his best to reform his diocese but in the end his good intentions accomplished nothing. Albert was a saint and a scholar, not a reforming administrator. After two unsuccessful years in office, he resigned as bishop of Regensburg and returned to Cologne.

In 1274 Albert was on his way to the Council of Lyons when word reached him that his friend, Thomas Aquinas, who had also been traveling to the council, had died suddenly at the Cistercian abbey of Fossanova. It was a painful blow. Albert told his friends that with Thomas' death, "the light of the Church has been extinguished."

Sometime in 1278, Albert was delivering a lecture when his memory failed. It was the onset of dementia, perhaps Alzheimer's disease. During the last two years of his life Albert's once-great mind became increasingly clouded. He died peacefully sitting in a large wooden chair, fully dressed in his habit, a throw rug over his knees. With his brother Dominicans gathered around him singing the *Salve Regina,* Albert the Great slipped away to eternity.

To Understand the Bible

St. Jerome (c.345-420) Feast day: September 30

Students of the Bible have as their patron St. Jerome. He spent nearly 40 years translating the Old and New Testaments and writing commentaries on the sacred books.

*J*erome is a paradox among the Doctors of the Church. Brilliant but thin-skinned, saintly yet combative, proud, resentful, irritable, and defensive, Jerome is a difficult man to like. Yet for all his faults, the Church owes Jerome a tremendous debt. He devoted almost forty years of his life to translating the Bible from the original languages into Latin, at that time the primary language of the Roman Empire. There have been many translations of the Bible since Jerome's time, but because he had at his disposal manuscripts of the Old and New Testaments that have long since vanished, his translation, known as the Vulgate, remains invaluable to biblical scholars.

Jerome's birth name was Eusebius Hieronymus Sophronius. He was born to Christian parents in the town of Stridon in what is now Croatia. His father sent Jerome to school in Rome where he mastered the Latin and Greek classics and showed a particular talent for rhetoric, the art of fashioning a compelling argument. It was a talent Jerome exploited skillfully throughout his life.

Like so many children of Christian families, Jerome had not been baptized at birth. His parents taught him the faith, and religious practice appears to have been a regular part of his life. Jerome himself tells us that while he was a student in Rome he spent his Sundays with friends visiting the catacombs to pray at the tombs of the martyrs. When he was twenty years old, Jerome requested baptism.

Not long after his christening Jerome decided to become a monk. With a handful of like-minded friends he set up a small monastery in Aquileia, a vibrant center of Christianity near Venice. There he met St. Chromatius and St. Heliodorus—two men of great learning and personal holiness who became Jerome's devoted friends and would latter help finance his translation of the Bible. Although committed to the monastic life, Jerome continued to study the pagan classics, and was especially devoted to the works of the Roman orator Cicero.

Jerome was not in Aquileia long before controversy broke out in the monastery. The community split, with several of the monks moving to an island in the Adriatic Sea, while Jerome and three friends traveled to Antioch.

In Antioch the little band was overtaken by illness. Two of Jerome's friends died and he himself became very ill. In a letter he wrote years later to St. Eustochium, Jerome tells of a dream he had while he was sick. He saw himself before the judgment seat of Christ. When the Lord asked Jerome what he was, Jerome answered, "I am a Christian." "Liar!" said Christ. "You are a Ciceronian. For where your treasure is, there your heart is also." Then Christ commanded his angels to whip Jerome.

When he awoke, Jerome was badly shaken. He resolved to give up pagan literature and to go live as a hermit in the desert. Jerome remained in the wilderness for four years, inflicting severe fasts on himself and suffering from hallucinations of Roman dancing girls. But in the desert Jerome also met a man who would change his life. One of the hermits living near Jerome had converted from Judaism to Christianity. Jerome asked this man to teach him Hebrew.

It was not easy for Jerome, who loved the polished phrases of the Latin and Greek classics, to adapt to the rough syntax of the Hebrew Bible. He said that initially he found Hebrew to be a language of "hissing and broken-winded words." He repeatedly gave up his study of Hebrew but always came back to it until at last he mastered the language.

About 380 Paulinus, bishop of Antioch, ordained Jerome a priest. It seems very odd since Jerome always said he had no vocation to the priesthood. He only accepted ordination under duress and with the understanding that he would not be required to fulfill any priestly office. It appears that he never even said Mass.

Soon after his ordination, Jerome traveled to Constantinople to study the Bible under St. Gregory Nazianzus, one of the great biblical scholars of his age. In Constantinople Jerome published his first biblical commentary, an analysis of the Vision of Isaiah.

When Pope St. Damasus called a council in Rome, Jerome accompanied Paulinus as the bishop's interpreter. Pope Damasus developed a high regard for Jerome and asked him to stay in Rome as his personal secretary. Jerome agreed, and the next three years were among the happiest of his life. Damasus encouraged Jerome's interest in biblical studies and urged him to create a standard Latin version of the Bible based, as much as possible, on the original manuscripts. Within three years Jerome produced new translations of the Psalms, the four Gospels, all the epistles, and the Book of Revelation.

At the same time Jerome became the spiritual director of a group of devout Roman women. They included St. Marcella, a noblewoman in whose house Jerome lived during his time in Rome; her sister, St. Asella, who took a nun's vows at age twelve; St. Fabiola who, before her conversion, had caused a scandal by divorcing her husband and then taking a lover; St. Paula, another aristocrat who became Jerome's most devoted friend and supporter; and Paula's two daughters, St. Eustochium, who acted as Jerome's assistant when he translated the Bible, and St. Blesilla, who practiced such extreme mortifications of the flesh that she died of her own self-inflicted penances.

When Pope Damasus died in 394 Jerome lost his protector. During his three years in Rome he had managed to offend both fashionable Roman society by lampooning its narcissism, and the Roman clergy by mocking its worldliness. With Damasus gone, Jerome's enemies struck back: they spread a rumor that he and Paula were lovers. Rather than stay and defend himself and Paula, Jerome left Rome for the Holy Land. He settled in Bethlehem and began to work on his translation of the Old Testament. It was a herculean labor that occupied the last 26 years of his life.

Paula and Eustochium, among others from Rome, followed Jerome to Bethlehem. Paula used her fortune to support Jerome, and to build a religious complex that included a monastery, three convents, a school, and a hospital for pilgrims. Jerome declined to move into Paula's monastery; instead he dug a cave for himself near the place where Christ was born.

He wrote to a friend, giving an idyllic description of life in Bethlehem. "Bread, our own vegetables, and milk—country fare—provide us with a plain but healthy diet. In summer the trees give us shade; in autumn the air is cool and the fallen leaves are restful; in spring our chanting of the psalms is made sweeter by the singing of the birds; and in winter, when it is cold and the snow falls, there is no lack of wood."

Of course, even in this Eden Jerome could not stay free from controversy. Paula's son-in-law, St. Pammachius, wrote from Rome that a man named Jovinian had published a book downplaying the need for asceticism, and asserting that the state of marriage is of equal rank with the state of consecrated virginity. Jerome published a withering rebuttal, worded so strongly that even orthodox Catholics thought he was maligning marriage.

Then Jerome picked a fight with St. Augustine because of a rumor that Augustine had published a book attacking Jerome's work. Augustine, exercising heroic self-restraint, assured Jerome that he had never attacked his work, but Jerome was not convinced. He fired off one sneering letter after another to Augustine. "I cannot at this time pronounce anything in your works to merit censure," Jerome wrote. "For, in the first place, I have never read them with attention."

Yet this irascible, often impossible man was devoted to his friends. When Paula died in 404 he was heartbroken; no one could console him. More dreadful news reached Jerome in 410. Rome had been sacked by the Goths and his disciple, St. Marcella, had been flogged to death by the barbarians. When the Holy Land was flooded with Roman refugees, Jerome did all he could for them. "I have set aside my commentary on Ezekiel," he wrote, "and almost all study. For today we must translate the words of the Scriptures into deeds."

In 416 Jerome's monastic complex itself was attacked by Pelagian heretics. They burned the buildings and beat the monks and nuns. Paula's daughter, Eustochium, never recovered from the attack. She died a few months later.

Jerome's health was also failing. He died peacefully in Bethlehem on September 30, 420. He was buried in the Church of the Nativity, beside Paula and Eustochium. Centuries later his relics were carried to Rome and enshrined in the Basilica of Santa Maria Maggiore.

In art Jerome is often depicted with a lion at his feet. It is a reference to a legend told about the saint. One day an enraged lion startled Jerome's monks as they worked in the fields. The beast pursued the monks to their monastery, but while everyone else sought safety, Jerome went out to confront the lion. Speaking softly, he calmed the lion, and found that it had a large thorn embedded in its paw. Jerome drew out the thorn, and the grateful lion spent the rest of his life at the monastery as Jerome's pet.

To Make the Best Use of Time
St. Alphonsus de Liguori (1696-1787) Feast day: August 1

Procrastinators can turn to St. Alphonsus de Liguori. Alphonsus once resolved never to waste time and he made good on his pledge. During his life St. Alphonsus founded the Redemptorist order, preached countless missions, wrote nearly one hundred books, and reformed one of the most troubled dioceses in Italy.

*F*rom a religious point of view the 18th century was a disappointing time that produced very few saints. One of the rare exceptions was Alphonsus de Liguori. God gave him 91 years of life. Alphonsus seems to have exploited every moment—bringing sinners back to God, founding and nurturing the Redemptorist order, writing classic works on moral theology, and, for twelve years, reforming the wayward clergy and instructing the unlettered laity of the diocese of St. Agatha of the Goths.

About eight o'clock in the morning on September 27, 1696, Anna Caterina de Liguori gave birth to her first child, a boy, in the family's country house at Marianella outside Naples. Two days later the infant was taken to the Church of Our Lady of the Virgins and baptized Alphonsus Mary Anthony John Francis Cosmas Damian Michael Gaspar (it was a custom among the Catholic nobility of Europe to give children a sonorous string of names). The parish register in which Alphonsus' baptism was recorded survives. In the 19th century, priests of the parish added these notations to Alphonsus' christening entry: "Beatified, September 1816. Canonized, 26 May 1839. Declared a Doctor of the Church, 23 March 1871."

Alphonsus' father, Don Joseph Felix de Liguori, was a captain in the Royal Navy of Naples, a post from which he derived very little income. Although Don Joseph's family had been members of the lesser nobility for 500 years, by the time Alphonsus was born the Liguoris were cash poor. Donna Anna had brought a substantial dowry when she married Don Joseph, and the family probably lived on that. Don Joseph was anxious to have a son who would restore the family's fortune. For a while it appeared that Alphonsus was the answer to his father's prayers.

As a Navy captain, Don Joseph spent much time aboard a galley rowed by slaves and condemned criminals. It made him a tough, intractable man. Don Joseph was not cruel to Alphonsus, but he was demanding. He arranged for tutors to teach his son at home, so he could more easily keep an eye on his progress. A squad of teachers came to the house to instruct Alphonsus in Latin, Greek, French and Spanish; mathematics, physics, and cosmology; history, philosophy, and even painting.

Don Joseph had a passion for music, so he hired Gaetano Greco, who had studied with the famous opera composer Alessandro Scarlatti, to teach Alphonsus the harpsichord. Don Joseph insisted that his son practice three hours every day. When he suspected that Greco and Alphonsus were not spending enough time at the keyboard, he locked them both in the music room. Don Joseph needn't have worried. Alphonsus' love for music rivaled his father's. In later years he would play to entertain the priests and lay brothers of his household, or to lead a congregation in hymns. Playing the harpsichord was the only worldly distraction Alphonsus permitted himself on his days of recollection.

Alphonsus' education was preparing him for what his father hoped would be a splendid and financially lucrative career. The path he had chosen for his son was the law, a guaranteed money-maker in litigious 18th-century Naples. By the age of 20, Alphonsus had completed his studies and was ready to practice.

Relatives and friends sent Alphonsus a steady stream of clients. Father Pier Luigi Rispoli, one of the saint's first biographers, says that Alphonsus won every time he went to court. It appeared that Don Joseph's investment was about to pay off. His next task was to find Alphonsus a wealthy woman to marry.

Don Joseph's first choice was a distant cousin, Teresa de Liguori, the daughter of a prince. The girl frustrated his plans by announcing her intention to become a nun. Don Joseph's next choice was the daughter of a duke, but by this time Alphonsus felt he had a call to the religious life. He refused to marry the young woman. Ironically, the catalyst that convinced Alphonsus to give up his life in the world arrived during a lawsuit.

Alphonsus had been retained by Don Filippo Orsini, the duke of Gravina, to sue the Grand Duke of Tuscany, Cosimo de Medici, for 600,000 ducats, money Orsini said was owed him for an estate in the province of Abruzzi. Alphonsus went into court confident that he had an air-tight argument. Actually he had overlooked a little phrase in the documents that revealed who had legal title to the land. The Medici lawyers exploited Alphonsus' oversight. They proved to the judges that the estate was indeed the property of the Medici family and the Orsinis had no claim to it. When the court ruled in favor of the Medicis, Alphonsus was stunned and humiliated. He returned home, locked himself in his room, refused to eat, and promised himself he would never practice law again.

Alphonsus' parents tried to persuade him to re-enter society, but the young man refused. He began making lengthy visits to churches and nursing the sick in a hospital for incurables. In a gesture that hearkened back to the Middle Ages, he laid his sword at the feet of a statue of Our Lady of Mercy. When he announced his determination to become an Oratorian priest, Don Joseph was not surprised, but he resisted anyway. For weeks, father and son were at a stalemate. It took the intervention of

Bishop Emilio Cavalieri, Alphonsus' maternal uncle, to break the deadlock. He suggested that Don Joseph let Alphonsus become a priest if Alphonsus agreed to give up the idea of joining the Oratorians and became a diocesan priest instead. Reluctantly, both men agreed.

After five years of study and preparation Alphonsus was ordained. There were 1,500 diocesan priests just in the city of Naples, and about 75,000 diocesan and order priests throughout the kingdom. By no means does this vast number of clergy suggest that Naples was in the midst of a golden age of selfless religious devotion. Many of the priests in the kingdom exercised no pastoral function, or were entirely unsuited to the religious life. At the root of the problem was the custom of passing all property to the eldest son, leaving nothing for his younger brothers to inherit. Under these circumstances many younger sons made the Church their career: as diocesan priests they took no vow of poverty and could accumulate wealth. Combine this with the immunity of the clergy from taxation and one had a system ready-made for scandal, abuse, and corruption.

Yet Naples was not completely bereft of good, holy, hard-working clerics. Alphonsus sought out some of the most active and dedicated priests in the city, including Father Matthew Ripa, who founded a college to prepare missionaries for China, and Father Thomas Falcoia, a man thirty years older than Alphonsus who was conducting retreats for nuns. Father Falcoia dreamed of starting a new order for men and women that would imitate as closely as humanly possible the virtues of Our Lord. While giving a retreat at the Scala convent, he met a young nun, Sister Maria Celeste, who told him she had received a series of visions about the birth of a new religious order. She even had revelations about what type of rule the order should follow. When Sister Maria Celeste showed it to Father Falcoia, he was amazed that it was exactly the rule he had planned.

In 1730 Alphonsus made a retreat at the Scala convent and, authorized by the local bishop, questioned Sister Maria Celeste about her visions and the rule. Rather than finding anything objectionable in either, Alphonsus was drawn to the missionary ideal of the prospective order. The nuns of Scala were the first to adopt the new rule: they were the first members of the Congregation of the Most Holy Redeemer. Another two years would pass before the male branch of the Redemptorists was founded by Alphonsus himself in a small guest house owned by the Scala convent.

The Redemptorists' mission was to bring sinners back to God and increase the fervor of practicing Catholics. They would arrive at a city parish or some remote rural village and, with the permission of the parish priest, preach for several days in the church. If the crowd was too large, they moved out to the town square and preached in the open. Between sermons the Redemptorists heard confessions and organized devotions to the Blessed Sacrament and the Blessed Virgin. Then they moved on to continue their work in the next parish.

Almost from the beginning the Redemptorists flourished. By 1735 bishops were inviting the order to their dioceses, and Alphonsus was building a monastery to serve as a retreat center and seminary to meet the growing demand for his missionaries.

For many years Alphonsus himself was frequently on the road giving missions. In his few spare moments he dealt with the administrative details of his order, studied moral theology, collected material for a great work he would publish years later, *The Glories of Mary,* and from time to time fended off efforts by Church or civil authorities who—believing there were more than enough religious orders—wanted to suppress the Redemptorists.

In 1762 Alphonsus' life became more complicated. Pope Clement XIII named him bishop of St. Agatha of the Goths, a small rural diocese between Naples and Capua. It proved to be

Alphonsus' greatest challenge. There were 35,000 souls in the diocese, few of whom had a command of Catholic doctrine. In too many cases, natural devotion had degenerated into superstition. Religious festivals often ended in drunken brawls. Alphonsus' biggest problem, however, were the priests: there were about 350 in the diocese and perhaps 100 more who had gone to Naples to pursue others careers. Alphonsus found priests who squandered their time drinking and gambling in taverns, semi-literate priests who could barely say Mass, priests who had gotten lucrative posts through bribery, priests who shamelessly flouted the rule of celibacy.

Within three weeks of his arrival Alphonsus sent a letter to every priest in his diocese. They were to say Mass reverently, following the rubrics, and they were to preach to the people in a plain, simple style their congregations would understand. Furthermore, he warned them against trying to use any outside influence to win lucrative benefices or important posts in the diocese. Alphonsus himself climbed into the pulpit to preach, bringing all the rhetorical firepower he had honed in his years as a lawyer. One Sunday, wearing a black stole and carrying a flaming torch in one hand, he preached a hair-raising sermon on Hell.

A particular embarrassment was the scandal of Father Marco Petti, a member of Alphonsus' own cathedral clergy. Petti had lived with his mistress, a married woman, for sixteen years. He did not blush to been seen with his three illegitimate children. Yet he had the effrontery to continue to say Mass. In a face-to-face meeting, Alphonsus invited Petti to move into the bishop's residence, the better to avoid temptation. Petti said he would prefer to build a little hut for himself on his estate and live there as a hermit. Alphonsus replied he had no trouble with Father Petti becoming a hermit; but he did worry that the priest might be joined there by a hermitess.

When Petti showed no sign of changing his life, Alphonsus

decided to turn the case over to the civil authorities. Petti was jailed for public immorality, then sent to a monastery to do penance for his sins. Some years later, Alphonsus restored to Father Petti the privilege of saying Mass, but only in private. He also brought about the return of Petti's mistress to her husband and arranged for the support of her illegitimate children.

For thirteen years Alphonsus labored in his diocese. He reorganized the seminary, reformed the convents, brought religious orders—including his own Redemptorists—into the diocese to raise the quality of preaching and religious education, and encouraged the study of moral theology among the clergy. He also wrote several books—so many in fact, that some of his critics complained that any bishop who wrote so much must be neglecting his diocese.

During this time Alphonsus suffered severe bouts of rheumatic fever, which produced the acute curvature of his spine that we see in so many portraits of the saint. Since he could no longer lift his head, he had to drink through a straw. At Mass he needed the support of an acolyte so he could drink from the chalice. In 1775, in consideration of Alphonsus' declining health, Pope Pius VI permitted him to resign the bishopric of St. Agatha. Alphonsus returned to Pagani, his favorite Redemptorist house, and made writing his full-time occupation. He imagined that he would die soon. In fact he had twelve more years to live, and one final crisis to face.

In 1779 the king of Naples issued a long-delayed royal decree recognizing the Redemptorists and granting them the right to open a novitiate and a house of study. But the king did not want another religious order in his realm, so he insisted that the Redemptorists must be secular priests. It was not all that Alphonsus had hoped for, but royal recognition was still a step in the right direction. Whether the Redemptorists were religious or seculars could be hammered out later. Then Alphonsus made a serious error in judgment.

Founders of religious communities traditionally look to Rome, or at least the local bishop, to approve the rule of their order. In 1779 the king of Naples and the pope were at odds. Rather than risk irritating his royal ally, Alphonsus agreed to submit his Rule to the king for approval. It was a tragic mistake that nearly destroyed the Redemptorists.

Alphonsus could not manage the negotiations himself. At age 83 his mind was still clear, but he tired easily, was hard of hearing, and his eyesight was so poor he could only read a few sentences at a time. He entrusted the task of getting approval for the Rule to two Redemptorists, Fathers Angelo Maione and Fabrizio Cimino. When they presented him with the Rule as approved by the king, Alphonsus could not read it. He gave it to his confessor, Father Andrew Villani, to review. Alphonsus didn't know that all three of his brother Redemptorists had betrayed him.

To please the king, Fathers Maione and Cimino had so altered the Rule that the Redemptorist community could barely be said to exist at all. The authority of the Rector Major—in this case Alphonsus himself—was restricted and the bulk of power given to two priests known as consultors. Unlike religious orders the Redemptorists would be under the authority of the local bishop. Worst of all, the solemn vows of poverty, chastity and obedience were rejected in favor of nebulous oaths.

Misled by Father Villani into believing that the Rule approved by the king was the Rule he had written, Alphonsus went ahead and signed the document. Publication of the new Rule provoked anger and outrage among the Redemptorists. A few blamed Alphonsus for permitting himself to be duped. Others took out their frustration on Fathers Maione, Cimino, and Villani. Many priests and lay brothers were certain that if Alphonsus signed such a mutilated rule he must be senile. Sadly, the affair was not settled and the original Redemptorist Rule was not restored until after Alphonsus' death.

During his last months Alphonsus suffered periods of dementia. Sometimes he thought he was on a mission, hearing confessions. In his final days he was afflicted by severe dysentery, gangrene, and uremia. At one point someone at the bedside held up before his face a picture of Gerard Majella, his late friend and fellow Redemptorist. In the years since his death Gerard had already become renowned as a great intercessor and saint. Alphonsus muttered, "Even he cannot cure me now."

On the evening of July 31 it became clear that Alphonsus was dying. The entire community crowded into his room, the overflow spilling out into the hall. Over and over they recited the prayers for the dying and the Litany of the Blessed Virgin. Sometime before noon on August 1, Alphonsus de Liguori passed away so peacefully that even those kneeling closest to his bed did not know he had died.

Models of Faith:
Saints for the Christian Life

BLESSED KATERI TEKAKWITHA

Models of Faith:
Saints for the Christian Life

*L*apsed Catholics are not a modern phenomenon—the life of St. Monica teaches us that. Her own son Augustine rejected the faith she had taught him as a child and joined the peculiar Manichean sect. A year or two after St. Monica's relics were rediscovered in Ostia in 1430, Pope Eugenius IV founded a confraternity in her honor. Members joined together to pray for family and friends who had fallen away from the Catholic faith.

As with lapsed Catholics, troublesome churchmen have also always been with us—the case of St. Joan of Arc being a particularly extreme example. This scrupulously Catholic young woman fell into the hands of a corrupt Church tribunal. In their eagerness to prove loyal to their English overlords these French clerics unjustly convicted Joan of heresy and witchcraft, then handed her over to the secular power to be burned. The outcry that followed Joan's trial, condemnation, and execution induced the pope to appoint a new panel of churchmen to review the case. They returned a verdict of not guilty.

Like St. Joan, St. John Mary Vianney encountered hostility from some members of the clergy. A handful of priests from

71

Vianney's own diocese complained to the bishop that the curé of Ars was unsophisticated, too rigid in his preaching, and possibly out of his mind. The bishop replied that he wished all his priests had a little of Father Vianney's madness. Sadly, contempt for St. John Vianney has arisen again in our day. When Pope John Paul II announced that he planned to personally conduct a retreat for priests, deacons, and seminarians at Ars, the parish St. John served for 41 years, a number of priests protested that Vianney was not a suitable model for contemporary Catholic clergy. The Holy Father gave the retreat at Ars anyway.

Some Christians are called to be faithful unto death like St. Joan, St. Tarsicius, and St. Stephen. Others, Blessed Kateri Tekakwitha for example, live their faith in spite of the mockery of their families. Some like Blessed Padre Pio endure the suspicions of their religious superiors. Most Christians, however, resemble St. Scholastica and St. John Berchmans—men and women who each day take incremental steps on their life-long pilgrimage toward God.

For First Communicants
St. Tarsicius (3rd century) Feast day: August 15

*First Communicants have as their patron St. Tarsicius, a youth
whose faith in the Real Presence of Christ in the Blessed
Sacrament was so unshakable he gave his life to protect the Host.*

Pope St. Damasus I (reigned 366-384) honored the martyrs above all other saints. Upon being elected pope he used his
office to encourage popular devotion to the men, women, and
children who had testified to the faith with their lives. He had
air shafts opened up to admit light and fresh air to the catacombs, widened the passageways to make it easier for crowds of
pilgrims to visit the graves of the martyrs, and constructed stair-
ways to the tombs of the greatest saints. The tomb chambers he
had adorned with marble and frescoes. Pope Damasus himself
wrote inscriptions that detailed the lives and merits of about
sixty martyrs, one of whom was St. Tarsicius.

Damasus says that Tarsicius was an acolyte, an altar server. At the time an acolyte was not a temporary office for young
boys but one of the minor orders, a step toward ordination to the
priesthood. Damasus does not tell us Tarsicius' age, but a tradition that dates back to at least the sixth century portrays Tarsicius as a boy in his early teens.

Tarsicius had been entrusted with the responsibility of
bringing the Blessed Sacrament to Christians in prison. Although
it was a dangerous assignment, the Roman clergy believed a boy
visiting prisoners would arouse less suspicion than a man. We
also know that it was the custom of the time for acolytes to carry

part of the Blessed Sacrament consecrated at the Pope's Mass to the other priests in Rome, and to take the Eucharist to those who could not come to Mass.

On the Appian Way outside the walls of Rome Tarsicius met a group of pagans. They could see that he was holding something concealed beneath his clothes, but when they asked what he had there Tarsicius refused to tell them or show them what he was carrying. St. Damasus' inscription puts it this way; he refused to "surrender the Sacred Body (of Christ) to rabid dogs."

Someone struck Tarsicius with a club, demanding that he reveal his secret. Still he refused, and now the crowd grew angrier. As they beat Tarsicius with clubs and stones he fell to the ground, face down, still protecting the Blessed Sacrament.

After he died several members of the mob rolled him over. They pried open Tarsicius' hands and searched his clothes but they found nothing. The Blessed Sacrament which the boy had been carrying had vanished.

The Christians of Rome retrieved the martyr's body and buried it in the Catacomb of St. Callixtus on the Appian Way, not far from the place where he had been killed. Centuries later St. Tarsicius' relics were moved to the Church of San Silvestro in Capite where pilgrims come to venerate a martyr who gave his life for the Blessed Sacrament.

For Help Making a Good Confession

Blessed Padre Pio Forgione (1887-1968) Feast Day: September 23

*Who better to invoke for the grace of a good confession than
Blessed Padre Pio? Every day for fifty years he heard confessions
from morning until night, read hearts, revealed to penitents their
most secret sins, and brought countless souls back to God.*

Pio Forgione was born on May 25, 1887, in the village
of Pietrelcina northeast of Naples. His parents, Grazio Forgione
and Maria Giuseppa Di Nunzio Forgione, were peasants who had
a small cottage with a dirt floor in the village and five acres they
cultivated outside the town. The day after his birth they carried
their newly born son to the Church of Santa Anna where he was
christened Francesco.

The Forgiones were a devout family. On Sundays and holy
days, most of the men of the village loitered outside the church
while Mass was being said, but not Grazio. He attended Mass with
his family, received the sacraments frequently, and made a habit of
visiting the Blessed Sacrament on his way to and from the fields.

In August 1875 Grazio took Francesco on a pilgrimage to
the shrine of St. Pellegrine the Martyr at Altavilla Irpina. They
were praying in the church when an ear-splitting scream drew everyone's attention. Up the aisle came a woman carrying her son—
deformed, retarded, and unable to speak. She pushed through the
crowd of worshippers until she stood in front of the statue of the
saint where she pleaded with St. Pellegrine to work a miracle.

Francesco and many others in the church prayed with her,
but when nothing happened the distraught woman dumped her

child at the statue's feet crying, "If you won't cure him, then you can keep him." Then she turned and headed for the door. A moment later the child stood up, called to his mother, and ran down the aisle after her. The crowd in the church erupted in an emotional frenzy. Padre Pio often told this story and always with tears in his eyes.

In 1903, when he was 16 years old, Francesco entered the Capuchin monastery at Morcone. He took the name Pio—Pius in English. Six years later when Brother Pio was ordained a priest he went home to Pietrelcina to celebrate his first Mass.

In 1910 Padre Pio, then only 23 years old, began to experience sharp pains in his hands and feet. He endured the mysterious affliction in silence until at last he admitted to his spiritual director that for over year he had been experiencing what he called "invisible stigmata." Padre Pio's Capuchin superiors sent him to their house in Venafro to undergo a series of medical examinations. At this time he admitted that he also felt the pain of Christ's crown of thorns and of his scourging, but there still was no physical manifestation of these pains. Then on August 5, 1918, Padre Pio experienced a mystical event known as transverberation. In a vision he saw someone he described as "a mysterious person." Suddenly Padre Pio felt as if he had been pierced by a lance, and a wound appeared in his side that bled continuously.

On September 20 Padre Pio was sitting in the chapel choir after Mass when he had another vision. The same "mysterious person" appeared to him, but this time the figure was bleeding from his hands and feet. When the frightening apparition disappeared Padre Pio found blood dripping from wounds in his hands, feet and side. He wrote to his spiritual director, "Dear Father, I am dying of pain because of the wounds and the resulting embarrassment....I am afraid I shall bleed to death if the Lord does not hear my heartfelt supplication to relieve me of this condition." The wounds, however, did not go away; they remained visible and seeped blood for the next 50 years.

Initially the Capuchins did not try to keep Padre Pio and his wounds out of the public eye. Thanks to photographers and to the mass media of the 20th century, Padre Pio's image and story spread throughout Italy and then around the globe. As word of Padre Pio's stigmata became known thousands of people descended on the town of San Giovanni Rotondo near Foggia in southern Italy, hoping for a glimpse of the friar's wounded hands. Immense crowds attended Padre Pio's Masses, which could last two or three hours since Padre Pio often went into ecstatic trances at the altar.

Meanwhile the Vatican sent Padre Pio to a series of medical specialists. There was no denying that the wounds were on Padre Pio's body; the question was what had made them appear. The Church has centuries of experience with people who claim private revelations and signs of divine favor. Some of these men and women have proven to be great saints. Many more were delusional or even frauds. Some had been victims of their families, their spiritual directors, or their religious communities who hoped to gain notoriety by being connected with a "stigmatist." The fact that the Capuchins had permitted great crowds to see Padre Pio made the cautious Roman Curia suspicious.

After studying Padre Pio's case Cardinal Merry del Vall sent the Capuchins these instructions: Padre Pio was to be kept under observation; he was not to say Mass at a fixed time, and it was preferable that he should say Mass in private; he was not permitted to bless people, nor to show his wounds, nor to let anyone kiss them. Nearly a year later the Holy Office declared "it has not noticed any supernatural phenomenon" relating to Padre Pio and ordered the faithful to act accordingly. A few days later the Capuchin Father Provincial forbade Padre Pio to say Mass in public.

The outcry from the faithful was immediate. The mayor of San Giovanni Rotondo, Francesco Morcaldi, led 5000 protesters through the streets. The demonstration nearly degenerated into a riot when some of the protesters threatened to burn down the house of the parish priest, who had testified against Padre Pio. Only the intervention of Mayor Morcaldi saved the rectory. That night a torchlit procession marched on the Capuchin monastery. The next day Padre Pio appeared in church to say Mass.

Two weeks later the Capuchin superiors issued another order transferring Padre Pio to a monastery in Ancona on the other side of Italy and far from the near-hysterical atmosphere of San Giovanni Rotondo. That order lasted a week before pressure from the faithful once again forced the Capuchins to back down. To his credit, Padre Pio never commented on the "triumphs" of his followers over the Church authorities. All he would say was that his strange experiences made him a mystery to himself, but he hoped that they might prove to do some good for others.

Crowds continued to come to San Giovanni and many of the visitors left gifts of cash with the Capuchin friars. In 1925 Padre Pio opened a small hospital and dedicated it to an earlier great stigmatist, St. Francis of Assisi. For the rest of his life Padre Pio worked to build ever finer medical facilities in the neighborhood of San Giovanni. He achieved his greatest ambition when he opened the House for the Relief of Suffering in 1956.

In 1931 the Holy Office took the drastic measure of suspending Padre Pio from all his pastoral functions. He was forbidden to hear confessions and could only say Mass privately inside the friary with one altar server and no congregation. These restrictions remained in place for three years.

Then in the late 1930s a new series of troubles plagued Padre Pio and the Capuchins. Father Raffaelle of St. Elias, the Father Guardian of the friary at San Giovanni, began receiving a stream of anonymous letters accusing Padre Pio of sneaking women into his cell at night. To satisfy himself that the charges were not true Father Raffaelle watched outside Padre Pio's cell night after night. He pasted bits of paper over the door jam that would have torn if anyone had tried to go in or come out of the cell—every morning the paper was intact. Finally Father Raffaelle felt confident that these malicious letters were the work of a crank.

It is said that Padre Pio had the gift of bilocation, a supernatural ability to appear in two places at the same time. His superior Father Carmelo da Sessano told this story. One evening there was a concert at the Capuchin monastery and Padre Pio was among the friars who attended. During the intermission he folded his arms on the chair in front of him and rested his head. His brother friars assumed he was tired and did not disturb him. When the intermission was over Padre Pio sat upright and gave his attention to the rest of the performance.

The next day Father Carmelo stopped to see a sick villager. He found the patient recovered and the family jubilant because Padre Pio had visited them the night before. Father Carmelo said it was not possible. Padre Pio had not gone out at all; he had attended a concert in the monastery. The family insisted that Padre Pio had come to see them, and they specified the time of his visit. It was during the intermission.

Padre Pio became such a popular confessor that by 1948 it was necessary for penitents to make reservations. The penitents "came from all parts of the world," writes the Most Rev. Paola Carta, retired bishop of Foggia. "They waited days and days for their turn...After which they left happy, to tell everyone of the privilege they had received and to keep in their hearts all their lives the memory of the Padre's words sealed in Confession."

What was it about "the Padre's words" that attracted such throngs of penitents? Countless pilgrims recount that Padre Pio revealed their hidden sins in the confessional, paving the way for a true Reconciliation with Christ and His Church. The situation was not always pleasant; if Padre Pio discerned that someone was not sincerely repentant he would roar a command to leave the confessional. Not infrequently, this would spark a crisis in the penitent, who would then return to Padre Pio with true contrition. Those who were truly sorry Padre Pio always welcomed with open arms, giving words of personal encouragement that often seemed divinely inspired.

In 1947 a Polish priest who was studying in Rome, Father Karol Wojtyla, traveled to San Giovanni to confess to Padre Pio. There is a story that Padre Pio told the young priest he would be elected pope and would shed his blood for Christ. While this anecdote is impossible to confirm, much more certain is another encounter Father Wojtyla had with Padre Pio.

In November 1962 Wojtyla was archbishop of Cracow. A friend, Wanda Poltawska, was diagnosed with stomach cancer and given 18 months to live. Archbishop Wojtyla wrote to Padre Pio asking him to pray for Wanda. On the day his friend was scheduled for surgery Archbishop Wojtyla called Wanda's husband Andrzej to see how the operation had gone. Andrzej reported that there had been no surgery. The pre-operation examination found that Wanda's cancerous tumors had inexplicably vanished.

On September 20, 1968 enormous crowds gathered at San Giovanni to celebrate the fiftieth anniversary of Padre Pio's stigmata. The church where he said his 5 a.m. Mass was filled with hundreds of red roses, gifts from admirers from around the globe. Although the church was filled with a congregation of 2000, and an enormous crowd stood in the square outside, no hysterical displays marred the anniversary Mass. Everyone displayed profound reverence for the solemnity of the occasion.

Two days later, when he was saying what would be the last Mass of his life, Padre Pio held up his hands to the congregation. The stigmata was gone. At 2:30 the next morning, September 23, 81-year-old Padre Pio died. More than one hundred thousand mourners attended Padre Pio's funeral, and an endless river of pilgrims has visited his tomb since the day of his burial. Today some 5 million faithful come every year.

For Altar Servers

St. John Berchmans (1599-1621) Feast day: August 13

The patron of altar servers is St. John Berchmans. As a young boy St. John volunteered to serve two or three Masses every day.

John Berchmans was born in Diest in what is now Belgium. His father made his living as a shoemaker, but was held in such high esteem by his neighbors that he was named a burgher, or member of the Diest town council.

Father Peter Emmerich, a monk of Tongerloo Abbey, was John's first teacher and the most important influence on his religious development. He taught John how to write Latin verse, took him on pilgrimages to local shrines, and let the boy accompany him on visits to priests and prelates in the area.

John enjoyed his studies and road trips with Father Emmerich, but acting was his passion. We are told that he gave a memorable performance in a production of *Susanna and the Elders*, a kind of Old Testament court room drama. John played the part of Daniel and brought real enthusiasm to his role as he defended the innocent Susanna from her lecherous accusers.

By now John had expressed an interest in entering the priesthood. The thought that their son had a vocation pleased John's parents. They sent him to the pastor of Diest's Church of Our Lady, where a number of other boys were receiving the rudiments of a clerical education.

When John was thirteen his father sat him down to deliver some bad news. The family had fallen on hard times. John would have to quit school and find work. John became so downcast that his father instantly regretted the idea of taking him out of school. Since the family still had friends in the town, John's father asked around to find John a position that would enable him to continue on the path to the priesthood.

A chaplain in Diest offered a solution to the Berchmans' problem: John could work as a servant in the house of a canon of the cathedral of Mechlin. The boy would receive no pay, but he would be permitted to pursue his priestly studies, for free, at the cathedral school. John accepted the offer immediately.

For two years John juggled schoolwork and housework. What might have exhausted other boys made John blissfully happy. A decisive event occurred in 1615 when the Society of Jesus opened a school in Mechlin. John met the Jesuits and was impressed by what he saw. Over the objections of the canon John transferred to the Jesuit school in 1616. John's father was especially disappointed by the boy's choice. If John had become a diocesan priest he would have had an income he could have used to help his family. As a Jesuit bound by a vow of poverty John would be of no use at all to the family finances.

John loved the rigorous life of the Jesuits, and he was delighted to find that the school staged sacred dramas. Among the Jesuits John developed a religious philosophy that would be made famous almost 200 years later by St. Therese of Lisieux. "Prize little things most of all," he used to say, and then set about the most mundane tasks as if they were the most important jobs in the world. Where other saints practiced extreme penances, John was satisfied if he followed the Jesuit Rule faithfully. Nor did he long for sublime mystical experiences: his favorite religious devotions were prayer before a crucifix and saying the rosary.

In 1616 news from home informed John that his mother had died and his father had entered the diocesan seminary. Eighteen months later John's father was ordained a priest. John was preparing to go to the Roman College for further study but he received permission from his superiors to visit his father before he left Belgium. Sadly the elder Berchmans died suddenly before John arrived.

In Rome John enjoyed a brilliant career as a philosophy student, finishing the course in three years. Just before his final exams, John's superiors asked him to participate in one of the public disputations that were a regular part of Jesuit life at the time. He performed so well he was appointed to the team of Jesuit students slotted to debate students from the Greek College.

On the day after the disputation with the Greek College John fell ill with dysentery. A fever followed, then inflammation of the lungs. It became obvious to everyone at the Roman College that John Berchmans was dying. On August 11 the entire Jesuit community of the Roman College walked in procession to escort the Blessed Sacrament to John's sickroom. After he had received Holy Communion for the last time, he asked for the Last Rites.

The next day a steady stream of priests, lay brothers, and classmates paraded into John's room to say good-bye. He died at 8:30 in the morning of August 13, 1621.

Immediately after his death, John Berchmans was hailed as a saint in his home country. Engravers could not produce enough portraits of the young hero to meet demand. Within a few months of his death 24,000 copies of John Berchmans' portrait had been sold just in the Low Countries. His youth, his down-to-earth piety, and his devotion to the Mass combined to make St. John Berchmans the patron of altar servers.

For a Good Retreat

St. Ignatius Loyola (1491-1556) Feast day: July 31

The Church is rich in spiritual classics but the most influential work of the last 400 years has been St. Ignatius Loyola's Spiritual Exercises. *It is the cornerstone of Jesuit religious formation and the basis of the contemporary retreat movement.*

*I*gnatius Loyola was born into a family of Basque nobility in the family castle of Azpeitia in summer or autumn of 1491, the youngest of the thirteen children of Beltran de Loyola and Marina Saenz de Licona. From his earliest years Ignatius was enchanted by dreams of chivalry and adventure. His own father Beltran had performed deeds of valor in the final years of the *Reconquista*, the Christian reconquest of Spain from the Moors. His oldest brother Juan sailed with Columbus on the discoverer's second expedition to the New World. Other Loyola brothers fought—and some died a hero's death—in France, Naples, the Low Countries, and the Americas. With these models before him it is no wonder that Ignatius longed to sacrifice himself for a great king, serve faithfully a beautiful lady, and win immortal fame in the eyes of the world.

As a young man he tried to live out his notion of the gallant cavalier. He was ambitious, vain, prickly about his honor, a gambler, a fighter, and a sexual adventurer. He longed to prove himself in battle, and to this end at age 26 Ignatius entered the service of Antonio Manrique de Lara, Duke of Najera and viceroy of Navarre, a province which both the French and the Spanish claimed as their own. Ignatius was in Pamplona when the

French attacked the city with an army of 12,000 men and batteries of heavy artillery. The city council surrendered, but Ignatius and the rest of the garrison of the citadel refused to give up. The French attacked and for six hours Ignatius led a desperate defense of the stronghold until finally under the relentless battery of the French cannons a portion of the fortress wall collapsed. Ignatius, sword in hand, stood at the breach, ready to fight to the death, when a cannonball passed between his legs, shattering one and wounding the other. As Ignatius fell to the ground, the garrison's courage gave way, too. They surrendered to the French commander, who spared the lives of the defenders and sent his own doctors to treat Ignatius.

Two weeks later a group of soldiers carried Ignatius in a litter home to Azpeitia to recuperate. The doctors whom the Loyolas summoned said Ignatius' leg had been badly set by the army surgeons: it would have to be broken and reset, a procedure Ignatius described in his autobiography as "butchery." When the wounds healed and the bone mended Ignatius found to his dismay that one leg was now shorter than the other. Worse still was the unsightly protuberance of bone just below the knee which would make it impossible for him to wear the tight-fitting hose and boots that were the fashion at the time. Ignatius commanded his doctors to saw off the offending lump of bone and stretch his leg—a gruesome operation performed without anesthesia.

To help him pass the time during the long weeks of convalescence Ignatius asked his sister-in-law Magdalena for some novels of chivalry to read. She had no such books. In fact the only two books in the house were a life of Christ written by Ludolph the Carthusian and Jacobus de Voragine's collection of saints' lives, *The Golden Legend*. As he read these books Ignatius' heart was touched by grace. He became ashamed of the vanity, pride, and lust that had ruled his life thus far. Ignatius had undergone a conversion, but he had not abandoned his chivalric ideals of suffering and self-sacrifice—instead he had shifted his focus from winning honor in this world to winning salvation in the next. His future course was confirmed for him one night in August or September 1521 when the Blessed Virgin and the Christ Child appeared in his room.

In February 1522 Ignatius began a penitential pilgrimage to Jerusalem, but first he traveled to the shrine of Our Lady at Montserrat. To a priest at the basilica he made a general confession of all the sins of his life. Then on the night before the Feast of the Annunciation Ignatius hung his sword and dagger on the grill before the altar of the Virgin of Montserrat and kept a nocturnal vigil, a deliberate imitation of the chivalric ceremony in which a gentleman prepared for knighthood by spending the entire night in prayer.

His next stop was the town of Manresa where he planned to stay only a few days. In fact Ignatius remained there for nearly a year. He lived in a cell in the Dominican monastery where the friars introduced him to such spiritual classics as Thomas á Kempis' *Imitation of Christ* and taught Ignatius the basics of religious formation—all lessons which he would apply later in his book, the *Spiritual Exercises.*

The *Spiritual Exercises* reflect Ignatius' own conversion experience. They urge the Christian to leave behind the old man, the one obsessed with comfort, respect, success, even his own good health, and become a new person eager to do God's will no matter how unpleasant, painful, personally demeaning, or even dangerous it may be. This theme is summed up in the prayer Ignatius composed to be said while performing the *Exercises*: "Take O Lord and receive my entire liberty, my memory, my understanding and my whole will. All that I am and all that I possess you have given me: I surrender it all to you to be disposed of according to your will. Give me only your love and your grace; with these I will be rich enough and will desire nothing more."

During the full 30 days it takes to complete the *Spiritual Exercises* the retreatant is challenged to examine his actions, his motivations, and his desires, and to give up all spiritually harmful attachments. While other spiritual classics are inspirational, the *Exercises* are practical. The principles discussed in the book are meant to be put into action, a distinction which has made Ignatius' *Spiritual Exercises* a vital force in the life of the Church for over 400 years.

When at last Ignatius arrived in Jerusalem on September 4, 1523, he was so deeply moved by the Holy Sepulcher, the Garden of Olives, the Mount of the Ascension, and other sites associated with the life of Our Lord that he decided to pass the rest of his life in the Holy Land. The Franciscan guardian of the holy places would not permit it: he had encountered zealous, naive souls like Ignatius before and they were nothing but trouble. If they did not get themselves arrested by the Turks, the Middle Eastern climate made them ill. When Ignatius declared that he was resolved to remain in Jerusalem nonetheless, the Franciscan guardian responded that the pope had authorized him to excommunicate disobedient pilgrims. So Ignatius returned to Spain, to Alcala where he applied for admission to the university, thus taking the first step toward his long-term goal, ordination to the priesthood.

In his zeal to bring souls to God Ignatius began to teach university students and adults how to pray and how to interpret the gospels. Since he was a layman with no formal training of any kind in theology or biblical studies, Ignatius' makeshift religion classes fell afoul of the Inquisition. He spent 42 days in an Inquisition prison before he was cleared of any suspicion of heresy. Nonetheless his examiners insisted that he stop teaching religion until he had a solid education in philosophy and theology. Instead Ignatius left Alcala for Salamanca where once again he preached in the streets, and once again the Inquisition had him arrested. This time he spent 22 days in prison before he was released with the understanding that he could teach children but not adults.

Two terms in Inquisition prisons finally made an impression on Ignatius. He decided to get a formal education at the University of Paris, regarded as one of the preeminent theology schools in Europe. In Paris he shared rooms with St. Francis Xavier and St. Peter Faber. Under Ignatius' influence both men abandoned their plans for worldly careers in favor of a life dedicated to God. In 1534 when the number of Ignatius' companions had grown to eight, the little band decided to take private vows of poverty and chastity. On the Feast of the Assumption they met in the crypt of the chapel of Saint Denis on Montmartre where Faber, the only priest among them, said Mass. Before they received Holy Communion they all recited their vows. The idea of forming a religious order had not yet occurred to them, but their private ceremony bound these men more closely together and strengthened their resolve to work for the greater glory of God.

Once all eight had completed their university education, perhaps inspired by Ignatius' tales of his own journey to the Holy Land, they decided to make a group pilgrimage to Palestine. They traveled to Italy to embark from Venice but the presence of Turkish warships in the Adriatic made it too dangerous to sail. Instead they began preaching and teaching in Padua, Siena, Bologna, and Vicenza. When people asked who they were, they said they were the *Compañia de Jesús*, or in Latin the *Societas Jesu*, from which comes the Jesuits' English name the Society of Jesus.

In November 1537 Ignatius, Faber and James Lainez set out for Rome to offer their services to Pope Paul III. In a chapel at La Storta a few miles from the Eternal City Ignatius had a vision of God the Father in which He promised, "I will be favorable to you in Rome." And He was; these zealous, university-trained men impressed Paul III. He assigned Faber and Lainez to teach theology and Scripture at Rome's Sapienza University while Ignatius carried out his own impromptu ministry of preaching, teaching, and bringing souls to God. In Rome Ignatius, now a priest, offered his first Mass on Christmas Eve. Fittingly, this Mass was celebrated at the Basilica of Santa Maria Maggiore in the Chapel of the Manger where a relic of Christ's crib is displayed.

By now Ignatius and his companions began to see themselves as a distinct religious congregation of teachers of Catholic doctrine, ready to do anything or go anywhere at the command of the pope. On September 27, 1540, Pope Paul III gave formal approval to the Society of Jesus. Ignatius was unanimously elected the first general of the order. For the last fifteen years of his life he directed the Jesuits, overseeing the expansion of his order from eight to 1000 members with 76 houses in 12 provinces across the globe—including Brazil, Japan, and India.

During a heat wave in July 1554 Ignatius became ill with a stomach ailment. On July 30 Ignatius asked his secretary Juan de Polanco to go to the pope with a request for his blessing on Ignatius and the Society of Jesus. Polanco did not think Ignatius was dying; he told Ignatius that he would go see the pope tomorrow. "I would be pleased more today than tomorrow, or the sooner the better," Ignatius said. "But do what you think best in the matter."

At dawn the next day the infirmarian visited Ignatius' room and was shocked to find him dying. Polanco raced to the Vatican but by the time he returned Ignatius Loyola was dead— without receiving the papal blessing or even the Last Rites.

He was buried in the little church of St. Mary of the Way. When that church was replaced by the magnificent Gesu, Ignatius' remains were transferred there. Pope Gregory XV canonized Ignatius on March 12, 1622, during the same ceremony in which he canonized Teresa of Avila, Isidore the Farmer, Philip Neri, and Francis Xavier.

When Mocked for Christian Living

Blessed Kateri Tekakwitha (1656-1680) Feast Day: July 14

*Christians have always endured mockery and scorn for
practicing a faith that is often at odds with the larger society.
Their patron is Blessed Kateri Tekakwitha who was so severely
abused by her relatives and fellow tribesmen that she could
find peace only by leaving her home in New York and
traveling 200 miles to a Christian Indian village in Quebec.*

If any place in the United States is holy ground it is the
site of the Mohawk village of Ossernenon in the Mohawk Valley
near Auriesville, New York. Three Jesuit martyrs died there: St.
Rene Goupil in 1642, and St. Jean de la Lande and St. Isaac Jogues
in 1646. Ten years later Blessed Kateri Tekakwitha was born in the
same village.

Her mother Kahenta was a Christian Algonquin who had
been captured near Trois Rivieres, Quebec, during the incessant
war between the Hurons and the Iroquois. She might have been
killed if a warrior of the Turtle clan had not volunteered to take
her into his lodge as his wife. Kahenta bore two children, a girl
whom they named Tekakwitha, and then a boy. We do not know
the names of Kateri's father and brother.

In 1660 when Kateri was only four years old a smallpox
epidemic struck Ossernenon. Smallpox, unknown in the Americas until the arrival of the Europeans, had a devastating effect
on the Native American tribes who had no natural resistance to
the disease. Kateri's mother, father, and baby brother all died in
the epidemic. Kateri also was infected and although she survived

the disease it severely weakened her eyesight and left her face badly scarred.

Her two aunts and an uncle gave the orphan a home, but for all the good intentions of her relatives Kateri grew up self-conscious and shy. As a very young girl she decided never to marry. Since she was not a Christian at the time and there was no Mohawk equivalent of the consecrated life of a nun, Kateri's biographers have wondered what prompted this unusual resolution. Some attribute it to divine intervention, a secret prompting of her heart that she did not yet understand. It may be that Christ was calling her to be His alone. It is also possible that Kateri, who felt awkward even among relatives who wanted to help her, could not imagine being intimate with a man, nor bear the anxiety of having children who might die in the next epidemic.

When Kateri was eleven years old there arrived in her village three French Jesuit priests. Fathers Jacques Fremin, Jacques Bruyas, and Jean Pierron had traveled with the Mohawk deputies who were returning home from Quebec after making peace with the French. These priests, whom her uncle welcomed as guests into his lodge, were the first missionaries Kateri had ever seen. No doubt the Jesuits discussed the basic principles of Christianity with their hosts, but no one in the family, Kateri included, converted. After three days the priests moved on. Nearly eight years would pass before another missionary came to the village.

It was during those years that Kateri's relatives and tribesmen learned of her decision never to marry. At first they were confused. Then their confusion turned to anger, and their anger to mockery.

By now repeated epidemics had forced the Turtle clan to abandon Ossernenon and build a new village, Caughnawaga, north of the Mohawk River near the modern town of Fonda, New York. Father Jacques de Lamberville, SJ, arrived in the new village in 1675. He baptized Kateri, his first and only convert, on

Easter 1676. It was at her baptism that she took the name "Kateri," Iroquois for Catherine.

Although Kateri was the only Christian in the village, she practiced her faith with fervent determination and devotion. Her uncle and aunts looked for any excuse to beat her. They refused to give her any food on Sundays because she refused to do any work on the Lord's day. When she walked outside her relatives' lodge, children threw stones at her. Once a warrior ran toward her brandishing a tomahawk; Kateri felt she was about to be killed. Life for this lonely convert had become unbearable.

Father de Lamberville urged her to leave Caughnawaga and go to the Christian Indian village of Saint Francis Xavier Mission at Kahnawake opposite Montreal on the St. Lawrence River. The mission was 200 miles away yet Kateri walked the entire distance alone. She left her home on July 14 and arrived in October 1677. A Christian Indian, Anastasia Tegonhatsihonga, who had known Kateri's mother, welcomed the girl into her cabin.

Safe at last among people who shared her faith and respected her vow of virginity, Kateri practiced her faith with new zeal. She attended two Masses every morning, and at the end of the day returned to the chapel for Vespers or Benediction of the Blessed Sacrament. In addition to the meatless Fridays that were customary at the time, she fasted on Wednesdays and Saturdays. On Christmas Day 1677, she made her First Holy Communion. Her spiritual director, Father Pierre Cholenec, said that for the last three years of her life Kateri tried "to preserve throughout the entire day the good sentiments she had experienced in the morning at the foot of the altar." She showed such profound devotion when she received the Sacred Host that other Christian Indians jostled each other for the privilege of kneeling beside her at the altar rail.

Kateri's genuine sanctity, combined with her desire for spiritual knowledge and her eagerness to apply as much of it as she understood, impressed not only the Christian Indians and the French colonists, but also the French missionaries. The priests worried how much of the Catholic faith the Indians understood and accepted. In Kateri they found a true believer. In 1679 she formalized her life long resolution never to marry by taking a private vow of perpetual virginity.

At the end of Lent Kateri became seriously ill and died on Wednesday during Holy Week, April 17, 1680 at Kahnawake. Father Cholenec who witnessed her death and remained in prayer beside her body testified that the smallpox scars that had disfigured Kateri's face disappeared "suddenly about a quarter of an hour after death, and [her face] became in a moment so fair and beautiful that noticing the change I cried out in surprise." Two French settlers also saw the miracle and honored the Mohawk saint by making a wooden coffin for her (usually the dead, French and Indian, were buried wrapped in a shroud). When the mission moved several years later the Jesuits considered the bones of Kateri too valuable to leave behind. The coffin enabled them to identify her remains.

Devotion to Kateri began immediately, but the process for Kateri's canonization has moved slowly. Pope John Paul II declared her Blessed on June 22, 1980, in the presence of hundreds of Indians from North America. She is the first Native American beatified by the Roman Catholic Church and a model for all those who endure ridicule for their faith.

For Lapsed Catholics
St. Monica (331-387) Feast day: August 27

*St. Monica prayed for seventeen years that her son, Augustine,
would give up his sinful life and return to the Church.
Catholics have asked St. Monica to intercede for
lapsed members of their families at least since
the mid 15th century when Pope Eugenius IV
established the Confraternity of St. Monica.*

St. Monica like most saints never told her own story. She
was fortunate however to have as her personal biographer her son,
the great St. Augustine.

Monica was born in the rural town of Thagaste, now Souk
Ahras in Algeria. It was a small place of only a few thousand inhabitants surrounded by farms. Monica and her family were Ber-
bers, the native people of the country. This part of North Africa
was religiously diverse. Roman paganism, the old Carthaginian
paganism (Monica's name was derived from that of the goddess
Mon), a host of cults, and various strains of Christianity all existed side by side.

As the daughter of Catholics Monica was brought up in
the old religious traditions of the Church in Africa, such as fasting all day Saturday in preparation for Sunday Mass, and attending banquets (which sometimes degenerated into drinking parties)
at the tombs of martyrs on their feast days. She remained loyal to
these acts of devotion for most of her life, even after they had
gone out of fashion among African Catholics.

As an adolescent girl Monica developed a taste for wine.

It was her responsibility to go to the cellar and bring wine to the table for her parents. She got into the habit of taking a few surreptitious sips before returning to the dining room. Soon she was downing a cup a day. A servant who caught her humiliated Monica, calling her a little drunkard. Monica felt the humiliation keenly and ever after was careful to restrict her consumption of wine.

Although this story may sound like the Roman version of the child caught with her hand in the cookie jar, in Monica's world it was a more serious infraction. Fourth-century Roman society believed wine was an erotic stimulant. A young girl who drank wine in secret was not keeping her passions under control and might even be in danger of compromising her virtue.

Sometime before the year 354 Monica's parents arranged a marriage for her to Patricius, a pagan, a Roman citizen, and a town councilor of Thagaste. St. Augustine always described his father as poor. Certainly Patricius was not an aristocrat (he was probably descended from freedmen, slaves who had been liberated by their master). Nonetheless Patricius owned land, a good house in town, and was comfortable enough financially that he never had to work to support himself and his family.

Patricius' own mother lived with him and his new wife. Initially Monica and her mother-in-law bickered. We know that some of the women slaves of the household took sides in the women's quarrel. On one occasion Patricius' mother asked him to have some of these slaves beaten because their gossip was only increasing the antagonism between herself and Monica. In time Monica and her mother-in-law made peace, and Monica even persuaded her mother-in-law to become a Christian.

A tiresome mother-in-law was not all Monica had to endure. Patricius had a violent temper. He never beat his wife, but his rages tested Monica's patience. Even more distressing were Patricius' infidelities. In his *Confessions* St. Augustine tells us that his mother never reproached her husband for cheating on her. Among her friends however Monica, who had a gift for sarcasm, described all Roman wives as "slaves" who dared not "withstand their masters."

Monica gave birth to Augustine on November 13, 354. She had other children, a son Navigius and a daughter Perpetua, but we are not certain about their birth order. Augustine was not baptized at birth. Since baptism washes away all sin many Christian parents postponed the sacrament. It was not uncommon for believers to wait until they were on their deathbed to be baptized. When Augustine was born Monica saw to it that he was marked with holy oil in the sign of the cross and had blessed salt, a sign of exorcism, sprinkled on his tongue. This ceremony would have made him a catechumen, one who was taking instruction in the faith, and Monica was Augustine's teacher.

Augustine was Monica's favorite. She breast fed him herself at a time when other mothers of her class would have given their child to a wet nurse. She liked to have her boy with her, "as is the way with mothers," Augustine recalled, "but far more than most mothers."

Patricius loved Augustine dearly. He was ambitious for his son. By the time Augustine was 15 his father had scraped together enough money to send him to school at Madaura, a university town located about 40 miles from Thagaste. The effort and expense Patricius incurred won him universal respect in town. After one year, however, the money ran out and Augustine was compelled to return home while his father tried to raise more funds so his boy could continue his education.

One day during Augustine's year of idleness father and son went to the baths together. For the first time Patricius realized that Augustine was on the verge of manhood. That night, overjoyed at the thought that soon he would have grandchildren and in celebration of Augustine's budding virility, Patricius got drunk.

Monica, however, was not ready to see Augustine marry.

She worried that if he married and started a family he would never finish his education nor have any chance of going on to a lucrative career. Instead of looking for a bride for her 16-year-old son she warned him against committing sexual sins, especially the sin of adultery. Augustine treated her "womanish advice" with contempt. He was, he says in his *Confessions*, "in the mood to be seduced." Later Augustine would blame Monica for not having married him off. If his mother had found him a wife, Augustine argues unfairly, he would not have lived in sin with his mistress for so many years.

Meanwhile Patricius came around to Monica's way of thinking. He put away his plans of becoming a grandfather and concentrated on getting Augustine back into school. Patricius called on Romanianus, the most prominent and wealthiest man in the district. A patron-client relationship existed between Romanianus and Patricius that was further strengthened by a distant blood tie. Romanianus made a generous offer: he would subsidize Augustine's entire education—not at Madaura, but at cosmopolitan Carthage, the city known as "Rome in Africa."

In 371 at age 17 Augustine went to Carthage to continue his studies. He had barely settled in when word came from home that Patricius was dead. Monica's grief at the death of her husband was compounded when word reached her from Carthage that Augustine had taken a mistress. A year later the woman (in none of his writings does Augustine ever mention her name) gave birth to a baby boy they named Adeodatus, meaning "gift from God."

Augustine returned home to Thagaste in 375 to take a post teaching literature. In Carthage he had joined the Manichean sect, a group that taught that the universe was ruled by two opposite powers which were constantly in conflict. One, the Father of Greatness, embraced all positive immaterial qualities such as light and intelligence. The other, generally called Satan, ruled over base matter and was the cause of all that was evil in the world. Every human being was a battleground between these immortal forces of good and evil. According to the Manichees, over the course of history several "Jesuses" had come to earth to assist humankind in its struggle against Satan, but none of these Jesus figures were saviors who would triumph over Satan.

To Catholics, especially to one as devout as Monica, Manicheism was the grossest of all heresies. When Monica learned what her son had become she barred the door and refused to let him in her house. So Augustine went to live with his patron Romanianus who was also a Manichee.

Monica turned to God, weeping for her son as if he were dead. She went to see a bishop who had been raised a Manichee but had converted to Catholicism. Monica asked him to go speak with Augustine to show him his errors, but the bishop answered that Augustine was still in the first flush of his conversion; he was not ready to listen to sound arguments against Manicheism. Monica would not take no as an answer. She pleaded and wept and made such a nuisance of herself that the bishop lost his temper. "Go away from me," he said. Then getting some of his composure back he added, "Don't worry. It is not possible that the son of so many tears should be lost forever."

One night God sent Monica a dream to console her. She saw herself standing on a narrow wooden beam with a handsome, radiant young man. The youth told her to dry her tears because some day her son would be with her. When she told Augustine her dream he said they could indeed be together if she became a Manichee. Monica's sarcasm served her again. She answered, "He didn't say I was to be with you. He said you were to be with me!"

In 383 Augustine announced that he was going to Rome to pursue his teaching career. His mistress and Adeodatus would accompany him. Monica wanted to go as well, but rather than refuse her outright Augustine did something very cruel. At the harbor he took her to see a small chapel dedicated to the martyr St. Cyprian. While Monica prayed Augustine hurried to the ship and sailed without her. By the time Monica came out of the chapel Augustine's ship was already out of sight. She stood alone on the dock, beside herself with grief.

Mother and son did not see each for two years. In the spring of 385 she decided to go to Rome, but Augustine was no longer there. He had come to Rome in hopes of making more money and winning recognition as a teacher and philosopher. Instead, a number of Augustine's students cheated him out of his fees. Furthermore, the city was becoming a backwater. The emperor had made Milan his capital where he welcomed to his court intellectuals and poets from across the empire. Augustine had even heard good things about the bishop of Milan, St. Ambrose, whose learned sermons were rooted in a sound classical education. Thus Augustine traveled north to Milan—and Monica followed him.

In Milan all of Monica's prayers and tears for Augustine bore fruit. Years earlier she had delayed arranging a marriage for him so he could finish his education. Now that education was working in Monica's favor. Augustine had become disenchanted with Manicheism. In a gloomy mood he began rereading the *Academica* by his favorite classical author, Cicero. In this book the old Roman orator derided impulsive schoolboys who claim to seek the truth but become beguiled by a peculiar sect. Augustine took Cicero's reproach to heart. He lost his faith in Manichean doctrine, and even confidence in his ability to discern what was good and true.

Monica had become a member of St. Ambrose's congregation. During Holy Week 386, when the Emperor Theodosius had surrounded Ambrose's basilica with troops because the bishop would not surrender any Catholic church to the Arian heretics, Monica had been one of the throng of Catholics who barricaded themselves with Ambrose inside the church. Then on Holy Thursday Theodosius backed down; the troops were returned to their barracks and the churches of Milan were left undisturbed. Ambrose had won his showdown with the emperor.

Ambrose's moral authority impressed Augustine almost as much as his erudition. Yearning for the truth, longing to be taught, Augustine accompanied his mother to any Mass where Ambrose was scheduled to preach.

Once Augustine began taking instruction in the faith from Ambrose, Monica felt confident enough to move against an aspect of her son's life which she had tolerated for years: his mistress. Augustine knew that as a Catholic he could not continue to live with this woman as his common-law wife. Since she was of low birth he was reluctant to marry her, and besides Monica was already negotiating his marriage to a Catholic heiress. Augustine would have to send away the woman he had lived with for 17 years. In the *Confessions*, Augustine wrote that sending away the mother of his son "cut and wounded" his heart. She returned to Africa, but left their son Adeodatus with Augustine.

On the night of April 24-25, 387, at the Mass of the Easter Vigil, St. Ambrose baptized both Augustine and Adeodatus. The prediction that the irritable African bishop had made to Monica so many years before had been fulfilled at last.

After his baptism Augustine resolved to return home to Thagaste. There he, Monica, Adeodatus, and a handful of like-minded friends would live as a kind of monastic community. They made their way to Ostia, the port of Rome, and waited for a ship that would take them back to Africa. One day while they were waiting Monica and Augustine stood beside a window discussing the joys the saints must experience in Heaven.

Suddenly mother and son were caught up in an ecstasy and were granted a glimpse of the beatific vision. When the vision had faded away Monica said, "Son, for my part I have no further joy in any thing in this life....There was only one reason I wanted to linger in this life—to see you become a Catholic Christian before I died. Now that my God has done this for me, what more is there for me to do here?"

Five days later, Monica fell ill with a fever. As she drifted in and out of consciousness, Augustine, Adeodatus, and Augustine's brother Navigius remained at her side. At one point she told her sons to bury her in Ostia. Navigius, trying to cheer her up, said he hoped she would recover so they could return to Africa, then some day far in the future they would bury her in her own country. Monica answered, "Lay this body anywhere; do not worry about this: I have only one request, that wherever you are you remember me at the altar of the Lord."

On the ninth day of her illness, Monica died. She was 56 years old. As Augustine closed his mother's eyes, Adeodatus collapsed in grief. When the boy had recovered himself everyone in the house gathered around Monica's deathbed to chant Psalm 100, "I will sing of loyalty and of justice; to thee, O Lord, I will sing."

In 1430 Monica's tomb was discovered in Ostia. Pope Martin V transferred her relics to Rome, enshrining them under the altar in a side chapel of the Church of St. Augustine. A fragment of the original inscription on St. Monica's tomb was discovered in 1945 by two young boys who were digging beside Ostia's Church of St. Aurea.

In the 15th century Pope Eugenius IV established a confraternity of St. Monica whose members prayed for lapsed Catholics. This pious organization was revived in 1850 in Paris by a group of French women who gathered together under the patronage of St. Monica to pray for sons and husbands who had left the Church.

For Deacons
St. Stephen (died c. 34) Feast day: December 26

Deacons have as their patron St. Stephen, one of the first seven deacons of the Church. He was ordained by the apostles to serve the Christians of Jerusalem.

Everything we know about St. Stephen, one of the first deacons and the first martyr, comes from chapters six and seven of the Acts of the Apostles in the New Testament.

Stephen came from a family of Hellenists, Jews who had emigrated from Palestine to one of the Greek-speaking provinces of the Roman Empire. Hellenists spoke Greek rather than Aramaic, and in the synagogues heard the Scriptures read in Greek rather than Hebrew. The sixth chapter of Acts tells us that tension arose between the Greek Jewish converts to Christianity and the Palestinian Jewish converts. The Greeks said that their widows and needy were being neglected in favor of the Hebrew poor. In an effort to resolve the problem the apostles ordained seven men as deacons to serve the poor and preach the faith. The first name on this list of seven is Stephen.

St. Luke, the author of Acts, tells us that Stephen was a handsome man with "the face of an angel...full of grace and fortitude," who in his zeal for the faith debated with members of four different Greek synagogues. When Stephen's eloquence got the better of the Hellenist Jews his angry opponents seized him and dragged him off to the court of the Sanhedrin. There false witnesses charged him with blasphemy, denouncing the Temple sacrifices, and reviling the Law of Moses.

The High Priest (perhaps Caiaphas, the same High Priest who tried Jesus) asked Stephen if he had anything to say. In answer to these accusations Stephen delivered a lengthy speech which traced the sacred history of the Jews from Abraham to their own day. He concluded his discourse with a denunciation of his accusers and judges: "You stiffnecked people, uncircumcised in heart and ears, you always resist the Holy Spirit. As your fathers did, so do you. Which of the prophets did not your fathers persecute?"

Oblivious to the commotion in the court, Stephen antagonized his audience further by characterizing them as "betrayers and murderers" who did not keep the Law of Moses. Then, suddenly filled with the Holy Spirit, he looked to Heaven and cried out, "Behold, I see the heavens opened, and the Son of Man standing on the right hand of God."

This was too much for the men in the court. They rushed upon Stephen, dragged him outside the city walls, and stoned him to death. One of the Jewish officials overseeing this brutality was a man named Saul—known to us as the Apostle Paul.

As the stones struck him, Stephen prayed, "Lord Jesus, receive my spirit." Then, down on his knees and near death, he prayed again, "Lord, do not hold this sin against them." After the mob had dispersed Christians removed Stephen's body for burial.

Although St. Stephen's feast day was observed by the ancient Church the location of his tomb was forgotten. In 415 a priest named Lucian learned through a vision that St. Stephen's body was buried in Caphar Gamala north of Jerusalem. With Bishop John of Jerusalem and several other bishops Lucian set out for the site where they found the relics of the first martyr. A large crowd of Christians had followed the clergy to the site, and when the tomb was opened 73 sick people were healed.

Bishop John formed a procession to escort St. Stephen's relics to Jerusalem where they were enshrined in the Church of Sion. In Book 22 of his *City of God*, St. Augustine, who was alive at the time, testifies to the discovery of St. Stephen's tomb and reports the miracles wrought by some relics of St. Stephen that were brought to Africa.

St. Stephen has always been venerated by deacons as their special patron. Today a network of deacon-intercessors who call themselves the Sons of St. Stephen pray daily for an end to abortion, for the protection of families, for the health of the Holy Father, and for all priests and bishops that they may be inspired by St. Stephen to be courageous in teaching and bearing witness to the truth.

For Cloistered Nuns
St. Scholastica (c.480-547) Feast day: February 10

*As her brother St. Benedict is the father of monks in the
Western Church, St. Scholastica is the mother of all orders
of cloistered nuns. From her convent on Monte Cassino,
the Benedictine sisters spread around the globe.*

An old tradition tells us that Scholastica and Benedict
were twins whose mother died giving birth to them. They were
born in the province of Nursia, near Assisi, in what is now Umbria. As landowners the twins' parents were well-off but the family was not part of the aristocracy.

While she was still a child, perhaps from the time of her
birth, Scholastica's father dedicated her to God. We do not know
when she left her home to live with other religious women. We
do know that when Benedict founded his monastery at Monte
Cassino, Scholastica moved there, too, and founded the convent
that became the motherhouse of all Benedictine nuns.

Scholastica's convent was located about five miles from
Benedict's monastery. Since men were not permitted inside the
convent and women were not permitted inside the monastery,
once a year Benedict and Scholastica met at a small house half-
way between their two religious communities. The story of what
happened the last time the brother and sister met comes to us
from Pope St. Gregory the Great; he testifies that he heard the
story from four of Benedict's disciples.

Benedict brought a few monks from the abbey to share his
visit with Scholastica. After passing a pleasant day in conversa-

tion and prayer, they had dinner together but lingered so long talking after the meal that before anyone became aware of the time it had grown very late. Benedict rose to leave but Scholastica pleaded with him to stay a little longer. "Please," she said, "do not leave me tonight. Stay, and we will talk about Heaven until morning."

Benedict was surprised that his sister would suggest that they break the Rule. "What are you saying," he said. "You know I can't stay away from the monastery all night."

Scholastica bowed her head and folded her hands on the table, the very picture of resignation. Benedict and his monks had barely stepped toward the door when a flash of lightning split the night sky and a violent storm shook the little house. Benedict turned on his sister whose head was still bowed. "God forgive you! What have you done?"

Scholastica looked her brother in the eye and said, "When I asked you for a favor you would not listen to me. So I asked God, and He heard my prayer. Go ahead—leave if you can. Leave me and return to your monastery." Seeing that he was defeated Benedict sat down and spent the rest of the night talking with Scholastica. The next morning the storm abated and brother and sister returned to their communities.

Three days later Benedict was looking out the window of his cell when he saw Scholastica's soul flying to Heaven in the shape of a white dove. He sent some monks to her convent to carry Scholastica's body to Monte Cassino where Benedict buried it in the tomb he had prepared for himself. Three years later when Benedict died he was buried in the same vault. Sister and brother are still enshrined together in the crypt of the Abbey of Monte Cassino.

While some Benedictine sisters pursue an active apostolate teaching or nursing, many Benedictine nuns follow the original charism of their order as it was laid down by St. Scholastica, living a life devoted to prayer and contemplation.

For Parish Priests

St. John Mary Vianney (1786-1859) Feast day: August 4

St. John Mary Vianney, the patron of parish priests, labored for 41 years to bring about the total conversion of his tiny parish.

St. John Mary Vianney is popularly known as the Curé of Ars. In France a curé is a pastor of a parish, the man who cares for souls. In fact the French word curé comes from the same root as the English word cure, and certainly there was a great deal in Vianney's time which needed to be made right.

He was three years old when the French Revolution broke out, sweeping away almost all of the old order—the good and the bad. The principles of liberty, equality, and fraternity still sound thrilling, but the sad truth is that the leaders of the Revolution betrayed their ideals almost from the beginning. The Church was targeted because the revolutionaries regarded it as a prop of the monarchy and the aristocracy. Contempt for God, hatred of the holy, worship of self and of material goods, the insignificance of the individual in the eyes of the state—these became part of the legacy Robespierre and his followers bequeathed to the world. In the confused and angry decades that followed, the Curé of Ars tried to draw people out of their selfishness, out of their hate-filled philosophies, and back to God.

John Mary Vianney was born into a family of peasants in the village of Dardilly not far from Lyons on May 8, 1786. During his childhood his family practiced the Catholic faith in secret. Among the other outrages the Revolution inflicted on the Church—from guillotining Carmelite nuns to setting up a prostitute costumed as the "Goddess of Reason" on the High Altar of Notre Dame in Paris—was an attempt to impose upon the Catholic faithful "constitutional" clergy, priests who had renounced their loyalty to the pope and given their allegiance entirely to the state. One such priest was sent to staff the parish of Dardilly, but the Vianney family and most of their neighbors refused to attend a church run by a schismatic priest who preached revolution instead of the gospel from the pulpit. On Sundays and holy days they slipped off to barns or farmhouses to hear Mass offered by outlaw priests who had remained loyal to Rome. It was dangerous to defy the Revolution. In nearby Lyon, Joseph Fouché, a government official who once had been an Oratorian priest, sent 130 Catholic priests to the guillotine.

Vianney was 18 when he resolved to become a priest. This was a difficult proposition since he had not had more than a few months of formal education. At age 20 his parents gave him permission to leave home for the preparatory seminary Father Charles Balley operated in his rectory in the nearby village of Ecully. After so many years without any schooling at all study came hard to Vianney. Latin proved especially difficult to master, so much so that he sought special heavenly assistance by making a pilgrimage on foot to the tomb of St. John Regis, sixty miles away. Vianney returned from the shrine with more confidence, although his seminary studies would always be difficult for him.

In 1809 Vianney received a draft notice for Napoleon's army, which had started conscripting even seminary students to fight its continual wars. Vianney reported as ordered but became desperately ill. After eight weeks in a military hospital he was ready for duty, but on the day his regiment set out Vianney missed roll call. He tried to catch up but the troops were far ahead of him. As he was resting beside the road a man came along, picked up Vianney's knapsack, and urged the young man to follow him. The stranger led Vianney to a hut in the forest where he introduced himself as "a fellow deserter." Poor Vianney didn't think of himself as a deserter, just a little slow. He called on Paul Fayot, the mayor of the village of Les Noes, for help in rejoining the regiment, but the mayor pointed out that by being so late Vianney would already be listed as a runaway. Then he offered Vianney refuge in the home of a widowed cousin.

Vianney remained at the home of the mayor's cousin for fourteen months, helping to work the farm and giving lessons to the children. The villagers must have grown fond of their refugee. When Napoleon issued an amnesty to all deserters and Vianney prepared to go home, the townspeople had the village tailor make Vianney a soutane.

Upon Vianney's return home Father Balley sent him to the minor seminary. There he had an especially difficult time with philosophy and with his old nemesis, Latin. During the summer break Father Balley gave him crash courses in both subjects, but at the end of the school term Vianney's grades were wretched. In near despair he went to his mother's grave in the churchyard and wept, begging her to pray for him so he could become a priest.

Before he could be ordained to minor orders Vianney had to pass an oral examination. When he sat before the examiners Vianney panicked and his mind went blank. Once again Father Balley came to the rescue. He convinced the chief examiner to test Vianney in French in the rectory of Ecully, where he felt at home. Under these circumstances Vianney did very well. He received the minor orders of acolyte, exorcist, lector, and porter, in the Cathedral of Lyon. For the next year he studied with Father Balley in preparation for ordination to the priesthood, which he received at last on August 12, 1815. He was named assistant to Father Balley since no other pastor would take him.

Vianney and Balley had two happy, austere, religiously intense years together before Father Balley died. The pastor who replaced Father Balley did not want Father Vianney as his assistant. The bishop then assigned him to the remote parish of Ars, a place with 260 inhabitants, 40 houses, and four taverns. It was the Siberia of the diocese.

The Revolution had been hard on religious life in Ars; two curés had left the priesthood and the local freethinkers had taken over the parish church and turned it into a temple for the goddess Reason. For years the village had been without the Mass, the sacraments, or catechesis. On Sundays the villagers met in the square for dances that always seemed to end in a drunken riot.

From the day he was installed as curé in 1818 Vianney set about recalling the lapsed to the faith. He launched a campaign against drunkenness and the madness of poor people who squandered what little money they had in taverns. He preached against obscene language, and to make certain his congregation didn't miss his meaning he repeated the offensive words in the pulpit. It took eight years for Vianney to bring Ars to strict observance of Sunday as a day of rest with Mass in the morning, Vespers in the afternoon, and no unnecessary physical labor all day. A harder fight, and one contemporary Christians find hard to understand, was Vianney's war against dancing. He considered village dances lewd, riotous, and occasions of sin—and he wasn't alone in this opinion. Throughout the 19th century both Catholic and Protestant clergy in Europe and the United States preached against dancing. To underscore his point, in the Ars church Vianney hung a sign over the statue of St. John the Baptist that read, "His head was the price of a dance!"

He set a personal example of holiness by living in a very austere style. His diet rarely extended beyond potatoes and milk. His furniture in the rectory was the plainest sort. Parishioners who came to church at dawn for the early Mass often found him on his knees before the Blessed Sacrament, arms stretched out like a cross, praying for his parish. His most frequent prayers were "My God, my all. You see how I love you and I do not love you enough" and "My God, here is all—take all but convert my parish."

Not everyone wanted to be converted. For 18 months an array of parishioners in Ars harassed their priest by vandalizing the rectory, throwing manure at the door, and sending complaints to the bishop that Vianney had fathered a child by a village girl. Even some of Vianney's fellow priests joined in the calumny. At a retreat of the diocesan clergy one priest described Vianney as a madman. The bishop said, "Gentlemen, I wish all my clergy had a small grain of the same madness."

At the command of his bishop Vianney traveled to neighboring towns to give parish missions. This is how he developed a reputation as an insightful, compassionate, but compelling confessor. At the town of Montmerle so many people came to confess to the Curé that he barely left the church for six days. Soon Vianney would be spending up to ten hours in the Ars confessional during winter, sixteen hours in summer. In the final years of his life 80,000 penitents a year, from all over Europe and from as far away as the United States, came to Ars to make their confession to Vianney. Father George Rutler, who has written a biography of the Curé of Ars, wonders "what the equivalent would be today, when travel is so much easier."

His sermons also drew crowds. At Limas he walked into the church on the first night of his mission to find the sanctuary crowded with clergy and the pews crammed with lay people. The size of the congregation unnerved him at first, but he climbed into the pulpit and preached on the love of God. Later he reported, "everything went well; everybody wept."

And then the miracles began to happen. In Ars Vianney had opened a school for destitute girls. One day the supply of wheat was down to nothing and there was no money to buy more. The Curé swept the remaining grain into a small pile and placed in it a statuette of St. John Regis, the saint who had helped him in his studies for the priesthood. Then he gathered the schoolgirls and they all prayed together. Later in the day he sent one of the teachers up to the loft; when she opened the door grain cascaded down the stairs. "The good God is very good," the Curé said. "He takes care of His poor."

If Vianney experienced the power of God, he also encountered the devil. For thirty years he endured such phenomena as thunderous noises in the attic of the rectory, violent physical attacks on himself, and the sound of voices that seemed to come from nowhere. He gave the devil the contemptuous name of *grappin*, French for a small rake. Over time Vianney noticed a pattern: the devil was especially active the night before a great sinner came to the Curé's confessional. "The grappin is very stupid," the Curé used to say. "He himself tells me of the arrival of big sinners."

After 41 years of pastoral activity Vianney was physically exhausted. Sometimes he even passed out in the confessional. He stopped reading the Divine Office on his knees, and began to permit himself an afternoon nap. When Corpus Christi—the Curé's favorite feast day—came on June 23, 1859, he was much too feeble to carry the monstrance in procession. His curates placed it in his hands and helped support it at Benediction of the Blessed Sacrament.

On July 30 Vianney did not leave the rectory to hear confessions. He told his housekeeper, "It is my poor end," and asked her to send for the curé from a neighboring parish.

As word spread that Vianney was dying, clergy and dignitaries hurried to the rectory of Ars and crowds of lay people packed the village streets. Ars was experiencing a blistering heat wave and the Curé's room was stifling from the crowd of visitors at his deathbed. The teenagers of Ars tried to make their pastor more comfortable by stretching wet canvas over the rectory roof. Meanwhile dignitaries admitted to the room requested that Vianney hear their confessions, while from outside baskets of medals were sent for Vianney to bless.

When the time came for John Mary Vianney to receive the Last Rites, a procession of twenty priests escorted the Blessed Sacrament from the church to the Curé's room. "How kind the good God is," Vianney said. "When we are no longer able to go to Him, He comes Himself to us." The priests knelt around the bed as Vianney took the Host on his tongue. Then he whispered, "How sad to receive Holy Communion for the last time." On August 4, a violent thunderstorm broke over the village and John Mary Vianney passed peacefully to eternity.

His body was dressed in a cassock, surplice and stole and then laid out in the parlor of the rectory. For two days an endless stream of mourners passed the remains of the Curé of Ars. Then a procession of 300 priests and religious and 6000 laity escorted the body to the village church for the Requiem Mass.

Pope Pius XI canonized John Mary Vianney in 1925, and named him patron of parish priests in 1929. In recent years some priests have complained that Vianney is not a suitable patron. He is derided as fanatical in his piety and inflexible in his teaching. Pope John Paul II answered these criticisms on October 6, 1986, when he personally conducted a retreat for priests, deacons, and seminarians at Ars in honor of St. John Mary Vianney.

When Hurt by the Church

St. Joan of Arc (1412-1431) Feast day: May 30

The calendar of the saints is filled with stories of faithful
Catholic men and women who suffered injustice from worldly
Church officials. No case is more famous than that of St. Joan
of Arc. She was the victim of a conniving tribunal of bishops and
priests that falsely condemned her as a heretic and a sorceress,
then turned her over to civil authorities to be burned at the stake.

The France into which Joan was born in 1412 desperately needed to be saved. Since 1337 the country had been more
or less continuously at war with England, whose kings were
determined to seize the French crown by force of arms. By the
time Joan was born this Hundred Years' War was winding down
—and it appeared that England would be the victor. Most of the
country was in English hands, including the city of Paris. The
rich and powerful Duke of Burgundy had allied himself with the
English. The French king Charles VI was dead and his spineless
son the Dauphin Charles had not yet been crowned. Moreover
it appeared unlikely that this prince would ever become king.
The Dauphin's own mother, Queen Isabeau, had hinted that
Charles' father might have been someone other than the late
king. Worse, Queen Isabeau had gone so far as to sign a treaty
that implied her son's illegitimacy and barred him from inherit-
ing the throne of France.

In this anxious, uncertain time Joan was born on January
6, the Feast of the Epiphany, in Domremy, a village located in the
Meuse valley. Her parents Jacques d'Arc and Isabelle Romée al-

ready had three children—two boys and a girl. At the baptismal font in the church of Domremy she received the name Jeanne, the French form of Joan. She had ten godparents, as was the custom in Catholic Europe until the number was limited to two by the Council of Trent in the mid-16th century.

The d'Arcs were a family of peasant farmers, albeit more prosperous than most of their neighbors. In recognition of Jacques d'Arc's reputation for prudence and good character, the local lord appointed him sergeant of Domremy, a position of importance ranking just below the mayor and sheriff. His office gave Jacques the authority to collect taxes from his fellow villagers.

Joan's parents did not spoil her. They were conscious of their standing in the village and worried that their children might do something to shame the family. Time and again Jacques told Joan that if she lost her virtue she deserved to be drowned, and if her brothers proved unwilling to toss her in the water he would drown her himself.

Joan never learned to read or write. Once she began her mission, however, someone taught her how to write her name—we have several documents that bear her signature.

One day when Joan was fourteen years old, as she stood in the family's vegetable plot about noontime, she saw a bright light and heard the voice of St. Michael the Archangel telling her that she had been chosen by God to save France. Then he said that soon she would be visited by St. Margaret of Antioch and St. Catherine of Alexandria. For the next two years Joan was visited by these three saints. At her trial she testified that they came in dazzling light, gave off a lovely perfume, and even permitted her to embrace them. When one of her judges asked if the saints spoke to her in English, she gave the scornful reply, "Why should they speak to me in English when they are not on the English side?"

Theatrical and film versions of Joan's life have distorted

her personality. They depict her as mild and ladylike, attributing to her a degree of social polish she did not possess. The transcript of her interview with a panel of churchmen at Poitiers and the transcript of her trial at Rouen show us that Joan could be prickly, defensive, abrupt and even sarcastic. She routinely used mild oaths, most commonly "by the name of God" and "by Saint Mary." What deference she possessed she reserved for her "gentle Dauphin."

In 1428 the great archangel told Joan it was time for her mission to begin. He commanded her to go to Robert de Baudricourt, captain of the fortress of Vaucouleurs, who would help her reach the Dauphin. Joan was reluctant to leave home. Three visits from St. Michael in one week were necessary before she agreed to do as he commanded.

Joan needed an excuse to leave Domremy. One of her first cousins, Jeanne Lassois, and Jeanne's husband Durand lived two miles from Vaucouleurs, so she asked her parents' permission to visit them. Once safely away from home Joan told Durand her secret. He must have thought her naive at the least, but when they arrived in Vaucouleurs Joan identified de Baudricourt immediately although she had never seen him before. At her trial she told the judges that St. Michael had pointed him out to her.

De Baudricourt humored the girl as she described for him her mission from the King of Heaven to relieve Orleans, to see the Dauphin crowned king, and to drive the English from France. When she finished speaking, de Baudricourt laughed at her and told Durand to take the girl home and give her a good whipping. Joan's first attempt to begin her mission ended in failure.

In January 1429 cousin Jeanne Lassois was to give birth to a child. Under the pretext of helping her cousin Joan managed to get away from Domremy again. Once again she presented herself to Robert de Baudricourt, requesting an escort of armed men to take her to Chinon, the residence of the Dauphin. This time, inexplicably, de Baudricourt gave in and agreed to send her to the prince.

Cousin Durand bought her a horse and a black suit of men's clothing for the journey, so she could pass through the countryside without attracting attention. She also cut her hair short. With her escort she left for Chinon, sending ahead a letter to the Dauphin saying that she was coming to save France.

The Dauphin whom Joan longed to see was not a storybook prince. He was painfully thin, knock-kneed, with nervous, darting eyes and an unattractive face. Behind his back his courtiers called him "the Clown." He was also out of money. He had pawned the crown jewels, yet still was so short of cash he was forced to wear patched clothing.

Joan aroused Charles' curiosity but he did not really welcome her visit. By temperament the two were opposites. He was nervous and hesitant; she was resolute. He was not even sure if he was the Dauphin; she believed absolutely that she was the ambassador of the King of Heaven. Relatives, counselors, and flatterers pulled Charles in a dozen different directions; Joan's one direct path admitted no distractions.

It was by no means a given that the Dauphin would agree to see Joan. There were many self-proclaimed mystics and visionaries in medieval Europe, the vast majority of whom were either deluded or fraudulent. Yet because that stalwart, down-to-earth soldier Robert de Baudricourt had sent Joan to Chinon with two of his own lieutenants as escort, Charles thought twice before dismissing the girl as another peasant with religious delusions.

Charles agreed to see Joan but he also laid a trap for her. He had one of his vassals dress as the Dauphin while Charles, in less magnificent attire, stood among the crowd that filled the Great Hall of his chateau. Joan entered the hall, took one look at the imposter, and asked the assembly of 300 nobles, courtiers, and clergy why they tried to deceive her. Then she waded into the crowd until she stood before Charles. She curtsied (which must have looked odd since she was in men's clothes) and said, "Gentle Dauphin, my name is Joan the Maid. The King of Heaven sends me to you with the message that you shall be anointed and crowned in the city of Rheims."

Charles made one last effort to mislead her. "I am not the king, Joan," he said. Pointing to the imposter he said, "There is the king." Joan would not be deceived. "In God's name, Sire," she said, "it is you and no one else."

At last Charles gave up the charade. He took Joan aside for a private conversation. To prove that she had been sent by God she told the Dauphin three things he had prayed for on All Saints' Day 1428. Then she set his mind at rest about his legitimacy: he was indeed the son and heir of the late King Charles VI. Queen Isabeau may not have been sure who her son's father was, but God knew.

Charles was impressed but still cautious. Joan wanted him to give her an army to lead to Orleans. Instead he gave her a room in the chateau, a little boy to be her page, and also introduced her to his handsome 23-year-old cousin, the Duke d'Alencon. The Duke and Joan liked each other at once. Throughout her brief career he would be Joan's loyal ally.

For six weeks the Dauphin dawdled, undecided about how to proceed. Meanwhile Alencon gave Joan a war horse, and the priests at the Church of St. Catherine in Fierbois sent Joan a sword they found buried behind the altar. An armorer made white armor for her, and Hamish Power, a Scottish painter living in France, made a banner according to Joan's design: white satin fringed with silk and painted on it an image of Our Lord attended by two angels with the words "Jesus Maria."

At the Dauphin's command Joan submitted to an examination from a panel of churchmen at Poitiers. The surviving record of the examination reveals Joan's impatience with anyone, regardless of rank, who did not share her absolute certainty that she was an instrument of Heaven. Her answers to the churchmen's questions were curt, even insulting. When she was questioned by Carmelite Father Pierre Seguin what language her voices spoke, Joan answered, "A better language than yours." Father Seguin, who came from the south of France, spoke a Limousin dialect that would have sounded rough and rustic to Joan whose dialect was closer to standard French. Impertinence, however, is not heresy. Father Seguin and his colleagues reported to the Dauphin that Joan was a good Catholic, that they believed she had been sent by God to give new hope to the people of France.

In April 1429 Joan set out at last for Orleans. She rode at the head of about 3500 fighting men in her white armor, the sword of St. Catherine sheathed at her side, her white banner in her hand. Joan's brothers Jean and Pierre marched with her—they had come from Domremy to join her army.

In fact Joan was not the military commander of this force; she was its inspiration. Nonetheless she interfered in all the military councils. She also demanded that the commanders dismiss the army's female camp followers and with all their men go to confession. Many of Joan's biographers express surprise that these proud, rough fighting men did as they were told. It is not surprising at all. Joan's army was waiting for a miracle. Leaving the camp followers behind and going to confession was a small price to pay to see the hand of God strike the English.

Orleans had been besieged for six months when Joan arrived. The commander of the town, Jean the Bastard of Orleans (so-called because he was the illegitimate son of the Duke of Orleans), came out to greet Joan and then to escort her into his beleaguered city. As she rode through the city gate, the crowds pressed forward to touch her armor, her banner, even her white horse. She was their deliverer, their saint.

It took eight days of bloody fighting before Joan's army

finally drove the English from Orleans. Joan herself was wounded in the fight, struck by an iron-tipped arrow above her left breast. On the night of her victory, while the church bells rang and all the citizens of Orleans celebrated their deliverance, Joan returned to her lodging, had her bandage changed, ate a few slices of bread dipped in diluted wine, then went to sleep.

With Orleans liberated Joan moved on to her next task— bringing the Dauphin to Rheims for his coronation. Charles was truly delighted that Joan had driven off the English, but making the journey to Rheims was another matter. He complained that the way was not safe, that the English held too many towns between Chinon and Rheims.

To reassure their nervous prince, Joan, the Bastard of Orleans, and the Duke d'Alencon led an army into the Loire Valley to clear out every English stronghold along the road to Rheims. With each town that fell to Joan French morale increased, while the English assured themselves that they were not battling a peasant girl but a disciple of the Devil, "a limb of the Fiend," as the Duke of Bedford called her.

Once the road was as secure as Joan and her allies could make it, Charles consented to ride to Rheims.

On July 17, 1429, a magnificent procession led Charles through the city streets to the cathedral where the archbishop was waiting. Inside the church a vast assembly of knights, nobles, and prelates escorted Charles to the altar. But none of them attracted as much attention as Joan. Dressed in her white armor, her banner in her hand, she stood beside her gentle Dauphin as the archbishop placed the crown of France on his head. Only five months had passed since she had left her parents' cottage in Domremy in obedience to her voices.

With Orleans safe, the Loire Valley free of the English, and the crown firmly on his head, Charles felt at ease perhaps for the first time in his life. Joan pleaded with him to send her to

Paris to drive the English out of the French capital, but Charles put her off. He had a letter from the Duke of Burgundy, England's most powerful ally in France, offering a truce, possibly a permanent peace. A peace treaty appealed to Charles' cautious nature, but it filled Joan with dismay. Her voices had commanded her to drive the English out of France entirely, not to arrive at some accommodation with them. Meanwhile the English were busy reinforcing Paris.

At the end of August, when Charles finally granted permission for Joan and d'Alencon to attack Paris, the English position was stronger than ever. To no one's surprise, the French army was driven back.

After Joan's first defeat her friend d'Alencon returned home to his wife. Joan's army disbanded. Over the next year she was permitted to wage a few small battles, but it was clear to everyone, Joan included, that Charles had lost interest in her. He wondered what to do with a saint once she had served her purpose; the problem was solved for him outside the walls of Compiegne.

Directly across the river from the French-held city of Compiegne was a small fortress manned by Burgundian troops. Joan and two or three hundred men tried to capture the outpost, and it appeared that they would succeed when a larger Burgundian force arrived. The French retreated to the safety of the city walls, with Joan and a few others, including her brother Pierre, covering the retreat. Before Joan and her small party could reach safety, someone inside Compiegne raised the drawbridge. Joan was trapped outside the city. In seconds she was surrounded by several Burgundian soldiers, each one shouting, "Yield to me!" Ultimately it was an archer who dragged Joan to the ground and won the honor of having captured the Maid of Orleans. We don't know who the man was; the chroniclers who recorded the archer's exploit failed to write down his name.

Philip the Good, Duke of Burgundy, was jubilant when he

learned that his men had taken Joan prisoner. He locked her in
a tower of Beaurevoir Castle, the home of his vassal John of Luxembourg. John's wife Jeanne de Bethune, his elderly aunt Jeanne
de Luxembourg, and his step-daughter Jeanne de Bar were all
kind to Joan and tried to make her comfortable. Perhaps urged
on by the ladies, John of Luxembourg gave Joan access to the flat
roof of her tower where she could get some fresh air and enjoy
the sunlight. The three Jeannes tried to persuade her to put on
women's clothes, but she declined as politely as she could, saying
the King of Heaven had not yet instructed her to stop wearing
men's attire.

The kindnesses of her jailers did nothing to assuage Joan's
two constant anxieties: what would happen to her, and what
would happen to Compiegne now that it was threatened by the
Burgundians. One night she climbed to the roof of the tower,
commended herself to God and the Blessed Virgin, and jumped.
It was a seventy foot drop to the ground. When morning came
the castle guards found Joan lying crumpled and unconscious in
the dry moat: she had survived with only a concussion.

When Joan regained consciousness and found herself back
in her tower room, she nearly despaired. She refused all food.
Only after St. Catherine came to her with the assurance that
Compiegne would not fall did Joan take comfort and begin to eat.

The Duke of Burgundy had set a ransom of ten thousand
livres for his prisoner. When the money arrived it was not from
Charles, but from the English. After seven months of relatively
comfortable captivity among the Luxembourgs Joan was taken to
Rouen, a city which was still in English hands.

In Rouen she was treated like a common criminal. Leg irons
hobbled her movements. It is not clear if she had a bed. Her guards
were five English soldiers of the lowest sort who harassed her end-
lessly. She endured further humiliation by having her virginity
verified in an examination conducted by the Duchess of Bed-

ford and several midwives. And she was forbidden to hear Mass.

The indictment against Joan was religious rather than civil in nature. French prelates and theologians who had given their support to the English would examine her on charges of sorcery, idolatry, and heresy. Joan's primary judge was Pierre Cauchon, Bishop of Beauvais. In the best of times he was a cold man, and he nursed a special grudge against Joan. The year before, the French had retaken Beauvais and Bishop Cauchon had been forced to flee to Rouen. In Beauvais he had lived as a prince of the Church; now he lived as an exile and refugee dependent on the charity of strangers. To Cauchon it must have appeared miraculous that the one person he blamed for his current galling situation should have been captured in his diocese and sent to him for sentencing.

Although she could not go to Mass Joan was given a confessor. The priest appointed could not have been worse. Nicolas Loiselleur passed himself off as a fellow countryman, the better to win Joan's confidence. Not only did he repeat to the lawyers for the prosecution what Joan told him in confession, he concealed notaries and other witnesses in an adjoining room where a spy hole let them hear everything the poor, frightened prisoner said.

The scandalous conduct of Father Loiselleur was only one facet of that mockery of justice that passed as Joan's trial. Under Bishop Cauchon a majestic ecclesiastical court was assembled in Rouen. The judges were Cauchon and John Lemaistre, prior of the Dominicans in Rouen. Five other bishops, three abbots, and the English cardinal, Henry Beaufort, Bishop of Winchester, also attended, while 48 doctors of theology, 42 doctors of canon and civil law, 7 physicians, and 55 priests, religious lay brothers, and clerics participated in the process. For her part Joan had no canon lawyer arguing her defense. She was not permitted to call any witnesses to testify on her behalf, nor were any of the churchmen in the court permitted to explain the difficult questions of law and theology put to her during the trial.

The entire procedure was a farce, with Cauchon shouting down any churchman in the hall who insisted that Joan be treated fairly. One of the judges, the Dominican prior Lemaistre, hated the whole affair; Cauchon commanded him to do as he was told. When a doctor of theology, Jean Lefevre, objected to one of the questions put to Joan, Cauchon ordered him to "be silent in the Devil's name." Jean de la Fontaine, one of the canon lawyers prosecuting Joan, had to leave Rouen abruptly after he gave her some advice on how to defend herself against her accusers.

Cauchon was not the only menace in the court. On one occasion when Joan was asked if she would submit herself to the judgment of the Pope, she replied yes. Father Isambart de la Pierre, a Dominican, advised her to correct herself and say that she would submit to the judgment of the General Council at Basel since there she would find many members of her party. The Englishmen in the room closed in on Father de la Pierre, threatening to throw him into the Seine if he didn't keep his mouth shut.

Joan had no hope of justice in such a court. Her judges described her visions as diabolical and the theology faculty of the University of Paris weighed in with the opinion that everything Joan had said about her mission was poisonous to Christian souls. Bishop Cauchon's court handed down the decision the English wanted to hear. Joan was a heretic, a sorceress, a schismatic, and an apostate.

On May 24 an enormous crowd crammed itself into the cemetery adjacent to the Abbey of Saint Omer. Two platforms had been erected in the graveyard. On one stood Bishop Cauchon, Cardinal Beaufort, and a host of churchmen and English lords. On the other platform stood Joan, still in men's clothes. Alone and surrounded by people who hated her, Joan heard the churchmen excommunicate her and deliver her over to the secular authorities to be burned alive. In terror for her life, with no friends or advisors to help her, Joan abjured everything she had said about her voices and her mission and signed a recantation. She agreed to wear women's dress again. In return Cauchon lifted the excommunication and sentenced Joan to life imprisonment.

A repentant Joan was not what the English wanted. Once she was back in her cell one of the guards tore the dress off Joan and threw men's clothes at her. That was all it took to declare Joan a relapsed heretic and to sentence her to the flames.

The one act of charity Joan's judges showed her was to send Father Martin Ladvenu to hear her confession and give her Holy Communion on the morning of her execution. Afterward he accompanied her to the stake.

The English were so eager to burn Joan they did not even wait for Bishop Cauchon to formally hand her over to the secular authorities. No sooner had he pronounced her a heretic than soldiers seized her, dragged her to the top of the pyre, and bound her to the stake. She begged for a cross, and while Father Isambart de la Pierre ran to the nearby Church of the Holy Savior to fetch a processional crucifix, an English soldier took a stick, snapped it into pieces, and made a cross for Joan. She took it from his hand, kissed it, then slipped it under her gown between her breasts. As the flames rose around her, Joan cried, "Jesus! Jesus!" while Father Isambart held the cross as high as he could so she could see it in her final agony. When the fire had burned itself out, the ashes were collected and dumped into the Seine.

Twenty-five years after Joan's death her mother Isabelle and her brothers Jean and Pierre petitioned Rome to revisit the case. In 1456 Joan's cause was heard once again, this time in Paris' Cathedral of Notre Dame. An enormous crowd of Joan's friends and supporters filled the church as witness after witness testified that Joan was pious, orthodox, and as true a daughter of the faith as the Catholic Church had ever known. Her vindication was pronounced at Rouen where she had been wrongly executed. Her brother Jean and Father Ladvenu who had heard Joan's last confession were present on the day the Archbishop of Rheims read a public statement denouncing the sentence against Joan as "tainted with fraud, calumny, iniquity, contradiction and manifest errors of fact and of law."

From the day of her death Joan was widely venerated in France as a visionary, a hero, an innocent crushed by corrupt and malicious men, both lay and clerical. Her rehabilitation was complete in 1920 when Pope Benedict XV canonized Joan. In 1922, his successor Pope Pius XI named Joan patron of France.

Heavenly Mentors:
Saints for the Workplace

SAINT ISIDORE THE FARMER

Heavenly Mentors:
Saints for the Workplace

The custom of assigning patrons to trades and professions has passed down to us from the Middle Ages when every guild had its saint. In those days guild members celebrated the feast day of their patron by taking the day off from work, attending a Mass celebrated in the saint's honor, and perhaps walking in a public procession. These devotional practices ran so deep in the life of tradespeople that even the Reformation had a hard time uprooting them. In 1539 Bishop Veysey of Exeter in England complained that working people were practicing a kind of passive resistance to Henry VIII's edict against saints' days. On the feast days of their patron saints fishermen would not go out fishing and blacksmiths would not shoe a horse.

The tradition of assigning patron saints to various professions continues to be very popular. At this writing Pope John Paul II has just named St. Thomas More, already the patron of lawyers, patron saint of statesmen and politicians.

As in the case of St. Thomas, some of the saints in this chapter received their designations by papal proclamation. These patrons include St. Michael (for police officers); St. John Baptist de la Salle (for teachers); St. Camillus de Lellis (for nurses); St. Francis de Sales (for writers). But in most cases working people adopted as their own a saint who worked at their profession. Physicians took Ss. Cosmas and Damian as their patrons because these two martyrs were medical men. Booksellers took St. John of God as their patron because at one point in his erratic career he peddled religious books from town to town.

Other trades chose their patron on the basis of some episode in the saint's life. Chefs took as their patron St. Lawrence because he was roasted to death on a grill. Hairdressers invoked St. Mary Magdalene, who wiped Christ's feet with her luxurious hair. Funeral directors resorted to St. Joseph of Arimathea, who removed Christ's body from the cross, prepared it for burial, and laid it in a new tomb.

The process of seeing a connection between an event in a saint's life and our own still goes on. Just by her nickname, "the Little Flower," St. Therese of Lisieux was the obvious choice as patron saint of florists. Likewise it makes sense that spacewalking astronauts would take as their patron St. Joseph Cupertino, a 17th-century Franciscan who floated through the air.

For Advertisers
St. Bernardine of Siena (1380-1444) Feast day: May 20

*A dynamic preacher, St. Bernardine's favorite topic was the
Holy Name of Jesus. While he preached he held up in front
of his congregation a tablet inscribed with the letters IHS.
Because of its resemblance to a logo, or even a miniature
billboard, St. Bernardine became patron of advertisers.*

As a young man Bernardine of Siena went to hear St.
Vincent Ferrer. During his sermon the Dominican preacher predicted that there was someone in the crowd who one day would
take his place. Bernardine was that man.

As an Observant Franciscan priest Bernardine traveled
the entire length of Italy preaching against gambling, usury, and
superstition, and urging his listeners to recommit themselves to
Christ. He had a powerful voice which sounded strong and clear
in churches, but also carried well when he preached from out-
door pulpits. Like other Franciscan preachers of the time Bernardine wove stories and jokes into his sermons, the better to
keep his audience's attention. He is most famous, however, for
his favorite visual aid—a wooden tablet on which was painted
the initials IHS, the symbol for the Holy Name of Jesus.

Inspired by Bernardine's preaching, noble families replaced the coats of arms they had hung on the walls of their palaces and favorite churches with a panel bearing the emblem IHS.
Almost overnight there developed a tremendous demand for
objects that bore the sacred monogram. In Bologna a card-maker
complained that his business had been ruined by Bernardine's

131

sermons against gambling. Bernardine suggested he take up a new trade painting the Holy Name on placards. The former card-maker took the preacher's advice and made a small fortune.

It was Bernardine's custom to end his sermons by inviting the crowd to come forward to kiss the sacred monogram. In 1427 one of his rivals, a Dominican named Manfred of Vercelli, gave Pope Martin V a grossly distorted account of what Bernardine was doing, even going so far as to accuse Bernardine of encouraging idolatry. Bernardine's first meeting with the pope did not go well. Martin was cold and suspicious. He forbade Bernardine to preach or to display the IHS emblem until a tribunal had examined his writings.

On June 8 the opposing parties gathered in St. Peter's Basilica for a formal hearing before the pope. St. John Capistrano spoke on Bernardine's behalf. By the end of the session Manfred's spite was exposed and Bernardine was cleared of all charges. Martin V not only endorsed devotion to the Holy Name of Jesus, he urged Bernardine to preach in Rome.

Bernardine kept traveling and preaching to the end of his life. He was on his way to give a mission in Naples when he fell ill with a high fever and died in Aquila on May 20, 1444. He was canonized six years later.

Bernardine's fellow Franciscans continued to promote the Holy Name devotion after his death, and soon the IHS symbol cropped up everywhere—from papermakers who used the sacred initials as a watermark to St. Joan of Arc who had the Holy Names of Jesus and Mary inscribed on her banner. In the 16th century IHS became the emblem of the Jesuits. Veneration for the Holy Name of Jesus endures today, especially in the Holy Name Society which is a regular feature of parish life in the United States.

For Members of the Armed Services
St. George (died c.303) Feast day: April 23

Nearly a thousand years ago the Crusaders adopted St. George as their patron saint, but devotion to him as the guardian of fighting men (and women) may go back much farther.

*P*eople who can't tell the difference between an archangel and an anchorite recognize St. George. The heroic image of George in full armor mounted on a white charger spearing a dragon appears on everything from Orthodox icons to British military medals to boxes of pasta. He is the patron saint of Genoa, Portugal, Catalonia, Armenia, Hungary, and most famously of England. Georgia, the former Soviet republic, was named for him.

According to the church historian Eusebius, Emperor Diocletian's empire-wide persecution of the Church began in 303 with the publication of an edict that outlawed Christian worship, expelled Christians from all public offices and the army, and ordered the destruction of churches and Christian books. In Nicomedia an unnamed Christian man tore down the edict and publicly destroyed it. He was arrested, tortured, and beheaded. Hagiographers believe that this anonymous martyr is the real St. George.

Beginning in the 5th century the most extravagant legends grew up around George—a sure sign of his popularity. He was said to have been tortured for seven years, to have risen from the dead three times, to have raised from the grave seventeen people who had been dead for centuries. And of course there is the story of his battle with the dragon.

Devotion to St. George was already widespread throughout the Christian world when the Crusades gave fresh impetus to his cult, especially as the patron saint of fighting men. Crusaders told how at the siege of Antioch in 1098 the military martyrs, St. George, St. Demetrius, St. Theodore, and St. Mercurius, rode down from Heaven to fight on the side of the Christians. St. George appeared again at Jerusalem: as a knight in white armor marked with a red cross he was the first to scale the city walls, and led the Crusaders into the Saracen-occupied city. King Richard the Lionheart (reigned 1189-1199) placed his army under the protection of St. George. In 1348 Edward III established his Order of the Garter with St. George as the knights' patron.

The English military turned again to St. George for inspiration during World War I. He was depicted on recruiting posters and soldiers in the trenches claimed to have seen him on his charger leading them against the Germans. After the war his image was often featured prominently in memorials to the fallen. Today St. George is still an emblem of courage and chivalry.

For Astronauts

St. Joseph Cupertino (1603-1663) Feast day: September 18

The patron of astronauts is St. Joseph Cupertino,
a remarkable Franciscan priest whose levitations and movement
through the air resembled the space walks of astronauts.

The Church does not know what to do with St. Joseph Cupertino. What are we to make of a priest who according to reliable eyewitnesses levitated and "flew" (or at least was propelled by some invisible power) through the air on at least 70 occasions over the course of 17 years?

When the Father General of the Franciscans took Joseph to a private audience with Pope Urban VIII, Joseph levitated in the presence of the Holy Father. (Pope Urban said if he outlived Joseph, he would promote Joseph's cause for canonization and personally testify to this miracle). On yet another occasion when Joseph was living in Assisi, Spain's ambassador to the papal court brought his wife and a large retinue to see Joseph. As he entered the church to greet his visitors Joseph saw a statue of Mary. He floated off the floor and flew over the heads of the ambassador and his party to the statue, where he remained suspended in the air. Then he floated to the church door, landed gently on the floor, and returned to the friars' residence. The Inquisition heard about Joseph and commanded him to appear before a tribunal. On October 21, 1638, while the inquisitors were questioning him, Joseph levitated.

His Franciscan superiors responded to the phenomena by banning Joseph from saying Mass in public, from joining the fri-

135

ars in the choir for the Divine Office, from eating with them in the refectory, from walking in processions and from taking part in any public religious function. They moved him from one Franciscan house to another. They sent him to live in obscure corners of Italy. At one point, for reasons that are still not clear, the Inquisition even insisted that he be transferred from the Franciscans to the Capuchins. To his superiors, even if Joseph's levitations were neither diabolical in origin nor the work of some undiscovered fraud, they were seriously disruptive to the day-to-day life of a religious community.

At the end of his life Joseph was living in a Franciscan house in Osimo. As he lay on his deathbed he heard the sound of the altar bell which announced that a priest was bringing Holy Communion to him for the last time—and for the last time Joseph levitated. He rose off his bed and floated out into the hall to meet the Blessed Sacrament.

When the cause of Joseph Cupertino's canonization was proposed, Prosper Lambertini was appointed "the devil's advocate." Lambertini was one of the Church's greatest experts on the saints and skeptical of reports of supernatural events. Yet even he had to concede that the witnesses who gave testimony of Joseph's levitations were of "unchangeable integrity." In the midst of the inquiry, Lambertini was elected to the papacy. As Benedict XIV Lambertini beatified Joseph.

For Booksellers

St. John of God (1495-1550) Feast day: March 8

*One of the jobs St. John of God held on his erratic
path to sainthood was peddler of religious books.
For this reason he is the patron saint of booksellers.*

*J*ohn was eight years old when a priest visiting his town,
Montemoro-o-Novo, Portugal, coaxed him to leave home and
go with him to Spain. We do not know the priest's reasons for
taking the boy away from his parents, but we do know that he did
not keep John long. At the town of Oropeza in Spain he left the
boy with the bailiff and vanished from John's life. Back in Montemoro-o-Novo, John's distraught mother died, perhaps of grief.
His father joined the Franciscans.

The bailiff who gave John a place to live treated him like
a member of the family. He sent him to school, put him to work
watching the Count of Oropeza's flocks, and eventually appointed John steward of the count's estate. At age 22, when John was
a strapping young man eager for excitement, King Charles V of
Spain declared war against France. John enlisted in the army
where he served for four years. He returned home to Oropeza in
time to join the count's troops and march off to a new war, this
one against the Turks in Hungary.

After the war with the Turks John drifted. He was a shepherd for a wealthy widow in Spain. He thought he would go to
North Africa to rescue Christian slaves and perhaps die a martyr.
When he met a Portuguese woman whose husband had become
an invalid John hired himself out to support the family. He must

have liked being on the road because his next career was peddling religious books and holy pictures from town to town.

Once he met a little barefoot boy. John offered the child his shoes, but of course they were too big, so John lifted the boy and carried him on his shoulders. Soon he was sweating and near exhaustion. He put the boy down beside a stream and knelt to drink and wash his face. When he looked up from the water he saw the boy was the Child Jesus. In his hand the Christ Child held an open pomegranate surmounted by a cross and inscribed with the words, "John of God, Granada will be your cross." (The pomegranate is the emblem of the city of Granada and a symbol of charity and fruitfulness.)

In obedience to his vision, John went to Granada. Since he had received no further instructions from the Christ Child he supported himself there by selling his books and sacred images. In January 1537 St. John of Avila, an impassioned preacher and mystic, came to Granada to give a mission. John of God joined the crowd in the church. In the middle of the preacher's sermon John began to wail, crying to God to have mercy on him. He ran from the church and stumbled through the city streets beating his breast, tearing his hair, howling with grief. After many days of this the town authorities had John locked in an asylum for the insane. Whenever he had an outburst the keepers of the asylum flogged John, or locked him in solitary confinement.

When St. John of Avila heard of John's plight he visited the asylum. He told John it was time to give up hysterics and find something useful to do for God. As the first step toward a productive life St. John of Avila recommended a pilgrimage to a shrine of Our Lady. At Spain's shrine of Guadalupe John of God had a vision of the Virgin and Child, who made him understand that his vocation was to feed the hungry, clothe the naked, and tend the sick and the dying.

Back in Granada John rented a house and turned it into a

hospital for the poor. With 46 beds the facility became a model of health care. Contagious cases were kept separate from the other patients; each patient had his or her own bed (rare even in private homes in 16th century Europe). The entire house was scrupulously clean; meals were served at set times; and John himself washed each patient each day.

In addition to the care of their bodies, John worried about the state of his patients' souls. He invited priests to come hear confessions and administer the Last Rites, and he led the hospital in morning prayers.

Initially John had to beg in the street for everything his hospital needed. Once his reputation was established, however, doctors and nurses volunteered to help him. The people of Granada donated food, wine, bedding, and other supplies. Men who joined him to serve the sick became the nucleus of his nursing order, the Congregation of the Brothers of St. John of God.

Many miracles stories are told about John of God. Probably the most famous is the story of the burning hospital. Granada's Grand Hospital was engulfed in a raging fire so intense that firefighters refused to enter the building. Someone said that there were sick people trapped inside. John pushed his way through the crowd, walked into the flames, and carried each patient to safety.

After twelve years of tireless service to the sick and the poor, John of God died while praying before the little private altar in his room. He was canonized in 1690 and named patron of the sick, of hospitals, and of booksellers.

For Chefs

St. Lawrence (died 258) Feast Day: August 10

St. Lawrence, the patron saint of chefs, was roasted alive on an
iron grill. In the midst of his torment he said to his executioners,
"Turn me over, I'm done on this side."

At the beginning of August 258, the emperor Valerian published an edict outlawing Christianity and commanding that all bishops, priests, and deacons be put to death. On August 6 Pope St. Sixtus II was arrested in the catacomb of Praetextatus on the Appian Way outside the walls of Rome. The pope had just finished saying Mass and was seated, addressing the congregation, when soldiers broke in. They seized Sixtus and four of his deacons, but for some reason they did not take the deacon Lawrence, who was also present.

As the soldiers began to lead their prisoners away, Lawrence tried to hold Sixtus back. "Where are you going, priest, without your deacon?" he asked. "Where are you going, father, without your son?" Divinely inspired, Pope Sixtus promised Lawrence that they would be reunited in three days.

While Sixtus and his deacons went to trial and execution, Lawrence hurried back to the city. Rather than see the Church's sacred vessels confiscated by the pagan state, Lawrence sold them and distributed the money to the poor.

Then Lawrence received a command to appear before the prefect of Rome. At the tribunal the prefect promised that he would not harm Lawrence if he handed over the treasures of the Church. The deacon asked for a little time to comply with this order; he was granted three days.

When Lawrence returned to the tribunal on August 10, he was followed by a large crowd of the lame, the blind, the poor, and the helpless, all of whom had been supported by the Church. "Here," he said, "are the Church's treasures."

The prefect was not amused. He commanded his guard to seize Lawrence, strip him naked, and bind him to an iron grill. Beneath the grill the executioners built a slow fire. As glowing coals broiled him alive St. Lawrence called out to his tormentors, "Turn me over! I'm done on this side." Minutes later Lawrence was dead.

The details of St. Lawrence's activities in the days following Pope Sixtus' arrest and his grisly martyrdom come to us from St. Ambrose (c.340-397) and the Christian poet Prudentius (348-c.410). While there is no doubt that these stories about St. Lawrence were current among Christians, especially in Rome, scholars continue to argue whether the details are authentic, carefully passed down by oral tradition, or legendary material that accumulated around a widely admired martyr.

Christians buried St. Lawrence on the Via Tiburtina outside the city walls. About the year 320, in recognition of the profound reverence in which the martyr was held by the Christians of Rome, Constantine built a fine basilica over St. Lawrence's tomb. The church still stands today, much enlarged and embellished over the centuries.

For Farmers

St. Isidore the Farmer (c.1080-1130) Feast day: May 15

*St. Isidore, the patron saint of farmers, used his long solitary
hours in the fields to deepen his prayer life.*

$\mathcal{I}$t is common for popes to canonize more than one saint
in a single ceremony, but St. Isidore the Farmer shared his canonization day with especially distinguished company: St. Ignatius
Loyola, St. Francis Xavier, St. Teresa of Avila, and St. Philip Neri.

The earliest biography of Isidore was written about 150
years after he died, so no doubt it is a combination of fact mixed
with legend. He was born into a peasant family in or near Madrid.
At the time Madrid was a small town, centuries away from becoming the capital of Spain. Isidore married a peasant woman,
Maria de la Cabeza, who is also honored as a saint. They had one
child, a boy, who died young. After their son's death Isidore and
Maria are said to have lived like brother and sister rather than
husband and wife.

The couple had no land of their own. Isidore worked on
the estate of Torrelaguna outside Madrid. Each morning on his
way to the fields he stopped at a church for Mass. During long
hours of plowing and harvesting he prayed. It is said that angels
were seen plowing with him and that he accomplished three
times as much work in a single day as any other tenant farmer.

Another story tells of his arrival at a confraternity dinner
accompanied by a large crowd of beggars. The host complained
that he did not have enough food for so many people, but Isidore
urged him to serve the meal and see what happened. In the kitch-

en the portions miraculously multiplied so there was enough for everyone and plenty left over besides.

Isidore died in 1130, several years before his wife. He was buried in the cemetery of St. Andrew's Church until 1170, when his grave was opened and his body found to be incorrupt. The relics were transferred to a shrine inside the church and devotion to St. Isidore began to spread.

He is said to have appeared to King Alfonso of Castile in 1211 to show him how to defeat the Moors in battle. In 1615, when physicians believed King Philip III of Spain was dying, the relics of St. Isidore were carried to his room. The king recovered completely and in thanksgiving petitioned the pope to grant Isidore a formal canonization ceremony.

St. Isidore's popularity remains widespread in Spain, but devotion to him among farmers has spread around the globe. In the United States he is the patron of the National Catholic Rural Life Conference. Every year the conference presents the Isidore and Maria Award to a married couple who exemplify a strong family life, sound stewardship of the gifts God has given them, personal integrity, and deep religious faith.

For Financial Professionals

St. Matthew, the patron of anyone who works in the financial professions, was a tax collector working on his accounts when Christ called him to be one of the twelve apostles.

Christ's call to Matthew to become one of his apostles is the only time the evangelist is singled out in the gospels. He was the tax collector of Capernaum, a job that would have earned him the contempt of his fellow Jews because he was collaborating with their Roman conquerors.

Matthew was at work in the customs house when Christ stood before him and said, "Follow me." Immediately Matthew left his money and his accounts. To celebrate his conversion Matthew invited Christ and the other apostles to his house where he threw a lavish dinner.

Ancient tradition says that Matthew preached the gospel first in Judea then in Ethiopia where he was martyred. According to tradition he had finished saying Mass and was making his thanksgiving before the altar when a soldier crept up from behind and stabbed him in the back.

It appears that the oldest surviving fragments of the New Testament come from St. Matthew's gospel. Three small bits of papyrus, preserved in the library of Magdalen College, Oxford, have been dated to the year 60 by Carsten Peter Thiede, a German papyrologist.

For Firefighters
St. Florian (died 304) Feast day: May 4

*Firefighters invoke as their patron St. Florian, a Roman
soldier who refused to deny Christ even when his
persecutors threatened to burn him alive.*

St. Florian was a high-ranking officer in the Roman army stationed in what is now Lorch, Austria, when the emperor Diocletian initiated the last and bloodiest persecution of Christians. Aquilinus, the governor of the province, made it his business to hunt down any Christians hiding in the mountainous regions of Austria. On the bridge outside Lorch Florian ran into a band of Christian-hunters, several of whom he recognized as former comrades-in-arms.

"Where are you going?" Florian asked his old friends.

"We are searching for Christians," answered a soldier.

"Friends," Florian said, "I am a Christian."

Reluctantly, the soldiers arrested Florian and led him to the governor.

The terms of the imperial edict dictated that a Christian could save his life by burning incense before statues of the Roman gods. Aquilinus offered Florian this option. When Florian refused to sacrifice to false gods, the governor condemned him to death.

One version of the martyrdom says that at first Aquilinus ordered his soldiers to burn Florian alive. "If you burn me," said Florian, "I will climb to Heaven in flames." So Aquilinus had Florian scourged, and then commanded that he be drowned. A troop of guards and executioners led Florian, bruised and bleeding, to a bridge over the River Emms, near the place where it flows into the Danube. They bound Florian's wrists, tied a millstone to his neck, and shoved him into the river. The weight of the stone dragged Florian to the river bottom where he drowned.

A Christian woman named Valeria retrieved Florian's body from the water and gave it a decent burial. Today his relics lie enshrined in the Abbey of St. Florian near Linz.

In art St. Florian often is depicted pouring water on a burning town. The image refers to a legend dating from the Middle Ages which tells how Florian, with a single bucket of water, saved an entire town from a conflagration.

Devotion to St. Florian has been on the increase since 1969 when the cult of St. Barbara, another saint traditionally invoked for protection against fire, was suppressed. Today St. Florian is honored by firefighters, as well as all those seeking to preserve their lives and property from flames.

For Florists

St. Therese of Lisieux (1873-1897) Feast day: October 1

*Florists have as their patron St. Therese of Lisieux, popularly
known as "the Little Flower." As she was dying of tuberculosis
Therese promised, "I will spend my Heaven doing good on earth."
Then she added that the graces she won for anyone who prayed
to her would cascade to earth like a shower of roses.*

The day her sister Pauline entered Lisieux's Carmelite
cloister nine-year-old Therese Martin could not stop crying.
Their mother, Azelie-Marie Guerin Martin, had died five years
earlier of breast cancer. Pauline, the second eldest of the five Martin girls and fourteen years older than Therese, had stepped in to
become her little sister's mother. Now she was leaving, too. "I
was going to lose my mother all over again," Therese said. "I
can't tell you what misery I went through at that moment."

Therese's solution to this wretched situation was to announce that she had a vocation to Carmel. Pauline humored her
sister (the Martins always humored Therese) and took her to see
the prioress, Mother Marie de Gonzague. Because she was still a
child Therese was permitted inside the grill to speak with the prioress privately in the convent parlor. To her credit Mother Marie
de Gonzague treated Therese seriously, but told the child she
could not accept a nine-year-old girl as a postulant. Therese
would have to wait until she was sixteen to enter—on this point
the prioress was firm. For the next six years Therese Martin de-
vised one scheme after another to enter Carmel early and speed
up her reunion with Pauline.

The Martin household in which Therese was born on January 2, 1873, resembled a cloister in some respects. The family was tightly knit; they did not mix much with anyone outside their circle of relatives. The parents, Louis and Zelie, were intensely pious: both had tried unsuccessfully to enter religious life before their marriage. On their wedding night Louis suggested that they commit themselves to a Josephite marriage—living together as brother and sister without ever making love, in imitation of the Blessed Virgin and St. Joseph. Now Zelie was as religious as her new husband, but she wanted a large family. No one knows what she said to Louis but over the next thirteen years Zelie gave birth to nine children, five of whom—all girls—survived to adulthood: Marie, Pauline, Leonie, Celine, and Therese.

Under Zelie's overzealous direction the five Martin sisters were encouraged to incorporate into their lives regular periods of prayer, a regimen of self-sacrifice, and a consciousness of personal faults. The one rebel was Leonie. Although she was as genuinely religious as anyone in the family, she resisted her mother's efforts to mold her devotional life. To make her conscious of her failings Zelie gave Leonie pieces of cork; every time she caught herself committing some fault she was to put a piece of cork in a special drawer. Leonie refused, and poor Zelie feared her rebellious daughter might be on the path to damnation.

Both Martins were self-employed. Zelie had a thriving business making Alencon lace and Louis was a clockmaker. In 1871 Louis sold his company. The money he received from the sale of his business coupled with an inheritance and the income from Zelie's business enabled Louis to live in comfortable retirement with his family. When Zelie died in 1878 Louis found comfort in his daughters, especially Therese, whom he called his "little queen." They went for long walks in the afternoon to visit the churches of Lisieux, and often on the way home Louis would buy Therese some little treat.

It is no surprise given the intense piety of the Martin family that one by one the sisters entered the convent. Pauline was first. She went to the Carmel. Marie followed her there. Leonie tried to strike out on her own by entering the convent of the Poor Clares but she proved unsuited and after two months was sent home. Therese described her return: "We saw those blue eyes of hers again often wet with tears." On Pentecost Sunday in the year Therese was fourteen she followed her father out to the garden to tell him she wanted to enter the Carmel like her sisters. Louis wept, but tried to convince himself that God was bestowing a singular grace on him by taking his daughters one by one.

Although she was too young Therese was determined to enter the Carmel in Lisieux. Louis took her first to see the superior of Carmelite men but the interview was not a success; Therese's request irritated him. He told her to wait until she was sixteen. Next Louis made an appointment with the bishop of Bayeux. He listened sympathetically to Therese but in the end the bishop also told her to wait. In her disappointment Therese wept so hard the bishop took her in his arms to comfort her.

Louis thought Therese needed some distraction. Father Reverony, a priest and acquaintance of the Martins, was leading a pilgrimage to Rome. Louis decided he, Therese, and Celine would join it. The highlight of the tour was to be a Mass said by Pope Leo XIII in his private chapel. After the Mass, each pilgrim would kneel individually before the Holy Father to receive his blessing. By this point in the pilgrimage Father Reverony had a good idea what type of girl he was dealing with in Therese. He gave strict instructions that no one was to address the pope. Nonetheless when her turn came Therese asked Pope Leo to let her enter the Carmel a year early. The pope gave Father Reverony a quizzical look, but the priest assured the Holy Father the bishop of Bayeux was looking into the matter. "Very well, my child," Leo said, "do as your superiors tell you."

Therese was not put off so easily. She grabbed the pope's knees and said, "But if you would say the word, Most Holy Father, everyone would agree."

Very gently Pope Leo gave a non-committal answer, "All is well. If God wants you to enter, you will." Therese was about to press her point, and Celine was chiming in, when the papal guards and Father Reverony physically lifted Therese to her feet and all but carried her out of the chapel.

Back home in Lisieux Therese waited for word from the bishop. It arrived on New Year's Day—he granted her permission to enter the Carmel a year early. The prioress, Mother Marie de Gonzague, however, would not admit Therese until Easter.

On April 9, 1888, Therese along with all her family went to Mass at the Carmel church. Afterward she and Louis bid each other a tearful good-bye. Then she walked through the door in the grill where her sisters Marie and Pauline were waiting for her with Mother Marie de Gonzague and the rest of the nuns.

In many respects Therese was already prepared for the rigorous life of a Carmelite. She had developed a profound relationship with God. On the other hand she was still a 15-year-old girl and the routine of prayer, work, and silence certainly clashed with her adolescent impulses. She admitted that during the early days she found "more thorns than roses" in the Carmel. In her father's house she had never washed clothes, scrubbed floors, or performed any other housekeeping chores. As a postulant she was expected to do all these things—and she was very bad at them. It was humiliating for Therese to be so clumsy at tasks others found simple.

At home she had been indulged and in the Carmel Marie and Pauline still tried to spoil her. They even went so far as to appeal to the prioress for dispensations from some of the more rigorous elements of the rule for their baby sister. (During winter, when the other nuns wore sandals, the Martin sisters wanted the prioress to give Therese permission to wear fur-lined boots.)

Word came to Marie, Pauline, and Therese that Louis had suffered a stroke, the first of several that would eventually rob him of his mobility and of his mind. When he died in 1894, Celine joined her sisters in the Carmel.

In the early hours of Good Friday 1896, as she lay in bed, Therese felt her mouth fill up with blood. It was the first sign that she had contracted tuberculosis. The Carmelite rule requires nuns to inform the superior whenever they are ill. Obediently Therese told Mother Marie de Gonzague what happened in the night but assured the prioress that she was in no pain and wanted to keep the Good Friday fast. Mother Marie gave her consent. For the next year, as her condition worsened, Therese never requested nor did Mother Marie offer any dispensation from the severity of Carmelite life. But by spring 1897 it was obvious that Therese was dying.

Therese suffered an excruciating death. Mother Marie de Gonzague would not permit the doctors to use morphine to ease the patient's pain. In addition Therese struggled with a dark night of the soul that at times she felt certain would crush her faith entirely. By God's grace she did not succumb to despair, but tuberculosis kept her in perpetual agony. "What is the good of writing beautifully about suffering," she said. "It means nothing, nothing!" On another occasion when she felt she was suffocating she gasped out an appeal to the Blessed Mother. "Holy Virgin," she said, "I can get no earthly air!"

Death came late in the evening of September 30. Her three sisters and the rest of the community knelt around her bed reciting the prayers for the dying. Therese looked at her crucifix and said, "O, I love him! My God, I love you!" A moment later she was dead. Therese Martin was 24 years old.

In the Carmel Therese had written a memoir of her life. Mother Marie de Gonzague decided to have the manuscript published. In 1898 it appeared under the title *The Story of a Soul* and by 1910 had sold 47,000 copies. By 1915 the number sold had soared to 150,000 copies. Therese's autobiography not only made her known and loved throughout the world, it also broadcast her particular spirituality, the Little Way, in which Therese assured her readers that even the least thing done for love of God can help one grow in holiness. The name, "the Little Way," may be a product of 19th-century sentimentality, but the method Therese advocated for advancing toward spiritual perfection was rooted in the writings of St. John of the Cross, St. Teresa of Avila, and Thomas á Kempis' *Imitation of Christ.*

As Therese's fame spread, thousands of people claimed to have received favors through her intercession. At one point the Lisieux Carmel was receiving 500 letters a day, all of them about Therese. Pope Pius XI canonized Therese in 1925. In 1997 Pope John Paul II declared the Little Flower a Doctor of the Church.

For Funeral Directors
St. Joseph of Arimathea (1st century) Feast day: March 17

*The patron of funeral directors is St. Joseph of Arimathea
who claimed Christ's body after the crucifixion, prepared
it for burial, and laid it in a new tomb.*

*E*ach of the four gospels refers to Joseph of Arimathea
as a wealthy man, a secret disciple of Our Lord, possibly a member of the Sanhedrin religious court. That first dreadful Good
Friday, when the apostles were scattered and in hiding, Joseph
found the courage to go to Pontius Pilate and request the body
of Jesus. Along with Nicodemus, another clandestine disciple, Joseph took Christ's body down from the cross, wrapped it in linen,
and carried it to a tomb hewn from a cave that he had prepared
for his own use.

Over the centuries many legends have been told about St.
Joseph. The most beautiful associates him with the Holy Grail.
In this story Joseph is the uncle of the Blessed Virgin Mary, a
merchant whose business interests take him as far as the island
of Britain. When Jesus was a boy Joseph took him along on one
of his voyages to England. The 18th-century poet William Blake
immortalized this legend in his poem "Jerusalem:"

> *And did those feet in ancient time*
> *Walk on England's mountains green?*
> *And was the holy Lamb of God*
> *On England's pleasant pastures seen?*

The legend continues that at the crucifixion Joseph stood at the foot of the cross. As the Precious Blood dripped from Our Lord's wounds, Joseph caught it in the same cup Christ had used at the Last Supper. He later transferred the Blood into two cruets. After Christ's Ascension into Heaven Joseph took the cruets and the cup, known as the Holy Grail, and traveled to France with the apostle St. Philip. From there he went with twelve priests to carry the gospel to England.

The missionaries settled in Glastonbury where Joseph built a chapel which he dedicated to the Blessed Virgin. In the chapel he placed the cruets of Christ's Blood and the Holy Grail.

A persistent tradition in England says that Joseph's chapel, known as "the Old Church," survived at Glastonbury until 1184 when it was destroyed in a great fire. In 1186 the current Lady Chapel was consecrated on the site of Joseph's church. Five years later, in 1191, the monks of Glastonbury claimed to have found the graves of King Arthur and Guinivere, a discovery which linked Joseph of Arimathea to the Arthurian legend.

In 1965, amid the ruins of the Glastonbury Abbey, Queen Elizabeth II erected a large wooden cross with an inscription that reads: "The cross. The symbol of our faith. The gift of Queen Elizabeth II marks a Christian sanctuary so ancient that only legend can record its origin."

For Hairdressers
St. Mary Magdalene (1st century) Feast day: July 22

For nearly 1700 years the unnamed sinful woman who washed Christ's feet with her tears and wiped them with her hair has been identified as Mary Magdalene. Based on this episode in St. Luke's gospel, artists depicted St. Mary with a luxuriant head of hair, and hairdressers took her as their patron saint.

*T*hanks to St. Jerome and to St. Gregory the Great, three separate women in the gospels have been conflated into one. Both Doctors of the Church asserted that the unnamed sinner who wiped Jesus' feet with her hair, the sister of Martha and Lazarus, and the woman who was the first to see the Risen Christ were all Mary Magdalene. The adulterous woman Christ saved from being stoned to death is also said to be Mary Magdalene.

Who was the real Mary Magdalene? She was one of the women who traveled with Christ and the twelve apostles. According to St. Luke Jesus cast seven devils out of Mary. Her surname, Magdalene, refers to her home, Magdala, a fishing village on the northwest shore of the Sea of Galilee. In the first century the residents of Magdala were notorious for their lascivious behavior, a reputation which may have been the source of the legend that Mary Magdalene had been a prostitute.

Mary Magdalene followed Our Lord to Calvary and witnessed his death and burial. On the first Easter morning she encountered the Risen Christ in the garden but did not recognize him until he spoke her name. Then the Lord sent her to tell the apostles that he had risen from the dead.

Because Mary Magdalene was granted the privilege of announcing the Resurrection, St. Hippolytus (c.170-c.235) gave her the title, "Apostle to the Apostles." The unique grace which Mary received is celebrated each Easter in the *Victimae Paschali Laudes*, when the Church asks, "Tell us Mary, what did you see on the way?" Mary answers, "I saw the sepulcher of the living Christ and the glory of his rising. I saw the angel witnesses, the linen that covered his face and the shroud. Christ my hope is risen!"

As with so many of the Lord's disciples, legend supplies the details the New Testament omits. The most persistent tradition claims that during the persecution of the Church in Jerusalem the Jewish authorities set Mary Magdalene, Martha, Lazarus, and Maximinus (one of the Lord's 72 disciples) adrift in an oarless boat. The wind and the current took the little group to the south of France. Martha and Lazarus went off to preach the gospel. Maximinus became the first bishop of Aix. But Mary Magdalene retired to a cave east of Marseilles and spent the rest of her life as a hermit. She lived there so long that her clothes became rags and fell off her body. To preserve her modesty God made her hair grow to such length and thickness that it covered her nakedness. The cave, known as La Sainte-Baume, has been visited by pilgrims at least since the 5th century.

The legend goes on to say that when Mary was dying angels carried her to the house of St. Maximinus so he could give her Holy Communion for the last time. She died there and Maximinus buried her in his chapel. Pilgrims still come to the crypt of the medieval abbey church that was built on the site to pray at the tomb of St. Mary Magdalene and to venerate her relics, including strands of her abundant hair.

For Highway Construction Workers

St. John the Baptist (1st C.) Feast days: June 24 and August 29

St. John the Baptist, who helped "make straight in the
desert a highway for our God," is invoked as
the patron of those who build highways.

St. John's patronage of highway construction workers is
based on Isaiah's prophecy concerning him, "A voice cries: 'In
the wilderness prepare the way of the Lord, make straight in the
desert a highway for our God.'"

As in the case of Jesus and Mary, the conception of John
the Baptist was made known by the message of an angel. After
many years of marriage his father Zachary, a Temple priest, and
his mother Elizabeth were still childless. One day when it was
Zachary's turn to offer incense in the Temple, the archangel
Gabriel appeared to him and announced that Elizabeth would
bear a son and they should name the boy John. Foolishly Zachary
doubted the angel's word. For his unwillingness to believe he was
struck dumb.

Six months later, when Gabriel made his great Annunciation to the Blessed Virgin Mary, he passed along the news that
her cousin Elizabeth, whom everyone had thought barren, was in
her sixth month. Mary hurried off to En Kerem to see her cousin.
At the very moment she greeted Elizabeth, the infant John leapt in
his mother's womb.

When Elizabeth gave birth there was dissension in the family as to what to name the boy. To settle the question, some of
Zachary's relatives brought him a writing tablet and a stylus and

asked him what name his son should have. Zachary wrote, "His name is John." At that moment his power of speech was restored.

We do not know if Jesus and John knew each other growing up. Before Christ began his public ministry John left home and went into the desert around the Jordan River. There he lived a penitential life dressed in a camel skin with a piece of leather cord as a belt, eating only locusts and wild honey. Crowds from Judea, Jerusalem, and the region around the Jordan made the journey out to the wilderness to hear John call for repentance. Those who repented John baptized in the river.

Jesus began his public life by going to John and asking for baptism. John must have recognized his cousin as the Messiah; he responded that it was more appropriate for Christ to baptize him. But Jesus insisted, so John led him into the river. Following the baptism of the Lord, John heard a voice from Heaven announce, "This is my beloved Son, in whom I am well pleased."

One day the Pharisees and Sadducees came to the Jordan to learn from John if he were the Messiah. He said he was not. When they pressed him to declare who he was, John described himself as, "the voice of one crying in the wilderness, 'Make straight the way of the Lord.'"

The next day John saw Jesus passing nearby and declared to the crowd, "Behold the Lamb of God! Behold him who takes away the sins of the world!" In preaching his message of repentance John denounced Herod Antipas. The king had violated Jewish law by marrying Herodias, his half brother's ex-wife and his niece besides. Herod held John in superstitious awe, but to please Herodias he had John arrested.

On Herod's birthday Herodias instructed her 20-year-old daughter Salome to dance for the king. Full of wine and inflamed by lust for the young woman, Herod swore in front of all of his guests that as a reward he would give Salome anything she asked for, even if it was half his kingdom. Salome said she wanted, on a dish, the head of John the Baptist.

Salome's request filled the king with anguish but he could not renege on his promise. He sent his executioner to John's cell. When the executioner returned he presented the Baptist's head to Salome, who in turn gave it to her mother.

Christ himself spoke John's eulogy. "What did you go out into the wilderness to behold? A reed shaken by the wind? What then did you go out to see? A man clothed in soft raiment? Behold, those who are gorgeously appareled and live in luxury are in kings' courts. What then did you go out to see? A prophet? Yes, I tell you, and more than a prophet. This is he of whom it is written, 'Behold I send my messenger before thy face, who shall prepare thy way before thee.' I tell you, among those born of women none is greater than John."

For Lawyers
St. Thomas More (1478-1535) Feast day: June 22

St. Thomas More, the patron of lawyers, was himself a lawyer renowned in his day for his integrity. The transcript of his trial for treason has come down to us. It not only demonstrates More's skill in oral argument; it also reveals his conviction that a nation's laws must be based on the law of God.

Thomas More was born on Milk Street in London on February 7, 1478. His mother Agnes was the daughter of Thomas Granger, who became Sheriff of London. His father, John More, was a lawyer who ended his career as a judge of the King's Bench. Among the comfortable, conservative, solidly middle-class Mores Thomas was an anomaly. Even as a small boy he was quick-witted and could make the adults around him laugh. He excelled in his studies; when he went to Canterbury College, Oxford, he joined the circle of students and teachers who pursued "the new learning," meaning they studied Greek and classical philosophy, particularly the works of Plato.

More was devout. He had just become a lawyer when he moved to the guest house of London's Carthusian monastery. Over the next four years he tried to discern his true vocation by participating in the religious life of the monks while also pursuing his law career. Erasmus, one of his closest friends, tells us that after this lengthy trial period More admitted that given his libido he was better off finding a wife than taking vows as a Carthusian.

When he was 26 More and Jane Colt were married. She was the sixteen-year-old daughter of Sir John Colt who owned a small estate in Essex. During the next six years Thomas and Jane had four children together. Then unexpectedly in 1511 Jane More died. A month later More married Alice Middleton, a wealthy widow eight years his senior. Dame Alice was plainspoken and down-to-earth, an eminently practical woman who proved to be an ideal counterpart to More and an attentive mother to his children by Jane Colt.

Meanwhile More's law practice prospered. Unlike other London lawyers who had to scramble for business, More was sought by new clients. His growing reputation as a lawyer and a scholar—particularly after the publication of his book *Utopia*—brought Thomas to the attention of Henry VIII and the king's Lord Chancellor, Cardinal Thomas Wolsey.

In 1517 More was appointed to the King's Council. His subtle mind, his learning, and his wit made him a favorite with the King and won him one post after another—diplomat, judge, royal secretary. When Wolsey died in 1529, Henry named Thomas More Lord Chancellor of England, saying he was delighted to have a friend as his chancellor. On one occasion when Henry visited More at his home at Chelsea the king walked through the More's garden with his arm draped around his friend's neck. More's son-in-law William Roper was exhilarated by this sign of affection but More had no illusions about the king. "If my head could win him a castle in France," he told Roper, "it should not fail to go."

The crisis between More and the king was not over a castle in France, of course, but over Henry's desire for a son. He and his wife Catherine of Aragon had only one living child, the Princess Mary, and Henry was convinced that no woman could rule England. In all of England's history there had been only one female monarch, Queen Matilda, during whose reign the country had been torn apart by civil war—not an encouraging precedent. In 1527 Queen Catherine was 42 years old and unlikely to produce any more children. At the same time Henry had developed an intense passion for 23-year-old Anne Boleyn.

In order to marry Anne, Henry would have to convince the pope to annul his marriage to Catherine. Henry took the position that by marrying Catherine, the widow of his elder brother Arthur, he had violated canon law. It is true that the Church forbade marriages between in-laws, but Pope Julius II had granted Henry and Catherine a dispensation to marry. Now Henry was asking Pope Clement VII to declare that his predecessor had no right to grant such a dispensation, that his marriage to Catherine was invalid from the beginning, and that Henry was free to marry Anne Boleyn.

The case dragged on for four years, and with each passing year Henry became more determined to be free of Catherine. In 1531, no longer willing to wait for the pope's consent, Henry assumed the title "Protector and Supreme Head of the Church in England." Initially Henry permitted a qualifying statement, "as far as the law of God allows," to be added to the definition of his new authority, but the direction the king was taking was unmistakable. St. John Fisher, bishop of Rochester, stood up in the House of Lords to argue against granting this new title to the king. If the English "leap out of Peter's ship" Fisher warned, the country would be "drowned in the waves of all heresies, sects, schisms, and divisions."

As Lord Chancellor it was More's duty to support the king's new title. This he could not do, and so he resigned his office and retired to Chelsea.

After More's resignation events moved very quickly. In February 1533 Henry married Anne Boleyn secretly (she was pregnant at the time). Immediately afterward the new Lord Chancellor, Thomas Cromwell, introduced an act to Parliament forbidding an English subject to appeal to Rome in any matter whatsoever—a piece of legislation which More said marked England's break from the Catholic Church. In April Thomas Cranmer, the new archbishop of Canterbury, pronounced Henry's prior marriage invalid. Anne was proclaimed Queen of England. Thomas More was conspicuously absent from Anne's coronation in May.

To the world More appeared perfectly calm and collected amid these upheavals. But he confessed that at night he often lay awake in his bed troubled by "night fears" and "forecasting all such perils and painful deaths" that he might suffer because he had opposed the king.

In 1534 Parliament passed the Act of Succession which declared Catherine of Aragon's marriage to Henry null and decreed that the children of Anne Boleyn would be the heirs to the English throne. Then the Act went on to deny that the pope had any authority or jurisdiction in England. Finally all subjects of the king were required to take an oath supporting the Act.

On April 12, 1534, More was ordered to come to Lambeth Palace the next day to take the oath. He spent most of that night in prayer. Very early in the morning he attended Mass and received Holy Communion. Then he walked with his family in the garden where he said good-bye. He would not let any of them see him to the dock where some of his servants were waiting in a small boat to row him to London.

At Lambeth a panel of the king's commissioners led by Thomas Cromwell and Thomas Cranmer asked More if he was ready to swear to the Act of Succession. Like a good lawyer he requested to see the document first. The commissioners sat in impatient silence as he read through the legislation. When he finished More said he would not condemn any part of the Act nor any person who swore to it. Furthermore he would happily swear that he recognized the right of Queen Anne's children to inherit the crown. Since there was more to the act than the succession, More said, "I cannot swear without the jeopardizing of my soul to perpetual damnation." For this qualm of conscience More was imprisoned in the Tower of London.

Initially More's confinement was not harsh. His room was high in one of the turrets, not in the dungeon; he was free to walk in the grounds, including its gardens; and he could go to Mass each day at one of the chapels within the Tower. As the months passed, however, and More showed no sign of giving in he was moved to worse quarters, forbidden to leave his cell, and his books and writing materials were taken from him. After fourteen months of confinement he was finally brought to trial for treason on July 1, 1535, at Westminster Hall.

The transcript of More's trial is extant and is the best source we have of his subtle mind and skill as a lawyer. He defended himself well until a false witness stepped forward. Sir Richard Rich testified that More had confided to him that he rejected the king's title "Supreme Head of the Church in England." When Rich had finished his testimony More said, "In good faith Master Rich, I am sorrier for your perjury than for my own peril." Then he asked the court how they could trust the testimony of Rich, "a man...always reputed as one of so little truth." And he asked his judges if it was probable that he, Thomas More, would tell Rich "the secrets of my conscience touching the king's supremacy?"

More's appeal fell on deaf ears. The jury retired for fifteen minutes before returning a guilty verdict. Now More stood and spoke his mind. He denounced Parliament's Act of Succession as "directly repugnant to the laws of God." Then he reminded the court that "as the blessed apostle St. Paul, as we read in The Acts of the Apostles, was present and consented to the death of St. Stephen and kept their clothes that stoned him to death, and yet be they now both twain holy saints in heaven and shall continue there friends forever, so I verily trust and shall therefore heartily pray that though your Lordships have now here in the earth been

judges to my condemnation, we may yet hereafter in heaven mer-
rily all meet together."

At the end of this impassioned speech the court sentenced
Thomas More to the gruesome death of a traitor: hanging until
half dead, then taken down alive, the intestines ripped out of his
body and burned before his eyes, his genitals hacked off, and finally the mercy of beheading.

None of More's family was present in the courtroom, but
his children were waiting for him at the Tower. John More knelt
in the street to receive his father's blessing. Margaret Roper el-
bowed her way through the guards and flung her arms around
her father's neck, weeping, kissing him, refusing to let him go.

During the six days between More's condemnation and
his execution Henry VIII commuted the sentence to simple
beheading. On the morning of July 7 More dressed himself in his
best clothes, took a small wooden cross in his hand, and walked
the 200 yards from the Middle Gate of the Tower of London to
Tower Hill. A large crowd had turned out to witness his execution. On the scaffold he asked them to bear witness that he was
giving his life "for the faith of the Holy Catholic Church" and to
remember that he died "the king's good servant, but God's first."
Then he knelt down and recited Psalm 51, the *Miserere*. When
he had finished praying More forgave, blessed, and kissed the
headsman. When he had placed his neck on the block and indicated that he was ready, the executioner beheaded Thomas More
with a single blow of the ax.

Some of More's family were present when his body was
buried in the Chapel of St. Peter ad Vincula in the Tower. His
head was boiled, impaled on a stake, and displayed on London
Bridge. More's daughter Margaret retrieved the head and buried
it in her husband's family vault in the Church of St. Dunstan
outside the walls of Canterbury, where it remains to this day.

For Nurses

*St. Camillus de Lellis, the patron of nurses, revolutionized
health care in 16th-century Italy. His hospitals were
scrupulously clean, the sick received healthy meals,
and the nursing staff were trained professionals.*

Camillus de Lellis must have made an intimidating nurse.
Six feet six inches tall and powerfully built, a man who had been
a soldier and a compulsive gambler, he did not look like the nurturing type.

Camillus came by his fearsome aspect honestly. His father
was a professional mercenary who had made a career of fighting
for the prince who paid his soldiers the highest rate. In 1527, as
a member of the army of the Holy Roman Emperor Charles V,
the elder de Lellis took part in the notorious sack of Rome.

Camillus was born in Bucchianeto de Chieti in Italy's
province of Abruzzi. He was his parents' only surviving child and
a source of anxiety for his poor mother. He grew up to be lazy,
short-tempered, bullheaded, and undisciplined.

At age seventeen Camillus enlisted as a mercenary for Venice in a war against the Turks. He was in the same regiment as his
father who taught him the rough ways of the military camp, especially gambling. For the next seven years father and son were soldiers of fortune together, until the elder de Lellis fell mortally ill
and died. Camillus' one consolation in later years was that on his
deathbed his father suffered a pang of conscience. He called for a
priest, made a good confession, and received the Last Rites.

Camillus was 24 when his father died. The young man was

unemployed and flat broke after suffering a run of bad luck at the gambling table. Furthermore, he had developed on one leg an open ulcer that would not heal. For a time he found shelter in a Capuchin monastery where he did odd jobs. Attracted by the stability of Capuchin life and moved by his father's deathbed repentance, Camillus asked to join the order. The superiors of the monastery did not believe he had a vocation, so Camillus returned to the life of a gambling vagabond.

Camillus was in Rome when the ulcer on his leg became so bad he required immediate medical treatment. Once again all his money was gone, so he struck a deal with the administrators of the San Giacomo Hospital: they would treat his leg and he would work as one of the hospital's servants.

Hospitals in 16th-century Italy tended to be wretched, filthy places. The "nurses" were often vagrants like Camillus who were taken in off the streets and put to work sweeping the floors, washing dishes, and cleaning and feeding helpless patients. Often these nurses neglected the sick; sometimes they robbed them.

In such company it was easy for Camillus to get a card game going. But losses at the card table bred resentment, and the resentments led to fighting. When San Giacomo's administrators traced the brawls that plagued the hospital staff to Camillus, they threw him out into the street.

At the city of Manfredonia Camillus was begging outside a church when a well-to-do gentleman famous locally for his good works spotted the tall young beggar. He gave Camillus a job working on a monastery he was having built outside the town. The work was pure drudgery. Camillus, who had no training as a builder, did the most tedious jobs: heavy lifting, driving donkeys, running messages, bringing meals to the craftsmen.

He could have left the construction site at any time, but he stayed and in time he found satisfaction in having at last acquired some discipline and self-control. When the monastery was fin-

ished Camillus returned to San Giacomo's Hospital in Rome. The
year was 1575; Camillus was 25 years old.

The hospital administrator at San Giacomo gave Camillus
a second chance. Meanwhile Camillus introduced himself to St.
Philip Neri, who agreed to serve as his spiritual director. The onetime mercenary and compulsive gambler had learned how hard
work could banish his old vices. Now he was learning that the
best reason to work was not for wages, but out of love for God
and for one's neighbor. Combining this inspiration with his experiences at the hospital, Camillus conceived the idea of founding
a religious society of laymen and priests dedicated to the loving
care of the sick.

Camillus converted a house in a bad part of town into a
tiny hospital, a decision which Philip Neri believed to be a serious mistake. Neri was certain that left to his own devices in a
neighborhood full of temptations Camillus would fall back into
his old habits. He urged Camillus to give up this idea of founding a nursing order and return to work at San Giacomo. Camillus
refused, and the once warm friendship between the two saints
turned chilly.

Camillus and his nurses went into the worst slums of
Rome to find the sick, the dying, and the abandoned. His hospitals set the standard for other institutions: wards were well ven-
tilated, the patients received healthy meals, and those suffering
from contagious diseases were quarantined. While many hospitals of the day tried only to make the sick comfortable until they
died, Camillus and his nurses sought effective treatments that
would restore the patients to health.

At the end of his life Camillus was tortured by memories
of his sinful past. When the general of the Carmelites visited him
Camillus begged the priest, "Pray for me, for I have been a great
sinner, a gambler, and a man of bad life." Before death came Camillus' confidence in God's mercy was restored. He stretched out

his arms so his body took the form of a cross, and giving thanks
for the Blood of Christ which had washed away his sins, he died.

Camillus was beatified in 1742 and canonized by Benedict
XIV in 1756. St. Camillus de Lellis lies buried in the little Church
of Santa Maria Maddalena in Rome. He was named patron of
nurses in 1930 by Pope Pius XI.

For Physicians

Ss. Cosmas and Damian (died c.287) Feast day: September 26

The patron saints of physicians, Ss. Cosmas and Damian, were doctors who never charged their patients a fee.

The twin brothers Cosmas and Damian were Christian Arabs who studied medicine at an academy in Syria. They opened a joint practice in the city of Aegeae near modern-day Iskendrun, Turkey. There the brothers made a name for themselves by treating the sick without charging a fee, and for teaching their patients about Christ. When a persecution of Christians broke out in Asia Minor, Cosmas and Damian were among its first targets.

They were arrested along with their three younger brothers Anthimus, Leontius, and Euprepius, and arraigned before the Roman governor who condemned all five to death. Legend says the brothers were chained hand and foot and thrown into the sea, but they floated safely to the surface. Then they were bound to stakes to be burned, but the flames billowed away from the martyrs. Next they were tied to crosses and bystanders and soldiers were invited to throw rocks and shoot arrows at them, but the missiles turned back striking the assailants instead. In the end Cosmas and Damian and their brothers were all beheaded.

By the year 400 a church had been built over the martyrs' grave. By the year 500 so many miracles were being wrought at the shrine that the custodians of the church began to record them (the record has come down to us). Since Ss. Cosmas and Damian were so popular in Rome, Pope St. Felix III (reigned 526-530) acquired their relics and enshrined them in a fine basilica which still stands overlooking the Forum near the Colosseum.

It was the custom for invalids seeking the intercession of Ss. Cosmas and Damian to spend a night in the martyrs' church. The saints would come to the sick in a dream and heal them by performing a miraculous medical procedure. The most famous case tells of a man whose leg was being eaten away by cancer. He was carried to the Basilica of Ss. Cosmas and Damian where he settled down for the night near their shrine. In a dream he saw the brother saints amputate his diseased leg and replace it with the leg of a Moor who had just died that day. The next morning the man awoke to find he was perfectly healthy and had a new leg, albeit a black one.

For Police Officers
St. Michael the Archangel   Feast day: September 29

Like the police officers whose patron he is, St. Michael the
Archangel enforces God's law and defends God's people from harm.

The name Michael means "Who is like God?" It was the war cry of the holy angels when they drove Lucifer and his rebel angels from Heaven.

Although it wasn't until 1950 that Pope Pius XII named St. Michael the patron of police officers the great archangel has been venerated as the guardian of God's people since ancient times. Devotion to him even predates Christianity, as we see in the biblical Book of Daniel. The author of Daniel, writing at the end of the second century before Christ during the persecution of the Jews under the tyrant Antiochus, assured the Israelites that in the archangel Michael they had a "great prince who has charge for your people" (Daniel 12:1).

As early as the age of the Apostles, the Christian Church, seeing itself as the New Israel, adopted St. Michael as its protector. The Book of Revelation (also known to as the Apocalypse) pauses in its graphic account of the final days of the world to return to the beginning of time when St. Michael, the captain of the angelic host, drove Satan and the other rebel angels from Heaven.

At approximately the same time the Book of Revelation was being written, St. Michael appeared in another early Christian work, *The Shepherd of Hermas*, written about the year 120, possibly by Hermas, the brother of Pope St. Pius I. In this mystical text Hermas describes the archangel as "the great and glorious angel Michael" who examines Christians at the end of their life to determine if they have kept the law of God.

In addition to the handful of places in Sacred Scripture where Michael is mentioned by name, Bible commentators in the early centuries of the Church speculated that God sent Michael on other missions as well. He is said to be the angel who guarded the entrance to Eden with a flaming sword (Genesis 3:24), the angel who blocked Balaam's path as he went to curse the Israelites (Numbers 22:22), and the angel who in the night struck down the Assyrian army that was besieging Jerusalem (2 Kings 19:35).

Elaborating on these interpretations, Jacobus de Voragine, author of *The Golden Legend*, records the medieval traditions that God sent St. Michael to inflict the ten plagues on Egypt, to part the Red Sea, and to lead the Hebrews safely through the desert to the Promised Land. Furthermore, at the end of time St. Michael will slay the Antichrist, and at the cry of the archangel the dead shall rise from their graves. Then at the Last Judgment St. Michael will stand before the vast assembly of the living and the dead bearing the tokens of Christ's Passion—the cross, the nails, the spear, and the crown of thorns.

In addition to his appearances in the Bible, St. Michael is said to have appeared to the faithful many times since the earliest days of the Church. In most of these early apparitions St. Michael came as a healer. At his ancient shrine near Constantinople, the Michaelion, sick pilgrims would keep vigil at night, waiting for St. Michael to come and heal them. An appearance of St. Michael in Normandy in 708 inspired the building of the great shrine of Mont St. Michel, and gave rise to St. Michael's title as patron of mariners.

Perhaps the most renowned of St. Michael's non-biblical appearances are centered around Monte Gargano, Italy. Here St. Michael is said to have appeared on four different occasions, beginning in 490, showing himself to be both a healer and a protector of the Christian faithful. A large shrine stands at Monte Gargano, built over the Grotto of St. Michael—an ancient chapel reputedly formed by the Archangel himself. Today this grotto is the only Catholic place of worship not consecrated by human hand, and is known as the "Celestial Basilica".

For Postal Workers

St. Gabriel the Archangel   Feast day: September 29

The archangel Gabriel, the patron saint of postal workers, is perhaps God's favorite messenger. He carried messages from Heaven to the Blessed Virgin Mary, St. Joseph, and St. Zachary.

In St. Luke's gospel Gabriel is the angel of two annunciations. First he appears to the priest Zachary and informs him that his wife will give birth to a son, John the Baptist. Then he pays a visit to the Blessed Virgin to announce that she has been chosen by God to be the Mother of the Savior. Gabriel's greeting to the Virgin, "Hail Mary, full of the grace, the Lord is with thee," is still recited daily by millions of the faithful.

In Hebrew Gabriel means "power of God," and Jewish tradition emphasizes the archangel's power: Gabriel is said to be the angel who destroyed Sodom. Christian tradition, however, emphasizes Gabriel the messenger. He is believed to be the unnamed angel who appeared to St. Joseph, announced the birth of Christ to the shepherds, and will blow the trumpet on the last day to announce the end of the world.

For Psychiatrists

St. Christina the Astonishing (1150-1224) Feast day: July 24

St. Christina's extreme behavior—possibly the result of schizophrenia—led psychiatrists to adopt her as their patron.

Christina was the youngest of three sisters who lived in the town of Saint Trond in Belgium. After the death of their parents the young women set themselves up as a little religious community in their parents' house. Their family "convent" had not been in operation long when Christina, then 22 years old, fell ill and died. At the Requiem Mass, Christina suddenly sat up in her coffin and levitated to the rafters of the church. All the mourners fled the church in terror except for Christina's eldest sister and the priest. When the funeral prayers were concluded he commanded Christina to come down from her perch. She obeyed.

She told her friends that when she "died" she visited Hell, Purgatory, and Heaven. In Heaven Christ offered her a choice: to remain with him now, or to return to earth and by her sufferings to bring many sinners to repentance. Christina chose to go back to earth and save souls. Then she warned her friends not to be surprised by anything she did since God had directed her to act in ways "never seen before among mortals."

Saying that she could not bear the smell of humans (some interpreters have taken this to mean Christina could smell sin on her fellow men), she fled to deserted places, or climbed to the tops of tall trees, or sought refuge in castle towers or church steeples—any place far removed from human contact. She threw herself into fires and thorn bushes, and stood for hours in a freez-

176

ing river. She went to graveyards and wailed for the dead who had died in their sins.

Christina was a constant source of embarrassment to her sisters and to her friends. They thought she was mad or possessed and locked her up, but she always escaped. Since confining her was useless they prayed to God to moderate Christina's actions, and He heard their prayer. One day Christina entered a church, climbed into the baptismal font, and completely immersed herself in the holy water. When she climbed out of the font she was calmer and content to live among people once again.

Christina made a point of begging from the hard-hearted. She said if she could move sinners to be merciful in this life, God would be merciful to them in the next. Once she walked into the house of a notoriously sinful man while he was enjoying a sumptuous meal. She begged for something to drink. To everyone's surprise the man gave Christina some of his fine wine. Afterward Christina said that by this single act of charity the man had ensured his salvation. She predicted that on his deathbed he would repent.

When Count Louis of Looz was dying he called Christina to his bedside. He told her all the sins he had committed since he was a boy and begged her to pray for his soul after his death. Christina did pray earnestly for the count, pleading with God to let her share half of the sufferings the count was enduring in Purgatory. Her prayer was granted; Christina's sisters were witnesses as she suffered first from fire, then from terrible cold.

When Christina felt she was dying she retired to a convent where her friend Beatrice was a nun. When Christina died before revealing certain secrets which Beatrice wanted to know, the nun threw herself on her lifeless body, calling on Christina to come back. Suddenly Christina's eyes opened. In a weary voice she answered Beatrice's questions. Then Christina made the sign of the cross over the nuns, settled back on her pillow, and died— for the third time in her life.

For Teachers

St. John Baptist de la Salle (1651–1719) Feast day: April 7

*St. John Baptist de la Salle's common sense approach
to classroom instruction has been adopted by parochial
and public schools around the world. In 1950 Pope
Pius XII named St. John patron of teachers.*

The teaching method St. John Baptist de la Salle advocated has become so well established in parochial, private, and public schools that it is difficult to imagine there was a time when some Church authorities in France considered de la Salle a dangerous radical. De la Salle's common sense classroom philosophy developed over decades and was based on his personal experience teaching children of vastly different social classes and intellectual abilities.

The heart of de la Salle's method was a curriculum which taught a set of skills ranging from the simple to the more complex. A student could not pass to a higher grade until he or she had mastered the course work in the current grade. St. John also believed it was wrong for a teacher to adhere rigidly to one way of teaching or explaining a subject; if the class was not grasping the material de la Salle insisted that it was the teacher's obligation to find another approach to make the lessons understandable.

De la Salle knew that students learn at different rates; he would not let his teachers leave slower learners behind. He insisted that children should be taught to read in their vernacular language first; they could learn to read Latin later. Finally St. John believed teaching by the question-and-answer method was better than lecturing or reading the textbook aloud to the class.

He called his teaching order Brothers of the Christian Schools because Christian doctrine and Christian practice were as important in de la Salle's curriculum as secular learning. Students and teachers prayed together at set times throughout the day. They attended daily Mass together. They studied the catechism in the classroom. Even lessons in good manners were given a Christian spin: since everyone was a child of God and a temple of the Holy Spirit, everyone, regardless of social class, deserved to be treated with courtesy.

John Baptist de la Salle did not set out to be an educational innovator. He was the eldest child of an aristocratic family from the French province of Champagne. His parents Louis de la Salle and Nicolle de Moet de Brouillet brought him up to be religious and self-disciplined, but also conscious of his rank. By age eleven he was already preparing for a career in the Church. He was ordained a priest in 1678 and settled into a comfortable life as a canon of the Cathedral of Rheims. He said Mass daily, was conscientious about participating in the religious functions of the cathedral, but he had no pastoral duties.

All that changed when de la Salle met Adrien Nyel, a layman who had opened four schools for poor children in Rouen and now wanted to open such a school in Rheims. Initially de la Salle was little more than a benefactor of the school. Drawing upon his large inheritance and upon the income he received as a canon de la Salle paid the teachers' salaries and even rented a house for them.

Nyel and de la Salle had no trouble finding students—the poor children of Rheims flocked to the schools—but finding good instructors was another matter, and Nyel had no talent for training teachers. A priest whom St. John respected told him the best way for de la Salle to train his teachers was to have them live with him. The idea made de la Salle cringe. He recalled later that he regarded these teachers as men who ranked lower than his servants. "The very thought of living with them," de la Salle said, "was unbearable." Nonetheless he overcame his snobbery, invited the teachers into his home, and by trial and error began formulating a new way to teach children.

In 1684 de la Salle resigned his office as canon and with twelve men formed the Brothers of the Christian Schools. De la Salle told his disciples that they were "ambassadors of Christ to the young." And he reminded them if they hoped to teach the faith to others, they would have to be steeped in it themselves.

The number of schools operated by de la Salle's brothers grew steadily in France throughout the 18th century. In 1789 there were 1000 Brothers of the Christian Schools in 121 communities. The French Revolution suppressed the order, and some of the brothers died on the scaffold, but in the 19th century the order was revived. Today there are about 8000 teaching brothers whose influence extends far beyond their own classrooms.

For Writers

St. Francis de Sales (1567-1622) Feast day: January 24

Many saints were prolific writers but St. Francis de Sales was persuasive. The leaflets he published on the truths of the Catholic faith—written in clear, polished prose—brought thousands of Calvinists back to the Church. For nearly 400 years his Introduction to the Devout Life *has been a beloved "how to" book on giving up sinful habits and growing closer to God. Pope Pius XI named him the patron saint of writers in 1923.*

Francis de Sales spent many years of his life laboring to turn back the chaos and bloodshed the Reformation and the Wars of Religion had brought to the Savoy region of Switzerland and southeastern France.

The de Sales family belonged to the minor nobility and were staunch Catholics, but Francis fell victim to the religious turmoil of his age. The question of predestination, the hottest point of contention between Catholic and Calvinist theologians, tormented him while a student in Paris. In his distress over the uncertain fate of his soul he cried out to God, "Whatever happens, Lord, may I at least love you in this life if I cannot love you in eternity." Francis credited the Blessed Virgin with saving him from falling into despair or heresy; he recited the *Memorare* day after day, and she did not leave him unaided.

After he completed his studies in Paris Francis went to Padua to take a doctorate in civil and canon law. His father expected him to become a statesman, but Francis was indecisive about what to do with his life. At his parents' chateau Francis met Claude de Granier, the bishop of Geneva who had been driven out of his city by the Calvinists. The bishop, impressed by Francis' knowledge of canon law, suggested he find his career in the Church. Inspired by the exiled bishop Francis began studying for the priesthood. He was ordained in 1593.

Almost immediately following Francis' ordination Pope Clement VIII appointed him provost of Geneva, an office second only to the bishop. His job was to make the diocese of Geneva Catholic again. It was a daunting assignment.

Calvinism had overrun the diocese in 1533. The Calvinists expelled the Catholic clergy, shut down monasteries and convents, desecrated churches and chapels, and outlawed all practice of the Catholic religion. The duke of Savoy reinstalled the bishop and clergy by force in 1564, but the Calvinists drove them out again in 1591. Pope Clement and Bishop de Granier expected Francis to reconvert 60,000 Calvinists to the Catholic faith.

Since it was impossible for him to visit every hamlet and farm in this mountainous region Francis fell back on a talent he had cultivated in the university; he wrote a series of leaflets explaining and defending the essentials of Catholic doctrine and had them distributed throughout the diocese. Meanwhile he and his cousin Louis de Sales, also a priest, traveled through the region preaching to and debating with the Calvinists.

Some Catholics thought Francis was rash traveling through the diocese without a military escort when Calvinist vigilantes were known to attack and kill Catholic priests. Others thought Francis should have asked the Duke of Savoy for troops to compel the Protestants of Geneva to return to the Catholic Church. But Francis did not want people to think he was afraid, nor would he accept any coerced conversions.

Success came slowly. In his first year Francis won 200 converts. In his second year he was able to have a weekly Mass said in public at Thonon, one of the main towns of the region.

Pope Clement sent Francis on a unique mission to Theodore Beza, a father of the Reformation in Switzerland, to persuade him to return to the Catholic faith. Beza received Francis and their discussions were cordial. He even went so far as to concede that the Catholic Church was an authentic church, but he would not renounce his Calvinism. As he walked Francis to the door at the end of their final meeting Beza tactfully commented, "If I am not on the right road, I do pray to God every day that His mercy will guide me to it."

In 1597, after four years of constant labor, Francis had revived Catholicism to the point where he could initiate the Forty Hours Devotion in the diocese. By paying public homage to the Blessed Sacrament Francis would underscore Catholic faith in the Real Presence, a doctrine the Calvinists rejected. He decided to hold the Forty Hours at Annemesse, and brought hundreds of Catholics to the town for the celebration. It was an impressive expression of faith. It did not convert any Calvinists, but it did strengthen the diocese's nervous Catholic minority.

In 1598 Pope Clement named Francis coadjutor, or assistant, bishop of Geneva. One of his first acts was to open a missionary center in Thonon for the purpose of training priests to reevangelize Savoy. He traveled to Paris to see King Henry IV about the political troubles of the region. The king and the bishop got along so well that Henry offered Francis a wealthy bishopric in France. "Sire, I have married a poor wife and I cannot desert her for a richer one," Francis replied. In 1602 Bishop de Granier died and Francis was named his successor.

By this time two-thirds of his diocese had returned to the Catholic Church, but the diocese of Geneva had many other problems. There were 450 parishes but not enough priests to administer them. There was no diocesan seminary. All the surviving monasteries in the region—with the exception of the Carthusians—were in need of reform. And Bishop de Sales was still exiled from his cathedral city, Geneva.

Since he had no seminary Francis taught theology courses himself and examined personally each new candidate for the
priesthood. He gave catechism classes to children. He preached
everywhere. He corresponded with hundreds of people seeking
his spiritual direction—over 2000 of his letters survive. And he
wrote treatises on everything from how to teach religion to how
to bring religious orders back to their original zeal.

Francis' most enduring legacy as a writer is his *Introduction to the Devout Life*. He wrote it, he said, "for those who live
in towns, in families, and at court [and are] obliged to lead out-
wardly at least an ordinary life." The aim of this practical, psy-
chologically astute manual was to help ordinary Christians give
up careless habits and old attachments to sin and bring them step
by step to a deeper love of God. The book became a best-seller
and the publisher made a fortune. Francis, to the horror of every
writer ever since, would accept no royalties.

Eventually, Francis' tireless preaching, his prayers and his
writing brought nearly the entire population of Savoy back to the
Catholic faith. But the gates of Geneva were never opened to him
nor was he ever enthroned in the city's Cathedral of St. Peter. In
autumn 1622 Francis' trouble with high blood pressure and a
weak heart caught up with him. Immediately after Christmas he
had a stroke. His doctors prescribed the barbaric "cure" of the
time—they burned the back of his skull with a hot iron, applied
a plaster that raised blisters on his bald head, then stripped it off
and applied the hot iron to Francis' raw skin. During the gruesome procedure tears rolled down his cheeks as he repeated,
"Jesus! Mary!" Francis died a few hours later on December 28.

The cause for the canonization of Francis de Sales opened
almost immediately after his death. In 1663 Pope Alexander VII
declared him blessed. Two years later the same pope proclaimed
Francis de Sales a saint.

Joy in the Lord:
Saints to Play With

BLESSED PIER GIORGIO FRASSATI

Joy in the Lord:
Saints to Play With

As the father of Gregorian chant, Pope St. Gregory the Great was the obvious candidate for patron of music and musicians. His position went unchallenged for 700 years until the proliferation of pipe organs in churches and a misreading of a line in the Divine Office pushed Gregory into the background and advanced St. Cecilia as the patron of all things musical.

The line that caused the shift is "*cantantibus organis illa in corde suo sui domino decantabat*," while the instruments were playing, she (Cecilia) would sing to her Lord in her heart. Apparently readers in the 14th century read *cantantibus organis* as "the organ was playing" and interpreted the rest of the phrase to mean that Cecilia herself was the organist. The image of a beautiful young woman seated at a pipe organ singing sweetly to God captured the popular imagination of the faithful in a way that St. Gregory the Great never did.

In the case of St. Sebastian and St. Bernard of Menthon the shift has been one of emphasis. Today archery is a sport; in the Middle Ages it was a military skill. When archers invoked St. Sebastian to guide their arrows, the targets in their minds were enemy troops, not a painted bull's-eye. In the same way, apprehensive pilgrims at one time invoked St. Bernard of Menthon to deliver them safely through the Alps. By 1923, however, when Pope Pius XI declared Bernard the patron of mountain climbers, modern highways had more or less eliminated the hazards of mountain travel. St. Bernard, the onetime protector of wayfarers who inched along dangerous mountain trails, has become the patron of hikers and rock climbers who seek out the most challenging peaks and sheer rock faces where they hope to experience the kind of adrenaline rush their ancestors tried to avoid.

Newly added to the list of patron saints is Blessed Pier Giorgio Frassati, an avid, sometimes reckless, mountain climber, hiker and skier. He is the logical choice for patron of today's extreme sports. In fact in Europe Pier Giorgio is often taken as the patron of Catholic athletic associations. At this writing Catholics in the United States have assigned Blessed Pier Giorgio a tamer designation—patron of World Youth Day.

It has taken a long time for patron saints of leisure activities to become part of the life of the Church. In earlier ages it may have seemed frivolous to ask Heaven to watch over swimmers or ice skaters. Yet it is part of the genius of Christianity to sanctify every aspect of life. Whatever can be put to a good purpose can be blessed—as anyone knows who has ever looked through the bewildering array of blessings that are contained in the Roman Ritual.

For Archers

St. Sebastian (died c.300) Feast day: January 20

In the Middle Ages archers took as their patron St. Sebastian,
the Roman martyr who was shot through with arrows.

The figure of St. Sebastian pierced by arrows is one of the most recognizable images in Christian art. With St. Agnes and St. Lawrence he is also one of the most revered of the Roman martyrs. Only a few years after his death a basilica was erected over his tomb on the Appian Way.

In spite of the antiquity of devotion to St. Sebastian and the obvious esteem in which he was held, we now possess very few facts about his life. All that we know for certain is what St. Ambrose tells us of Sebastian; he was a native of Milan who became a soldier and was martyred in Rome. This makes sense since Diocletian began his persecution of the Church by eliminating all Christians in the Roman army. By the fifth century, however, a richly detailed account of Sebastian's life circulated among Christian readers. Probably very little of it is accurate, but it is a fine legend nonetheless that is worth repeating.

According to this legend, Sebastian won the confidence of the co-emperors Diocletian and Maximian. They gave him command of the First Cohort of the Roman legions and then made him a member of the Praetorians, the bodyguards of the emperors. Sebastian used his rank to visit Christians in prison. He encouraged them to remain steadfast and bear their tortures with courage. Among the martyrs he visited were twin brothers, Marcellian and Marcus. These young men had been condemned to death but before the sentence was carried out the prefect of Rome permitted their parents, wives, and children to visit them in their cell in hopes that the grief of the family would persuade the brothers to renounce Christianity. At first it appeared that the prefect was correct; the weeping of their loved ones was unnerving the martyrs. As their resolution wavered, however, Sebastian spoke up. Addressing Marcellian and Marcus as "soldiers of Christ," he reminded them that the happiness of this world was nothing compared to the joys of eternal life in Heaven.

Their courage restored by Sebastian, Marcellian and Marcus rejected the pleas of their family to renounce their faith. The guards then led the young men to the place of execution, where their arms were bound behind their backs and their feet were nailed to wooden stakes. Then two executioners took up lances and ran the brothers through.

By encouraging Marcellian and Marcus, Sebastian had revealed himself as a Christian. When Sebastian was arraigned before the tribunal, Diocletian reproached him as an ingrate and a traitor who accepted honors from the emperor but secretly conspired against the welfare of the empire. Sebastian denied the accusation. "I have always prayed to Christ to save your soul and to uphold the empire," he said.

Because Sebastian had been a member of the imperial bodyguard he was sentenced by Diocletian to an especially cruel death. He ordered Sebastian's fellow Praetorians to take the prisoner to their camp outside the city walls, tie him to a stake, and shoot him to death with arrows. In obedience to the emperor's command the soldiers riddled Sebastian's body with arrows. Then they left him for dead.

After dark a Christian woman named Irene came to the camp to collect Sebastian's body for burial. As she cut him down from the stake she found he was still alive. Irene took Sebastian to her house where she nursed him back to health.

Once his strength returned Sebastian went straight to the imperial palace where he confronted Diocletian on the steps. The emperor was shaken when he saw Sebastian standing before him. "Isn't this Sebastian whom I sentenced to be shot to death with arrows?" Diocletian asked.

"The Lord kept me alive," Sebastian responded bravely, "so I could come back and rebuke you for your cruelty to the servants of Christ." Diocletian had heard enough. To his guards he said, "Kill him."

The Praetorians surrounded Sebastian. They beat him to death where he stood on the palace steps. When they were certain he was dead, they dumped his body in the Cloaca Maxima, Rome's main sewer.

That night St. Sebastian appeared to Lucina, who was a devout Christian woman. "In the sewer beside the Circus you will find my body," he told her. With a few Christian friends Lucina set out to retrieve the corpse. They found it exactly where the vision said it would be. The Christians washed the filth and blood from the body and wrapped it in a shroud. Then they bore it outside the walls of Rome down the Appian Way to a vault in the catacombs known ever since as San Sebastiano.

For Actors and Drama Students
St. Genesius (died c. 300) Feast day: August 25

*Actors and drama students venerate as their patron
St. Genesius, a Roman actor who converted to
Christianity in the middle of a stage performance.*

Tradition has it that Genesius was a comic actor in Rome during the reign of Diocletian. While performing a parody of baptism before the emperor, Genesius was unexpectedly touched by grace. He stopped delivering his sacrilegious lines and from his place on the stage rebuked the emperor for his cruelty to Christians.

Initially Diocletian thought the speech was part of the script. As Genesius went on, however, the emperor realized that the comedian was sincere. He stopped the performance, had Genesius arrested, and condemned him to be tortured to death.

As they tore his flesh with iron hooks and burned him with torches, the executioners urged Genesius to renounce his newfound faith and save his life. "Were I to be killed a thousand times for my allegiance to Christ," replied Genesius, "I would still go on as I have begun." In the midst of his agony the actor said that he regretted "sneering at the Holy Name," and "coming so late to worship the true King."

St. Genesius' relics are enshrined in the Church of Santa Susanna, the parish serving the American community in Rome.

Devotion to St. Genesius remains strong in the contemporary theatrical community, especially in Manhattan's theater district where St. Malachy's Church has a side chapel dedicated to the martyred actor.

For Fishermen

St. Peter (died c.64) Feast days: June 29 and February 22

St. Peter supported his family by fishing in the Sea of Galilee until Christ called him to leave his boat and his nets and become a "fisher of men." He has always been invoked both by commercial fishermen and those who fish for sport.

St. Peter, chief of the apostles and the first pope, began his working life as a fisherman. With his brother St. Andrew and the two sons of Zebedee, St. James and St. John, he formed a partnership to work the Sea of Galilee. He lived with his wife and mother-in-law a short walk from the seashore in a house in Capernaum that has been identified by archaeologists. While Peter and Andrew were casting their nets into the sea, Christ called them to follow him and become "fishers of men."

His given name was Simon, but Christ renamed his chief apostle Peter, saying, "You are Peter, and on this rock I will build my Church." The name is a play on words since Peter is derived from the Greek word for rock, petros.

There is a long-standing tradition of referring to St. Peter as the Prince of the Apostles, and if that title seems a bit grand for a fisherman it is nonetheless true that he ranked first among the Twelve. Whenever the gospel writers list the apostles Peter is named first. When the other apostles want to ask the Lord some question, Peter is their spokesman. At the first Pentecost it is Peter, full of the Holy Spirit, who speaks for all the others, delivering the first Christian sermon.

The Catholic Church believes that Peter's authority came

directly from Christ and has passed down to every pope since that day. This belief is derived from an episode recorded in the 16th chapter of St. Matthew's gospel, in which Christ asks the apostles: "Who do men say that the Son of man is?" The apostles answer, "Some say John the Baptist, others say Elijah, and others Jeremiah or one of the prophets." When Jesus asks what the apostles themselves think concerning his identity, Peter answers boldly, "You are the Christ, the Son of the living God."

After this confession of faith Christ declares Peter blessed, and tells him that this truth was revealed to him by God the Father. Then Christ says: "You are Peter, and on this rock I will build my church, and the powers of death shall not prevail against it. I will give you the keys of the kingdom of heaven, and whatever you bind on earth shall be bound in heaven, and whatever you loose on earth shall be loosed in heaven." (Matthew 16:18-19) Visitors to Rome can see this text inscribed in letters nearly six feet high around the interior of the great dome of St. Peter's in the Vatican.

Peter's outspokenness on this occasion is a good measure of his character. He was blunt and impulsive, an impetuous man. When he saw Christ walking on the Sea of Galilee, Peter climbed out of his fishing boat and tried to walk across the water to meet him. At the Transfiguration, as James and John cowered in terror before the vision of Christ in glory, Peter spoke up, offering to build three huts for Christ, Moses and Elijah so they could remain on the mountain top forever. On the night of the Last Supper Peter swore that he would follow Jesus anywhere, even to death itself. In Gethsemane when the mob laid hands on Jesus to arrest him, Peter drew his sword and sliced off the ear of Malchus, a servant of the high priest. But only minutes later in the high priest's courtyard Peter's bravado failed him. Three times he denied he had ever known Jesus.

After his Resurrection Christ appeared several times to

Peter. On one of these occasions he came to Peter and some of the Twelve as they were fishing in the Sea of Tiberias. After identifying himself by granting Peter a miraculous catch, the Lord asked Peter, "Do you love me more than these?"

"Yes Lord," Peter answered, "you know that I love you." Three times Christ repeated the question, as if to erase Peter's three denials. Peter, in an agony of conscience, wincing each time Jesus asked, tried to settle the matter once and for all. "Lord you know everything," said Peter, "you know that I love you."

After Christ's Ascension into Heaven, Peter performed the first miracle by an apostle, healing the crippled man at the Temple gate. In Lydda he cured Aeneas, a man who had been bedridden for eight years with palsy. He raised from the dead Tabitha, a woman famous for her good works. As word of Peter's power to heal spread, Jews from outside Jerusalem brought their sick into the city. They laid them on pallets along the streets in the hope that as Peter walked by his shadow might fall on them and restore them to health.

In many ways St. Peter remained a conservative son of Israel. He was faithful to the ancient customs of his people and uncomfortable with the party in the Church that wanted to sweep away the Law of Moses to make Christianity more attractive to the Gentiles. It took a voice from Heaven to convince Peter that Christians were not bound by Jewish dietary laws and the prompting of the Holy Spirit to teach Peter that God is no respecter of persons but wants the gospel brought to all nations. Peter put this lesson into practice immediately by baptizing the Roman centurion Cornelius and all his household.

Christians who converted from Judaism were scandalized that Peter broke Jewish religious law by consorting with the Gentile Cornelius, even eating with him. Although he defended himself the dispute troubled Peter; in the future he took pains to conceal from Jewish Christians all his meetings and meals with Gentiles.

Later, in a much uglier confrontation, St. Paul characterized Peter's discretion as hypocrisy, a charge which may have caused permanent harm to the friendship of these two great apostles.

After Herod Agrippa had executed St. James the Greater, he had Peter arrested and thrown into prison. Herod did not take any chances with his prize prisoner; Peter was bound with two chains. Two soldiers remained with him at all times in his cell while several more soldiers guarded the door.

In the middle of the night an angel appeared in the cell. He nudged the sleeping Peter and as the apostle stood up the chains fell from his wrists. The angel led him safely past all the guards, and when they got to the gate that led out to the street the massive iron door swung open by itself. Peter hurried to the home of a fellow Christian, where many had gathered to pray for him. Peter explained how an angel had delivered him. Then he entrusted the Church in Jerusalem to St. James the Less and left the city.

The theologian Origen (185-254) and the Church historian Eusebius (c.264-340) tell us that St. Peter founded the Church in Antioch. This appears very likely since in his letter to the Galatians St. Paul mentions that Peter was in Antioch.

We do not know exactly when Peter arrived in Rome. We do however know that he was arrested during Nero's persecution of the Church, and an ancient tradition says that he and St. Paul were incarcerated in the Mamertine Prison, a grim underground cavern beside the Roman Forum now converted into a chapel. Christ's cryptic words to Peter at the end of St. John's gospel are taken to be a prediction of martyrdom: "When you are old, you will stretch out your hands, and another will gird you and carry you where you do not wish to go."

The apocryphal *Acts of Peter*, written in the second century, records that when the persecution began the Christians of Rome urged Peter to save himself. He had left the city and was walking along the Appian Way when he saw Christ coming toward him. "*Domine, quo vadis?*" Peter asked, "Where are you going, Lord?" Christ answered, "If you desert my people, I am going to Rome to be crucified again." So Peter turned back.

Peter was crucified in an arena that stood where St. Peter's Square stands today. Origen says Peter asked to be crucified upside down, saying he was not worthy to die as his Lord had died. Christians buried his body in a cemetery on Vatican Hill. Around the year 80 Pope Cletus erected a shrine known as the Tropaion over St. Peter's grave. In the third century, during another persecution, the relics of St. Peter and St. Paul were moved for safety to the Catacomb of San Sebastiano. They remained there until the early fourth century when Emperor Constantine built the basilicas of St. Peter and St. Paul Outside the Walls.

In 1941, during excavations under the High Altar of St. Peter's, archaeologists found the apostle's tomb and the bones of an elderly, physically robust man. In 1968 Pope Paul VI announced to the world that after considerable study and examination he believed these bones were the bones of St. Peter. They remain today in their original grave directly under the High Altar of St. Peter's Basilica.

As keeper of the keys to Heaven St. Peter is the patron of locksmiths. As the first pope he is the guardian of the papacy. But St. Peter is most widely renowned as the much venerated patron of fishermen. The blessing of commercial fishing fleets in St. Peter's name is an annual event in places as varied as Stonington, Connecticut; Gloucester, Massachusetts; Ulladulla, New South Wales; and and the island of Pantelleria which is located off the coast of Sicily.

For Horseback Riders

St. Martin of Tours (c336-397) Feast day: November 11

St. Martin became patron of all riders because in works of art he is invariably shown on horseback dividing his cloak with a beggar.

The earliest writings celebrating heroes of the Church were concerned with acts of the martyrs. These writings recorded how Christians died. The life of St. Martin, written by his close friend Sulpicius Severus, is the first biography written in praise of how a Christian lived.

Martin was born in what is now Szombathely, Hungary. His father was a Roman soldier who eventually rose to the rank of tribune. Both of Martin's parents were pagans, yet when he was still a boy he was drawn to the Christian faith. At age ten he enrolled as a catechumen, an act which infuriated his father. By the time he was twelve Martin was imagining himself a hermit. He still had not been baptized when his father had Martin drafted into the military. Martin, fifteen years old at this time, resisted and tried to run away, but his father had the boy manacled and dragged to the recruiting station where he was compelled to take the military oath. Based on this event in Martin's life some have proposed Martin as the patron saint of those who resist the draft.

Sulpicius says Martin attempted to practice Christian virtues even in the army. He had only one servant whom he treated as an equal. They ate their meals together and even took turns cleaning each others boots. From his soldier's pay Martin kept what was necessary to sustain himself and his servant and gave the rest to the needy.

Martin was stationed at Amiens in France. Once, on a bitterly cold winter's day, Martin saw at the city gate a poor man dressed in rags, begging those walking by for some warm clothes. Martin's money was already gone and he had nothing of value on him, so drawing his sword he cut his own warm cloak and gave half to the shivering beggar. Some bystanders laughed at Martin, who looked foolish wearing half a cloak. Others felt a pang of conscience because they could have helped the man, too, but they had done nothing.

That night as Martin lay in bed he had a vision of Christ surrounded by a multitude of angels. The Lord was wrapped in half of Martin's cloak. "Look," Christ said to the angels. "Martin, who has not even been baptized yet, clothed me with this robe."

Martin was twenty when at last he received the sacrament of baptism. Soon afterward his company was called up to fight a barbarian tribe. The day before the battle all the soldiers lined up to receive combat pay. When Martin's turn came, however, he told the emperor, Julian the Apostate, that although he had been a soldier of Rome for five years he now served Christ and it was not right for him to kill. Julian took Martin's scruples for cowardice, but Martin denied that he was afraid. He offered to prove both his courage and his faith the next day. "I will take my stand unarmed before the line of battle tomorrow," he said, "and in the name of the Lord Jesus, protected by the sign of the cross, and not by any shield or helmet, I will safely penetrate the ranks of the enemy."

Julian was not impressed. He ordered Martin to be locked up until the next day when the Christian soldier would be exposed, unarmed, to the enemy. But the next morning the barbarians sent ambassadors to make a treaty with Julian. Sulpicius says that Christ granted Martin the victory without bloodshed.

After this confrontation with the emperor, Martin was released from military service. He went straight to Poitiers to live with the bishop, St. Hilary. In recognition of Martin's holiness St.

Hilary wanted to ordain him a deacon, but Martin demurred. So Hilary made Martin an exorcist instead.

In a dream Martin received a message to go home and bring his parents into the Church. With Hilary's permission he set out for Hungary where his mother and father had settled. Somewhere in the Alps robbers attacked Martin. Martin showed no fear to his attackers, and one robber in particular was impressed. The robber took Martin aside. "Aren't you afraid?" he asked.

"No," Martin replied. "I have never felt so safe; I know the mercy of the Lord is with me. If anything I am afraid for you because by living as a thief you prove that you are not worthy of Christ's mercy."

After more conversation the robber agreed to change his life and follow Christ. He released Martin and set him back on the road. Sulpicius says he knows for a fact that the robber gave up his wicked ways for a devout life—the robber himself told Sulpicius this story of his encounter with St. Martin.

At home Martin managed to convert his mother, but his father remained obstinate in his paganism. It was always painful for Martin to remember that although he had been able to bring many souls to God, he could not convert his own father.

By now the Arian heresy, which taught that God the Son was inferior to God the Father, was spreading and had become especially virulent in what is now Croatia. Martin went there to bring lapsed Catholics back to the faith. He met with fierce opposition from the Arian priests, who on one occasion even had Martin scourged.

After an absence of four years Martin returned at last to Poitiers. During the happy year he and Bishop Hilary spent together, Martin formalized his plan to start a religious community. In 361 Martin established the first monastery in France, near Poitiers at a place called Ligugé. The monastery still exists as a Benedictine house.

Over the next decade Martin's reputation for sanctity increased. The local people told stories, recorded by Sulpicius, that Martin had restored to life a slave who hanged himself, and raised from the dead a catechumen who had died before he could be baptized. More than simple tales of miraculous events, both stories are testaments to Martin's compassion. In Martin's day suicides and the unbaptized were thought to be automatically damned. By bringing these two unhappy men back to life, St. Martin gave each of them a second chance at salvation.

In 371 the bishop of Tours died and the people of the city asked Martin to accept the office. When he adamantly refused the citizens tried a different approach. A man named Ruricius called on Martin at his monastery, claiming that his wife was ill. He begged Martin to come to Tours to help her. Martin agreed, but as they approached the city he noticed the road was lined with people—all citizens of Tours sent out to intervene if Martin should try to run back to Ligugé. Once inside the city a massive crowd pressed around Martin demanding that he be their bishop.

The cry, "Martin for bishop!" was not unanimous. Some people in the town, and several bishops from surrounding dioceses, vehemently opposed Martin's candidacy. They said he lacked dignity, that his clothes were shabby and his hair unkempt. One bishop went so far as to describe Martin as disgusting. These men thought Martin would degrade the episcopal office. But their opposition was drowned out by the shouts of the overwhelming majority of Tours who forced Martin to become bishop.

In 371 most of France was still pagan, and as bishop Martin spent a great deal of his time trying to bring the faith to non-Christians. Sulpicius tells us that Martin and his monks destroyed many pagan temples, idols, and sacred groves. In contemporary societies where religious tolerance is enshrined in law such attacks are seen as abhorrent. In Martin's view, however, such religious toleration was misguided. He regarded all pagan practices as the work of the devil, and saw it as a bishop's duty to root out such wickedness.

Martin had no more patience for heresy than he had for paganism; but when bishops began calling on the emperor Maximus to arrest and execute heretics Martin, along with St. Ambrose, objected. They did not believe in capital punishment for heresy, and they thought it dangerous to bring the civil power into ecclesiastical affairs.

In the eyes of the people of Tours, Martin was not only a champion of the faith but also a worker of wonders. Sulpicius says Martin healed a little girl who had been born paralyzed and drove a demon out of the servant of a pagan proconsul (in gratitude the proconsul became a Christian). When his friend St. Paulinus of Nola went blind in one eye Martin restored his sight. At the gates of Paris Martin met a leper of such repulsive appearance it made his entourage shudder just to look at him. Martin, however, kissed the poor man and blessed him. Instantly the leper was made clean.

Sulpicius says that perfect calm was the predominant trait of Martin's personality. "No one ever saw him enraged, or excited, or lamenting," Sulpicius writes of his friend. The only thing that grieved him were the slanders he endured from his opponents who had never left him alone from the day he became bishop of Tours.

These opponents derided stories of Martin's miracles as superstitious tales, and charged that he preached clemency for heretics because he was tainted with heresy himself. Especially painful for Martin was the opposition of Brice, who had been a member of Martin's own monastery. Brice went about telling anyone who would listen that Martin was irrational, mad, senile, or all three. When the other monks urged Martin to send Brice away he answered, "If Christ could tolerate Judas, I can put up with Brice."

While Martin was visiting the town of Candes at the far end of his diocese, he became gravely ill and died suddenly on

November 8. His monks carried his body home to Tours where it was buried on November 11, the day that has been celebrated since then as his feast.

With his death the anti-Martin faction in Tours gained the upper hand, electing Brice to succeed St. Martin as bishop. As a sign of remorse, or perhaps to satisfy his predecessor's friends, Brice built a chapel over Martin's grave. Today a grand basilica stands on the spot. In the crypt near the saint's shrine pilgrims see a votive plaque that reads, "Angelo Giuseppe Roncalli, Apostolic Nuncio in France, client of St. Martin, the humble man of Tours. Blessed Martin preserve the clergy and people of Gaul. Look after your own everywhere." Angelo Giuseppe Roncalli, of course, is Blessed Pope John XXIII.

Sulpicius does not mention whether Martin was on horseback when he divided his cloak with the beggar, yet in paintings and sculptures of the scene the saint is always shown mounted. St. Martin is still associated with horses and riding. In Latin America he is invoked as San Martin Caballero—St. Martin the Horseback Rider. And at Golega, Portugal, the annual National Horse Show always coincides with St. Martin's feast day.

For Hunters

St. Hubert (died 727) Feast day: November 3

Hunters venerate as their patron St. Hubert, who had a conversion experience while chasing a magnificent stag through the forest.

Although Hubert was raised a Christian he grew up to be a worldly young man. His passion for hunting was so great it overshadowed all of his other obligations. One Good Friday, when he should have been in church, Hubert went deer hunting. In the forest he saw a magnificent stag and gave chase. The animal outran Hubert's horse, leading the hunter deep into the forest. In a clearing the deer stopped. When it turned around Hubert was astonished to see a crucifix between the stag's antlers. Then the stag spoke to him saying, "Hubert, unless you return to the Lord you will fall into Hell."

Hubert climbed down from his horse, dropped to his knees, and asked, "What should I do?"

"Go find Lambert, the bishop of Maastricht," the stag responded. "He will guide you."

This story of St. Hubert and the stag is colorful but not probable. However it came about, we do know that Hubert had a conversion experience, joined St. Lambert's household, and was ordained a priest by him.

As a man of deep piety, learning, and courage, Lambert was an excellent model for the clergy. He administered a vast diocese that embraced nearly all of Belgium and went out as a missionary to the pagan residents in neighboring regions. It is likely that Hubert accompanied his bishop on these missions.

As tokens of his admiration King Clovis III granted to Lambert small concessions such as exempting the bishop's Church of Our Lady from taxation. Dodo, a member of Clovis' household who harbored an irrational resentment against Lambert, murdered the bishop on September 17, 705. The clergy of Maastricht saw clearly that Hubert was the natural choice to succeed St. Lambert.

During the next twenty years Hubert continued his predecessor's good work. He was especially active in bringing the gospel to the residents of the Ardennes Forest in southern Belgium, a place where Christianity had not yet taken root. After a busy life as a bishop and evangelist, Hubert died peacefully on May 30, 727, and was buried in Liege. On November 3, 743, St. Hubert's body was moved to the Ardennes Forest, where he had labored so hard for the faith. He is enshrined in Andain Abbey, since renamed the Abbey of St. Hubert.

In 1568 Huguenots desecrated the abbey church, broke open St. Hubert's tomb, and destroyed his remains. A few fragments of the saint's relics which had been given to other churches before the sacrilege were returned to the abbey, and these are still enshrined in the abbey church today.

Devotion to St. Hubert as the patron of hunters remains strong in our day. Hunting lodges from Saskatchewan to Slovakia are named for St. Hubert; special Masses for hunters are offered on his feast day in places as diverse as Coaldale, Pennsylvania, and Warsaw, Poland. In the towns of the Ardennes as well as in Augusta, Georgia, hunters open the hunting season by bringing their hounds and horses to church to be blessed in St. Hubert's name.

For Mountain and Rock Climbers
St. Bernard of Menthon (died c.1081) Feast day: May 28

*Pope Pius XI, who was an avid mountain climber as
a young man, named St. Bernard of Menthon
patron of mountaineers in 1923.*

The castle of Menthon stands on Lake Annecy in Savoy, on the mountainous border between France, Switzerland, and Italy. In all likelihood, this is where Bernard was born into a noble family about the year 1000. His father's name was Richard, his mother's Bernoline.

When Bernard was old enough to begin his studies his parents hired a man named Germain to tutor the boy. This tutor taught Bernard to read and write, took him on rambles into the mountains, and encouraged the boy's religious devotion. One version of Bernard's story says his parents sent him to Paris to finish his education. While he was away his parents, who had no idea that their son had decided to enter religious life, arranged a marriage for him. When Bernard returned home he refused to marry, left the castle, and went to live with Peter the archdeacon of Aosta. Peter's house became Bernard's seminary where he prepared for ordination to the priesthood.

The diocese of Aosta extended into the Alps. Here many of the people were either pagans or practiced an odd combination of Christian and pagan customs. For the next 42 years Bernard traveled through the mountains preaching the gospel in large towns and on isolated farms. During these missionary expeditions Bernard came to know firsthand the dangers of travel in the Alps.

He had met pilgrims traveling from France or Germany to Rome whose companions had died of exposure in the mountains, or been swept away by an avalanche. He opened a monastery and hospice for travelers in what is known today as Great St. Bernard Pass, 8100 feet above sea level. A few years later Bernard opened a second monastery at the Little St. Bernard Pass, 7076 feet above sea level. The monks who staffed these houses, assisted by large dogs, dedicated themselves to rescuing lost or injured travelers and giving decent burial to those who died in the mountains. There is a legend that Bernard's own mother and father were among the wayfarers who found shelter in the monastery.

A handful of monks still staff the hospice in Great St. Bernard Pass, welcoming crowds of visitors, mountaineers, and hikers in the summer, and a few hardy pilgrims, climbers and skiers in the winter. The St. Bernard dogs are still on the site, although they are no longer used in rescue operations.

For Musicians and Singers

St. Cecilia (3rd century) Feast day: November 22

The fifth-century legend of St. Cecilia says that at her wedding banquet, while the musicians played profane songs, she sang a hymn to God in her heart. This incident inspired singers and musicians in the Middle Ages to take Cecilia as their patron.

*B*efore Constantine granted freedom to the Church, Christianity operated in secret in Rome. Generous, well-to-do Christians risked their lives by offering their homes as both church and community center. These house churches became known as *tituli*, a Roman term for an inscription which indicated who owned a piece of property. In the case of Christian *tituli*, a cross carved into a stone on the house indicated that it was the property of the Church. One of these was a mansion in Rome's Trastevere neighborhood that belonged to a Christian woman who was named Cecilia, probably the same Cecilia who was martyred in the 3rd century and who lies buried in the lovely basilica that was built over the house church.

From the time of her martyrdom St. Cecilia was immensely popular among the Christians of Rome. She was so highly regarded that her name was included in the list of Rome's best beloved saints and martyrs in the Roman Canon of the Mass.

An account of Cecilia's life and martyrdom was written in the fifth century. It is impossible to determine today whether it is entirely a work of romance intended to honor a famous saint, or was based in part on authentic events from her life. According to the story Cecilia's parents were patricians and Christians. When

208

she was old enough to marry her father betrothed her to Valerian, also a member of the patrician class but a pagan. Cecilia wanted to remain a virgin, to consecrate herself entirely to God, but she submitted to her father's will. At her wedding while the musicians and singers performed bawdy songs Cecilia sat apart singing to Christ in her heart.

That night when Valerian and Cecilia were alone in the bridal chamber Cecilia told her husband that as a young girl she had vowed her virginity to God. Since that time she had been guarded by an angel who would strike him down if he tried to consummate their marriage. Valerian was skeptical and asked to see this angel, but Cecilia insisted the angel would not appear until Valerian had converted to Christianity. Uncertain, but moved by Cecilia's sincerity, Valerian agreed to learn more about his wife's faith. The next day Cecilia sent Valerian to a house on the Appian Way, three miles outside the city walls, where Pope Urban would instruct him and baptize him.

Upon returning home Valerian found Cecilia in their bedroom with an angel standing at her side. In his hands the angel held two crowns, each made of roses and lilies, the emblems of martyrdom and virginity. As he crowned Cecilia and Valerian he instructed them to remain chaste. Then the angel said to Valerian, "Because you believed what Cecilia told you and have been baptized, ask whatever you wish and the Lord will grant it." Valerian said, "There is nothing dearer to me than my brother Tiburtius. Let him accept the faith, too." "Your request has pleased God," the angel said. "Your brother will join you in the faith and both of you will win the martyr's crown."

At that moment Tiburtius entered the room. He noticed a strong scent of roses and lilies, but could not see any flowers. Tiburtius was astonished when his brother told him he had been baptized that day. Tiburtius regarded Christianity with scorn and contempt, but persuaded by Valerian and Cecilia he went off to find Pope Urban and become a Christian.

After their conversion the two brothers devoted themselves to works of mercy. When an anti-Christian persecution broke out in Rome, Valerian and Tiburtius recovered the bodies of the martyrs and buried them. Their charity for the dead brought them to the attention of the authorities; both brothers were arrested and taken before the prefect, Almachius, who urged them to renounce Christianity and return to the gods of Rome. Both young men refused so Almachius condemned Valerian and Tiburtius to be beheaded the next day.

Maximus, one of the wardens who guarded their cell, was moved by the courage of two young men who were willing to sacrifice their lives for their faith. He converted to Christianity, too, and the next day all three men were executed together. Cecilia claimed the bodies and buried them.

Then Almachius sent soldiers to arrest Cecilia. When, like Valerian and Tiburtius, she refused to renounce her faith, Almachius condemned Cecilia to be suffocated in her own bath.

Soldiers led Cecilia home, locked her inside the bath, and built up the furnace until it gave off terrific heat. And yet Cecilia did not die. One of the soldiers went in to behead Cecilia, but he botched the job, only gashing her neck without severing it. Cecilia lingered for three days during which time she formally made her house over to the Church, entrusting it to the care of Pope Urban. When she died Urban had her buried in the Catacomb of St. Callixtus in a tomb next to the crypt of the popes.

In the 9th century Pope St. Paschal I (reigned 817-24) moved the bodies of St. Cecilia and Ss. Valerian, Tiburtius, and Maximus to the basilica he had built over Cecilia's mansion. During restoration work in 1599 the bodies of the saints had to be moved. When Cecilia's tomb was opened her body was found to be incorrupt. The excavators called the sculptor Stefano Maderno to the site to make a sketch of Cecilia's body exactly as it had been found. This drawing became the basis for a life-size sculpture Maderno made of St. Cecilia. The martyr's body did not remain intact; with exposure to the air, it crumbled to dust.

Since the 14th century St. Cecilia has been universally venerated as the patron saint of music. Rome's most renowned music school, the Accademia Musicale di Santa Cecilia, was named for her in 1584. Henry Purcell, George Friedrich Handel, and Benjamin Britten composed music in her honor. The poets John Dryden, Alexander Pope, and W. H. Auden have also written in praise of St. Cecilia. And throughout the world musical societies and concert series are named for her.

For Painters

Since the Middle Ages artists have placed themselves under
the patronage of St. Luke. According to a tradition that dates
back to the 6th century, Luke painted a portrait of the
Blessed Virgin and the Christ Child.

Of all the evangelists St. Luke provides us with the most information about the Blessed Virgin Mary. He alone tells us in detail stories of the Annunciation and Mary's visit to her cousin St. Elizabeth. He writes the only full narrative of the night Christ was born. Early commentators on the gospels suggested that Luke received these stories from Mary herself.

Luke was a Syrian born in Antioch. He was not Jewish, nor did he know Jesus. The claims that he was one of the seventy disciples of the Lord or one of the two disciples who met the Risen Christ on the road to Emmaus cannot be taken seriously. His translation of Hebrew and Aramaic terms peculiar to Judaism and his explanation of Jewish religious ceremonies and customs suggest that he wrote for a Gentile audience.

Luke's gospel makes known to us six miracles of Our Lord which occur nowhere else in the New Testament. These include the raising to life of the widow of Nain's son, the healing of the ten lepers, and the restoration of Malchus' ear after St. Peter had cut it off. Eighteen parables are also unique to St. Luke including such beloved stories as the Prodigal Son, the Rich Man and Lazarus, and the Pharisee and the Publican in the Temple.

St. Paul says in his letter to the Colossians that Luke was his friend and a physician. The Acts of the Apostles, also written by St. Luke, often reads like a memoir of the evangelist's adventures with Paul. Luke accompanied Paul on his first missionary journey to Europe. He was with Paul in Jerusalem when the apostle was nearly torn to pieces by an angry crowd. He was shipwrecked with Paul on the island of Malta. During Paul's final imprisonment in Rome Luke was the apostle's constant companion.

The Christian historian Eusebius (c.264-340) writes that after St. Paul's death Luke preached the gospel in Greece. It was there that he died at age 84, in the city of Thebes.

Based on the assumption that there was a close friendship between St. Luke and the Blessed Mother, there evolved the legend that as a special grace, Christ came down from Heaven in the form of a child so Luke could paint a portrait of the Virgin Mother holding in her arms her Divine Son. The most charming detail of this story is that Luke painted his picture on the kitchen table of the Holy Family's home in Nazareth.

Several pictures of the Madonna and Child are attributed to St. Luke. One likeness, in the Basilica of Santa Maria Maggiore in Rome, can be traced to 847 and is probably a copy of the icon which the Empress Eudoxia found at Jerusalem about the year 450 and sent home to Constantinople. The most famous painting attributed to St. Luke, however, is the Black Madonna of Czestochowa, the patroness of Poland.

Throughout the Renaissance artists' guilds were placed under the patronage of St. Luke. Leonardo da Vinci, Raphael, and Jan Vermeer are a few among the Old Masters who belonged to the Guild of St. Luke. In the 15th century a school for painters, the Academy of St. Luke, was established in Rome. The Academy is still in operation today.

For Skaters

The patron of skaters is St. Lydwina, a Dutch mystic who became
bedridden after suffering a fall while ice skating.

St. Lydwina was the only daughter in a family with nine children. Her mother's name was Petronella. Her father, Peter, was the night watchman of Schiedam, a small town near Rotterdam in the Netherlands. Lydwina was a devout girl. When she was about thirteen years old she made a private vow of virginity, but any intention she may have had to enter a convent was frustrated in winter 1395.

One day in January Lydwina went ice skating with friends on the frozen River Schie. Inadvertently one of her companions jostled her; Lydwina fell on the ice breaking a rib on her right side. Soon other complications set in. She suffered violent attacks of vomiting and chronic pain; she could not get out of bed. As she began to realize that she would never get well, this teenage girl, once so healthy, sank into depression.

Her parish priest, Father John Pot, who often visited Lydwina, suggested that she regard her sufferings as a special type of religious vocation. Devotion to the Passion of Our Lord was widespread in late 14th-century Europe, particularly in the Netherlands, and Father Pot urged Lydwina to imitate Christ on the cross and offer her sufferings to God for the salvation of sinners. Under Father Pot's spiritual direction Lydwina emerged from depression to begin a life of private prayer and contemplation. Once she began to view invalidism in a more positive light, Lydwina found her afflictions easier to bear.

In 1399, when Lydwina was nineteen, her symptoms became worse. Her face and limbs became distorted. She lost sight in one eye and the other became hypersensitive to light. A series of strokes left her whole body paralyzed and she could move only her left arm.

How could a simple broken rib cause such debilitating injuries? When Lydwina fell she must have struck her head on the ice. Her contemporaries make no mention of a head wound, but they do mention severe vomiting, an indication of a closed head injury. The blow to her head perhaps caused bleeding into certain areas of her brain. As a result, neurotransmission in that area of the brain could have been inhibited, explaining the blindness and contraction of her limbs.

Lydwina's physical condition attracted many physicians who wanted to study her case. Her Christlike patience drew visitors who sought Lydwina's spiritual advice. As Lydwina grew in holiness she began to experience supernatural favors. During periods when she appeared to be comatose her spirit traveled to Rome and the Holy Land. She had visions in which she spoke with Our Lord and the saints. Witnesses swore that for the last nineteen years of her life Lydwina consumed nothing but was sustained entirely by the Eucharist.

A new parish priest assigned to Schiedam, Father Andries, accused Lydwina of being a fraud and refused to give her Holy Communion. He told his congregation that she was possessed by the devil and urged them to pray that God would release her. The priest's denunciations caused such an uproar in Schiedam that Church authorities made a formal investigation of Lydwina. They found that she was orthodox, genuine, and guiltless of any fraud. The investigators also granted her the privilege of receiving Communion every two weeks, a very rare concession at a time when most Catholics did not receive more than twice a year.

Legend has it that shortly before she died, Lydwina's guardian angel appeared to her bearing a rose bush. He told her that when all the rosebuds had opened, her suffering would be at an end.

On her deathbed Lydwina was attended by Baudouin, her 12-year-old nephew. When she fell into her death agony the boy ran to fetch the priest to administer the Last Rites. Unfortunately, by the time the priest arrived Lydwina was already dead. The date was April 14, 1433.

Immediately, from the time of her death, Lydwina's grave became a place of pilgrimage. A 15th century woodcut that depicted her fall on the ice spurred devotion to Lydwina as patron of skaters. Although Lydwina was never formally canonized, Pope Leo XIII confirmed and sanctioned her cult in 1890.

For Swimmers
St. Adjutor (died 1131) Feast day: April 30

*St. Adjutor is venerated as the patron of swimmers because he
calmed a dangerous whirlpool in the River Seine.*

Adjutor was born to a family of knights in Vernon, Normandy. His father's name was John. His mother Rosamunde, famous for her piety and good works, was regarded by neighbors as a saint. When he was ready for school Adjutor's parents sent him to study with St. Bernard of Tiron at the monastery of Craon.

When Pope Urban II came to France in 1095 to preach the First Crusade to liberate the Holy Land from the Saracens, Adjutor responded to the Pope's call and with a company of 200 fighting men set out for Jerusalem.

The Crusade stalled for a time at Antioch where the Saracens besieged the city. One day Adjutor led a small scouting party outside the city walls. The party was ambushed by 1500 Saracens, and though Adjutor and his men put up a desperate defense, it seemed hopeless. Just as the Crusaders were about to be overcome, Adjutor called upon his favorite saint, Mary Magdalene. Through her intercession a violent storm broke over the battlefield. The terrified Saracens threw down their arms and fled.

Once the siege at Antioch was lifted Adjutor and his men joined the rest of the Crusaders in the conquest of Jerusalem. For seventeen years he remained there as part of the garrison of the Holy City.

While on patrol outside Jerusalem one day Adjutor fell into another ambush. The Saracens dragged him off to one of their strongholds and loaded down his wrists and ankles with heavy chains. From time to time his jailers took him from his cell to torture him, but Adjutor never lost his faith or his courage.

Adjutor knew he had no earthly hope of rescue. In his distress he prayed once again to St. Mary Magdalene and to his old teacher St. Bernard. The legend of St. Adjutor recorded in the Bollandists' *Acta Sanctorum* says the two saints appeared in Adjutor's cell and transported him home to Normandy. We know that Adjutor escaped his dungeon. There is no reason to doubt that his favorite saints helped him, but the miraculous transit back to France seems a bit much. In whatever manner he escaped, Adjutor was still wearing his chains upon his arrival back in Crusader territory. Back in Normandy Adjutor built a chapel honoring St. Mary Magdalene and became a Benedictine monk.

The stretch of River Seine that flowed near Adjutor's abbey was troubled by a whirlpool that had claimed many swimmers and boats. Adjutor sent a message to his bishop to come help him deal with the whirlpool.

The bishop came, and after saying Mass in the abbey, the two men rowed a boat out to the whirlpool. At the whirlpool's edge the bishop sprinkled holy water and gave his blessing. Then Adjutor took a piece of the chain with which the Saracens had bound him and cast it into the water. "It is as easy for God to free people from this whirlpool as it was for him to free me, through the intercession of St. Magdalene and St. Bernard, from my chains," said Adjutor. Immediately the whirlpool became calm.

When St. Adjutor died he was buried in the chapel he had built for St. Mary Magdalene. He has always been venerated by the people of Vernon as a favorite local saint and the guardian of swimmers and yachtsmen.

For All Lovers of Sport
Blessed Pier Giorgio Frassati (1901-1925) Feast day: July 4

Blessed Pier Giorgio Frassati was a born athlete who excelled in hiking, mountain climbing, and skiing. Many Catholic athletic associations in Europe have taken him as their patron.

*P*ier Giorgio Frassati was born on Holy Saturday, April 6, 1901 into one of the wealthiest and most influential families of Turin, Italy. His father, Alfredo, had served a term as senator, was the founder and director of the liberal newspaper *La Stampa*, and eventually was named Italy's ambassador to Germany. His mother, Adelaide Ametis Frassati, was a cultured woman and an amateur painter.

Pier Giorgio's parents, while seeing to his baptism, took little interest in his religious formation. Alfredo was an agnostic and Adelaide was only nominally Catholic. It was Adelaide's mother, Linda Copello Ametis, who first taught her grandson the essentials of the Catholic faith.

In school it became obvious that Pier Giorgio was not a brain, but an athlete. He excelled in sports and failed miserably at classwork. His parents transferred him to a Jesuit school where the priests and brothers gave students individualized instruction. Thanks to the extra attention, the boy's grades improved. Later in life he would study to be a mining engineer, hoping to "serve Christ better among the miners."

Pier Giorgio grew up to be a handsome, charismatic young man. Photographs show him with a head of dark, thick hair that he parted in the middle, deep-set eyes, a strong chin, a long prominent nose, very broad shoulders, and a muscular torso and arms. He surrounded himself with other young men who were as boisterous, energetic, and athletic as himself. They called themselves "The Shady Characters," and went on long hikes, strenuous mountain-climbing expeditions, and ski trips that featured reckless races down the slopes.

His friends knew Pier Giorgio was daring, but they also knew he was devout. He said the rosary as he climbed mountain trails, offering to take on the dirty job of greasing the boots of any of his friends who joined him in prayer. Mass and Holy Communion were essential to his daily routine. He had a particular love for nocturnal vigils before the Blessed Sacrament. Where others would sign up to watch before the tabernacle for an hour or two, Pier Giorgio often spent the entire night in prayer before Christ in the Eucharist.

At seventeen Pier Giorgio joined the St. Vincent de Paul Society, the international Catholic organization dedicated to helping the poor. He threw himself into the work, but since his father did not give him much spending money Pier Giorgio's acts of charity became distinctly personal. When an elderly woman was evicted from her apartment he found her a new place to live. On a bitter winter night Pier Giorgio saw a poor man shivering on the street, so he took off his own fine overcoat and gave it to him. He helped a man fresh out of prison get a job by going along with him to the factory and persuading the foreman to hire the ex-convict. So he wouldn't forget anyone, he kept a small notebook in which he jotted down the names, addresses, and particular needs of sick and poor individuals who had come to depend on him.

He often said, "Charity is not enough, we need social reform." To that end Pier Giorgio joined Catholic action organizations that promoted social reform within the framework of the teachings of the Church. He wanted to see a state truly based on

Christian principles rather than on some secular theory.

Like his father Pier Giorgio was vehemently anti-Fascist. Upon one occasion he went to Rome to participate in an anti-Fascist demonstration that turned into a brawl when the police attacked the demonstrators. It would have been wiser to run, but instead Pier Giorgio grabbed a pole that had been used for a banner and clubbed the police with it. He was arrested and spent the night in jail.

Alfredo Frassati was equally fearless. Even as Mussolini's power increased he continue to criticize him in *La Stampa*. One evening in June 1924 five Fascist blackshirts broke into the Frassati house in Turin and started smashing up the place. Pier Giorgio threw himself on the intruders, managing to land a few punches before the five ran away from the house and down the street where a getaway car was waiting for them.

In the early summer of 1925 Pier Giorgio's beloved grandmother was dying. He felt sick, but he tried to ignore it to be with his grandmother during her last days. At the wake and at the funeral, following her death, he appeared distracted and self-absorbed. His mother complained bitterly that he had been almost no help during this difficult time. After the burial Pier Giorgio admitted that he was ill. The doctor who diagnosed his condition as a virulent strain of polio suggested he might have contracted it in the Turin slums. To the Frassati family it was incomprehensible. Pier Giorgio was young and strong. How could he be dying?

Even on his deathbed Pier Giorgio still worried about the poor. He gave his notebook to his sister, Luciana, instructing her how to continue his assistance to his friends in the tenements and hospitals. In the early evening of July 4, 1925, Pier Giorgio Frassati died. He was 24 years old.

On the day of Pier Giorgio's funeral his family was stunned to see nearly a thousand men, women, and children from some of the poorest neighborhoods of Turin line the streets to see his coffin pass. The Frassatis knew that Pier Giorgio had performed many works of charity, but they had no real idea how wide-ranging his efforts had been.

Pope John Paul II beatified Pier Giorgio Frassati in 1990, hailing him as "the man of the eight Beatitudes," urging Catholic youth to take him as their model. In Europe, Italy and France especially, many Catholic athletic associations place themselves under the patronage of Blessed Pier Giorgio, while in the United States he is venerated as the patron of World Youth Day.

Thirsting for Justice:
Saints for Social Action

SAINT GERMAINE COUSIN

Thirsting for Justice:
Saints for Social Action

Homelessness, child abuse, and violence against women have always been with us. But there have also always been heroic, compassionate individuals who tried to help the victims. A classic case is St. Peter Claver, a Spanish Jesuit priest who dedicated his life to the African slaves of Colombia. He could not stop the slave trade, but he could comfort the bodies and souls of the enslaved Africans.

Unlike Peter Claver, who was never in danger of becoming a slave himself, most of the saints in this chapter actually experienced the specific social problem of which they are now patron.

St. Maria Goretti, patron of the sexually abused, was not quite 13 years old when her 20-year-old neighbor attempted to rape her. When Maria fought off her would-be rapist, he stabbed her to death.

St. Germaine Cousin, patron of abused children, was born with a withered right arm and a disfiguring skin disease. Her father and stepmother could not stand the sight of the girl. They excluded her from family life, barely fed her, made her sleep in an opening under the stairs, and while she was still a child they sent her out alone to take care of the family sheep.

The Nazis arrested St. Maximilian Kolbe in their round-up of Polish priests and intellectuals. St. Chad was obliged to give up the distinguished office of archbishop of York when the evidence revealed that his consecration was invalid. As an immigrant to the United States St. Frances Xavier Cabrini learned about discrimination first-hand, and she experienced all the usual difficulties of settling in a new country—from trouble trying to master a new language to attempting to fathom an alien culture.

The link between the saints in this chapter and their clients may be especially close. Here are men and women—and one child—who have intimate knowledge of many social troubles.

For the Homeless

St. Benedict Joseph Labre (1748-1783) Feast day: April 16

*"Foxes have holes, and birds of the air their have nests, but the
Son of man has no place to lay his head." Inspired by this text
from St. Luke's gospel, St. Benedict Joseph Labre left his parents'
home and spent the rest of his life as a wandering pilgrim.*

The story of Benedict Joseph Labre teaches us that an eccentric can be a saint. Born in the village of Amettes in France, Benedict Joseph was the eldest of fifteen children, the son of respectable shopkeepers. When he was twelve years old the boy's parents sent him to live with his uncle, the curé of a parish about forty miles from Amettes. There Benedict Joseph continued his education with the hope of becoming a priest.

Benedict Joseph was an intense boy, an avid reader of the Bible and lives of the saints. By the age of eighteen he had resolved to join the strictest religious order he could find. He applied first to the Trappists but they turned him away because he was too young. The Cistercians rejected him because his personal eccentricities made him unsuited to life in a religious community. The Carthusians sent him home after a six-week trial period.

Once Benedict Joseph realized that he was not suited to monastic life he hit upon a fresh course of action: he would become a permanent pilgrim, living as a solitary, having no belongings except the clothes on his back, keeping silent as much as possible on the road, praying incessantly. Like Christ he wanted to be a man who had no place to lay his head.

He set out on foot to the great pilgrimage centers of Western Europe: the shrines of St. James at Compostela in Spain, of the Sacred Heart at Paray-le-Monial in France, of Our Lady at Loreto in Italy, and of Ss. Francis and Clare at Assisi. He never begged but relied entirely on whatever strangers were moved to give him. If he received money, more often than not he gave it to others he judged needed it more than himself.

Benedict Joseph is not a romantic figure. He never bathed or washed his clothes. He was infested with lice. Some custodians, offended by the smell and look of him, drove him out of their churches. Often he was mocked; sometimes he was beaten.

In 1774 Benedict Joseph settled in Rome and remained there except for an annual pilgrimage to Loreto. He lived in the Colosseum, attended Mass every morning at Santa Maria dei Monti near the Forum, and kept busy the rest of the day visiting churches. If a church was holding Forty Hours Devotions in honor of the Blessed Sacrament he would spend his day there.

After years of sleeping in the open in all kinds of weather, Benedict Joseph's health became so bad he was compelled to move to a shelter for the homeless. Yet he still continued his rounds of church visitations. On Wednesday of Holy Week 1783, while hearing Mass at Santa Maria dei Monti, he collapsed. He died later that day; he was 35 years old.

Immediately Benedict Joseph became the focus of a grass-roots cult. The priests at Santa Maria dei Monti had a death mask made of his face and preserved his filthy ragged clothes as relics. After an especially rigorous investigation of his life and merits (to make certain that he was neither mentally disturbed nor a fraud), Blessed Pope Pius IX canonized Benedict Joseph Labre in 1883. His tomb is in Santa Maria dei Monti, the church he loved.

The English hagiographer Donald Attwater described St. Benedict Joseph Labre as an "example of those who, at all times in Christian history, have refused in the name of Christ to be 'respectable.'"

For Immigrants

St. Frances Xavier Cabrini (1850-1917) Feast day: December 22

*St. Frances Xavier Cabrini was herself an immigrant who came
to America for the express purpose of serving Italians who were
trying to make a new life for themselves in the New World.*

As a little girl Francesca Cabrini's favorite book was a
collection of stories about St. Francis Xavier's missionary jour-
neys in Asia. She cherished the idea of becoming a missionary in
China but as Pope Leo XIII told her, her destiny was not in the
East but in the West.

Francesca was born the tenth of eleven children (only four
of whom survived to adulthood). Hers was a family of reasonably
well-off farmers in the town of Sant' Angelo Lodigiano near
Pavia in northern Italy. She was educated by the Daughters of
the Sacred Heart and trained to be a schoolteacher.

In 1876 Francesca took the first step toward realizing her
dream of becoming a missionary. With seven other women she
founded the Missionary Sisters of the Sacred Heart, an order
that balanced an active ministry in the world with regular periods of prayer and contemplation. As a nun she took the name of
her favorite saint, Francis Xavier. In 1887 when she received
Vatican approval for her order Mother Cabrini thought she
would soon be on her way to China. In fact the call came from
an unexpected direction.

A grim economic depression combined with political up-
heaval drove hundreds of thousands of Italians to leave their
country. Between 1899 and 1910 nearly two million Italian im-

229

migrants arrived in the United States, and about 77 percent of these were *contadini*, landless farmers from southern Italy who were completely unprepared for life in urban America. As if to add to the immigrants' misery, even the Church in America was ambivalent about the newcomers. On the one hand the hierarchy welcomed a new influx of Catholics to the country. On the other hand the emotional piety and colorful saints' festivals that were integral to Italian Catholic life made many American priests and bishops—most of whom were Irish or of Irish descent— extremely uncomfortable. Some pastors consigned their Italian parishioners to church basements for Mass. Most pastors refused to sponsor the festivals. The archbishop of New York City, Michael Corrigan, was just one American bishop who petitioned Rome to send him some "good Italian priests." Pope Leo XIII did send Italian priests to America, but he also sent Mother Cabrini with six of her sisters.

They arrived in New York on March 31, 1889. No one in the chancery had any idea that the Italian nuns were coming. Archbishop Corrigan could not have been more disappointed upon meeting Mother Cabrini. He wanted strong, experienced clerics to help with the Italians; instead he got a nun who was not even five feet tall. The archbishop told Mother Cabrini candidly that he did not believe nuns were suited to work with the immigrants. Since her ship was still docked in New York, he suggested that she return to the harbor and sail back to Italy. Mother Cabrini replied, "I have letters from the pope." And she stayed.

Since Mother Cabrini and her nuns would not do as they were told, Archbishop Corrigan washed his hands of them. He would not authorize any diocesan funds to help them. Following their archbishop's lead, the male religious orders also declined to help the Missionary Sisters. Consequently their first home was a squalid apartment crawling with cockroaches and bedbugs. In order to support themselves the nuns begged door to door until female religious orders in New York heard of the new arrivals and offered their help. The Sisters of Charity and the Bon Secours Sisters were especially generous to Mother Cabrini and her nuns.

The sisters began work at once among the immigrants they had come to help: visiting the sick, feeding the hungry, educating children, caring for orphans. Their heroic efforts and the good it produced even won over Archbishop Corrigan, who became the Missionary Sisters' chief benefactor in New York.

But with success came increased demands for help. Mother Cabrini brought more of her nuns over from Italy and sent them to new establishments in Buffalo, Chicago, Cincinnati, St. Louis, New Orleans, Denver, San Francisco, and Seattle. She opened her first hospital in 1892. It was the 400th anniversary of Christopher Columbus' arrival in the New World so she named it after the Italian explorer. Thereafter every hospital Mother Cabrini founded was named Columbus Hospital.

She was a determined woman and she was intensely passionate about her vocation. Mother Cabrini once defined a missionary as someone who carries "the Name of Christ to all people—to those who as yet do not know Him, and also to those who have forgotten Him."

During some 29 years of missionary work Mother Cabrini crossed the Atlantic Ocean 25 times and founded 67 schools, orphanages, and hospitals around the world—one for each year of her life. In 1916 she retired from active life for a six-month retreat. She was in Chicago before Christmas 1917 helping get the new Columbus Hospital there in operation. When she woke up on the morning of December 22 Mother Cabrini felt too weak to go to Mass. A sister brought her breakfast, helped her dress, and got her into her rocking chair. Then she left Mother Cabrini alone. About noontime the same sister returned to serve lunch, and found Mother Cabrini dead of a cerebral hemorrhage.

In 1946 Pope Pius XII canonized Mother Cabrini and

named her patron of immigrants. On July 7, 1946, Cardinal Samuel Stritch of Chicago celebrated the first American citizen to be named a saint, saying, "If Americans are known throughout the world for getting things done with efficiency and with the utmost dispatch, Mother Cabrini is indeed a typical American....She left nothing undone to accomplish the Divine Will, once it was known to her, even though the task seemed far above human strength."

To Save the Environment

St. Francis of Assisi (1182-1226) Feast day: October 4

*Devotion to St. Francis as the special guardian of the
natural world dates from the Middle Ages. In recognition
of the man who saw the glory, the beauty, and the wisdom of
God reflected in all creation, in 1980 Pope John Paul II
named Francis of Assisi patron saint of ecology.*

Francis, recognized by history for his embrace of absolute poverty, grew up in a family that wanted nothing to do with it. His father Pietro di Bernadone was a well-to-do cloth merchant who had met his wife Pica on one of his business trips to France. The couple lived above their shop near the Piazza del Commune in Assisi. That is where Francis was born in 1182. He was christened Giovanni, John, but his father nicknamed him Francesco, the Frenchman.

Pietro had a prosperous business and fully expected Francis to follow in his footsteps. But the sober, respectable life of a cloth merchant did not appeal to Francis. The saint's first biographer, Thomas of Celano, says he ran with a crowd that was vain, silly, and extravagant with money. During festivals Francis and his friends were the life of the party, dancing and singing in the streets all night long, and sometimes brawling when they had drunk too much wine. All this waste and frivolity irritated the serious, frugal Pietro.

When Francis was twenty years old Assisi went to war. For years there had been rivalry between the old aristocratic families who wanted Assisi to remain a feudal city and the rich merchant families who wanted a republic. In 1202 the long-simmering feud erupted in civil war, with Assisi's old rival Perugia throwing its support behind the nobility. Francis, who appears to have thought war was an adventure in fancy dress, enlisted on the side of the merchant class. He got his one and only taste of battle at Collestrada where the men of Perugia scattered the men of Assisi and took many prisoners—Francis among them. He spent a year in a dungeon with his fellow prisoners of war. The filth, the rats, the bad food, the crowding, the smells, the confinement all took their toll on Francis. When he was released he was in the middle of a profound depression.

Back home he tried to run the streets at night with his friends as he had before the war, but in secret he often slipped away to an unseen corner to pray. He was torn between the pleasures he had enjoyed as a young man and the promptings of his heart that were leading him away from them. One day while out riding Francis had an experience that convinced him he was undergoing a genuine religious conversion. He saw a leper on the road. The old Francis held a deep-seated horror of leprosy and certainly would have galloped away from the poor man. But the new Francis got down from his horse, kissed the leper's hand, and gave him some money.

In the fall of 1204 Francis went to pray outside the city in the little tumbledown church of San Damiano. Over the altar hung a painted wooden Byzantine-style crucifix that depicted Christ gazing directly at the congregation. As Francis prayed he felt a strange sensation that knocked him face down on the floor. When he raised himself, he saw the lips of the figure of Christ move and heard a voice say, "Francis! Rebuild my church which as you can see has fallen into ruins."

Taking the message from the cross literally, Francis ran back to his father's shop where he gathered up some of the finest cloth, mounted his horse and rode to the city of Foligno to sell it. With the coins weighing heavily in his purse, he rode back to San Damiano and gave all the money to the priest assigned to the church. It was a generous gift; the only difficulty was the cloth had not belonged to Francis.

When Pietro learned of his son's act of "charity" he dragged Francis to Guido, bishop of Assisi, and demanded restitution. Seated in the piazza outside his palace the bishop heard the case then ruled in Pietro's favor; Francis would have to return the money. Since the priest of San Damiano had not spent one penny of it this was easy to accomplish, but Francis went a step farther. Standing in the public square he stripped off all his clothes and handed them to his father. Conversion had not diminished Francis' taste for the flamboyant. While Pietro stood in stunned silence and the crowd in the square buzzed with excitement, Bishop Guido hurried down the palace steps, pulled off his mantle, and wrapped it around the naked young man.

For the next three years Francis was a source of shame for his parents. Dressed in a long rough tunic, he begged in the streets for food and for alms to rebuild San Damiano. To the Bernadones this was no religious vocation at all. Once again Heaven intervened to direct Francis. On February 24, 1208, Francis heard Mass at the little church of St. Mary of the Angels (now known as the Portiuncula). The gospel reading of the day instructed the disciples of Christ to own neither gold nor silver, nor a wallet for their journey, nor two coats, nor shoes, nor a staff, and that they were to exhort sinners to repentance and announce the Kingdom of God. Francis must have heard these words many times before, but on this day they pierced his heart.

Now Francis' religious life had a direction. He began to preach in the streets of Assisi with the kind of exuberance and contagious joy he had demonstrated when he stayed out all night singing troubadour songs. Thomas of Celano tells us that Francis always began with the words, "May the Lord give you peace."

Then he preached Christ's message of repentance and salvation in terms so clear and moving that he caused a sensation among the people of Assisi. Within a few weeks half a dozen men had joined Francis as disciples. They called themselves the *frati minores*, or lesser brothers.

Francis taught a way of life that emphasized the humanity of the poor, abandoned, crucified Jesus. For this reason Francis and his disciples carried the love of God first to lepers, the destitute, the sick, and all sinners. Previously a man or woman with a religious vocation left the world by entering a monastery or convent. Under Francis' inspiration, one left the world by turning away from all possessions and living as poor as the Son of man who had no place to lay his head.

Francis' devotion to the humanity of Jesus spilled over into profound reverence for the Mass and love for the Blessed Sacrament, the true body and blood of Christ. It also revealed itself one Christmas at Greccio where Francis assembled the first Nativity scene—the better to underscore the poverty and vulnerability of the Holy Family.

Just as he saw Christ in all men, Francis saw the power and the splendor of God in all creation. When he saw birds and lambs and flowers he marveled over the goodness of God, but he felt the same way when he contemplated worms. He celebrated the beauty of the universe in his renowned Canticle of the Sun. Some enthusiastic but misguided souls interpret the canticle as if Francis were a pantheist who worshipped the sun, moon, wind and fire as gods. Francis would have recoiled at such a suggestion: his canticle is a hymn the natural world sings to its Creator.

The Franciscan movement exploded. By the year 1220 it had grown to 5000 members across Europe. People admired these preachers for the austerity and holiness of their lives, but also because, unlike the monastic orders which drew away from the world, the Franciscans plunged into the thick of it. Living among the people made it easier for the friars to offer religious counsel, to hear confessions, and to foster devotions to the Passion of Christ, the Infant Jesus, the Blessed Sacrament, and the Blessed Virgin—all especially dear to St. Francis' heart.

Wherever Francis went people told of the miracles he performed. He tamed a savage wolf that had been terrorizing the citizens of the Gubbio. At his request a large flock of swallows fell silent so a congregation could hear St. Francis preach. He restored sight to a blind woman and healed a woman whose hands were so crippled with arthritis she could not hold anything. When some Franciscan brothers had lost patience with a leper who blasphemed against God for his disease, Francis visited the man and healed both his sick body and his raging spirit. Yet these miracles pale to insignificance compared to the stigmata.

In August 1224 Francis along with a few companions traveled to an isolated cave on La Verna, a rugged mountain north of Arezzo, for a forty-day retreat. On or near the Feast of the Exaltation of the Holy Cross, September 14, Francis had a vision of a seraph. The angel's six wings burned like fire and its hands and feet were fixed to a cross. No one knows how long the vision lasted, but when Francis came out of his ecstasy he found on his hands, feet, and side the marks of Christ's Passion. This is the first recorded instance of the stigmata.

Eyewitnesses all gave the same description of Francis' stigmata. It appeared as if nails were embedded in Francis' hands and feet. The palms of his hands and the tops of his feet bore large dark protuberances of flesh that resembled the heads of large iron nails. On the back of his hands and the soles of his feet were short, tapering lengths of flesh that resembled bent nails.

As one would expect the wounds were painful. Once a brother inadvertently brushed his hand against the wound in Francis' side. The saint cried out and slapped the hand away. The wounds also oozed blood from time to time, especially the one in Francis' side.

Fearful that attention from the curious and even the devout would lead him into the sin of pride, Francis tried to conceal the stigmata. He started wearing socks and shoes, wrapped bandages around his palms and let his sleeves fall down over his hands. If he had to wash his hands in the presence of others, he only dipped his fingers into the water.

Toward the end of September 1226 Francis was dying. He asked his brothers to carry him to the Portiuncula church so he could die in the place he loved best. While on his deathbed he composed a new verse for the Canticle of the Sun, praising God for "Sister Death." Then he dictated to a letter to an old friend who lived in Rome, Lady Jacoba dei Settisoli, asking her to come quickly and bring a shroud, candles, and incense for his funeral, and a sweet almond pastry she used to make for Francis. The saint had barely finished dictating the letter when Lady Jacoba appeared at the door asking "What is the news? Is Father Francis still alive?" At home she had heard a heavenly voice telling her to hurry to Assisi if she wanted to see her friend again. She had brought everything necessary for the Requiem with her. And she had Francis' favorite pastry, too.

On the night of October 3 Francis of Assisi died. At the urging of Lady Jacoba the friars agreed to uncover the stigmata so mourners, especially St. Clare and her nuns, could see the miracle. Two years later Pope Honorius III declared Francis of Assisi a saint.

To Save the Whales

St. Brendan (c.486-575) Feast day: May 16

An incident recorded in the legendary Voyage of St. Brendan *tells how he became patron saint of whales. While searching for the Promised Land of the Saints, Brendan and his monks came ashore on a bare island. When they lit a cooking fire the island began to heave and head out to sea. Brendan and his monks had unwittingly anchored their boat beside a whale.*

Monks in Ireland in the early Middle Ages were great ones for travel. Some were tireless missionaries and teachers who carried the gospel and the legacy of Greco-Roman civilization back to the Continent to repair the wreckage of the barbarian invasions. Others were holy hermits who sought a "white martyrdom" by leaving family, friends, and home to live only for God in the solitude of such far-flung places as the Faroe Islands, Iceland, or Greenland. The *Voyage of St. Brendan* emerged out of the intense desire of Irish monks to sing God's praises in a place where no other human had set foot.

The *Voyage of St. Brendan* was enormously popular in the Middle Ages. There are 116 manuscript copies of it extant, in Latin and in various vernacular languages. The legend was so influential that until Columbus' voyage to the New World maps routinely labeled an island in the Atlantic as "St. Brendan's Island of the Promise," or "The Island of the Blessed."

St. Brendan was born near Tralee in County Kerry when Christianity was still new in Ireland—St. Patrick had died only twenty-five years earlier. Legend says that on the night the saint

239

was born thirty cows gave birth to thirty calves and a host of angels hovered around the house. The bishop of Kerry St. Erc (he had been a druid until St. Patrick converted him) baptized Brendan, took charge of his education, and eventually ordained him a priest.

As were so many Irish monks of his time, Brendan was a great founder of churches and monasteries. He founded Annaghdown and Clonfert in County Galway, Inishglora on an island off the coast of County Mayo, Adrfert in County Kerry and a chapel atop Mount Brandon on the Dingle Peninsula.

The *Voyage of St. Brendan* says Brendan was abbot of his monastery at Clonfert—popularly known as "Brendan's Meadow of Miracles"—when the monk St. Barinthus arrived one evening for a visit. He told Brendan a marvelous story of how he had sailed across the Atlantic to the Promised Land of the Saints. It was an earthly paradise where every tree bore rich fruit, every rock was a precious stone, where the sun never set, and no one was ever hungry or thirsty or cold or weary. Barinthus said he had fed so well in the Promised Land of the Saints that once he came home to Ireland two weeks passed before he felt hungry or thirsty again.

Enchanted by Barinthus' story, Brendan resolved to find this promised land for himself. He chose seven monks to go with him, and together they built a *curragh*, a wooden-framed boat covered with oxhide.

The *Voyage of St. Brendan* reads much like an Irish Arabian Nights tale. In the bowels of a mountain Brendan and his monks find a grand hall where some invisible power has prepared a fine meal for the wanderers. On Easter morning they come ashore on a barren island only to discover, when they light a cooking fire, that their "island" is actually a whale. As the monks sing Vespers, a flock of birds joins in. They mistake an iceberg for a floating mountain of glass. When a sea monster attacks the *curragh*, another sea monster appears from the deep to defend Brendan and his monks. Sitting on a barren rock battered by wind and waves they find Judas. And at the end they arrive in the Promised Land of the Saints. There they stay for forty days, eating and drinking their fill.

Of course most of the events described in the *Voyage* are imaginary, but it is true that Brendan made voyages to Scotland, Wales, and Brittany, and Irish monks who sailed to the Faroes or Iceland were likely to encounter whales and icebergs. For decades some historians have speculated that St. Brendan actually reached North America. To prove that such a voyage was possible, an Oxford scholar, Tim Severin, built a *curragh* much like the one Brendan would have used and sailed successfully from Ireland to Newfoundland in 1977.

To End Abortion

Our Lady of Guadalupe   Feast day: December 12

The right to life movement has taken as its patron Our Lady
of Guadalupe, whose miraculous image drew nine million
Mexican Indians into the Church and away from a form
of paganism which demanded human sacrifice.

efore dawn on Saturday December 9, 1531, Juan Diego, a 57-year-old Nahua Indian peasant, was on his way to Mass. As he passed a hill known as Tepeyac he heard the sound of unearthly voices singing so sweetly that for a moment he thought he must have died and was now in Heaven. He climbed up the hill to find the source of the music and at the summit saw a Lady whose garments shone like the sun. Around her feet the earth and even the humblest weeds glittered like precious stones.

Speaking in Nahuatl, Juan Diego's native language, and addressing him affectionately as "Juanito" the Lady introduced herself as "the ever-virgin Holy Mary, Mother of the True God." She told Juan Diego she wanted a church built on the site. "I am your merciful mother," she said, "to you and to all the inhabitants of this land and to all the rest who love me, invoke and confide in me." Then she told Juan Diego to take this message to the bishop in Mexico City.

The bishop at that time was Juan de Zumarraga, a Franciscan with a reputation for kindness to the Indians. The bishop's servants, however, were not eager to permit a poor Indian peasant to see their master. Juan Diego waited for hours before he was finally granted an audience.

Bishop de Zumarraga listened patiently to Juan Diego's story but promised only that he would think about this request for a church. Disappointed, Juan Diego returned to Tepeyac where the Blessed Mother was waiting for him.

Juan Diego believed that the bishop had put him off because of his low status. "I am a small rope," he told Our Lady, "a tiny ladder, the tail end, a leaf." Then he urged her to send someone important, well-known, and well connected to accomplish her will. But Mary would not let him off so easily. She conceded that she had many servants she could call upon to deliver her message, but for this mission she wanted Juan Diego to be her emissary. She commanded him to return to Bishop de Zumarraga the next day, repeat the request for a church, and declare firmly "that I, in person, the ever-virgin Holy Mary, Mother of God, sent you."

The next day was Sunday. After Mass Juan Diego walked to the bishop's palace and saw de Zumarraga again. On his knees, with tears in his eyes he repeated the Virgin's message. Bishop de Zumarraga questioned him closely about the appearance of this lady, and any other phenomena that accompanied the apparition. Finally the bishop said he would need a sign to convince him that the lady Juan Diego saw was truly the Mother of God.

Following this conference Juan Diego reported to Our Lady everything the bishop had said. "Well and good," she said. Then she commanded Juan Diego to come to Tepeyac again the next day when she would give him a sign so convincing the bishop would no longer doubt the truth of the message or question from whom it had come.

Juan Diego returned home, but when he arrived at his house he found his uncle Juan Bernardino desperately ill with smallpox, a disease that had come to the New World with the Europeans and had devastated the Indian population. When a doctor could do nothing for him, Juan Bernardino asked Juan

Diego to fetch a priest.

The way to the rectory lay over Tepeyac hill. Juan Diego was afraid that if Our Lady stopped him his uncle would die before the priest arrived. Rather than cross the top of the hill, he went around the side, but the Blessed Mother met him on the path. "What's this, my son," she said. "Where are you going?" Juan Diego told her his uncle was dying, that he was hurrying to fetch a priest, and he begged her to excuse him for the day—he would deliver her sign to Bishop de Zumarraga the next day.

"Am I not here?" Mary replied. "Am I not your Mother?" She assured Juan Diego that his uncle was already cured. Then she instructed him to climb to the top of Tepeyac, gather the flowers he found there, and bring them to her.

At the summit of the hill he discovered Castillian roses blooming inexplicably out of season. He gathered them in his tilma, an Aztec cloak woven of cactus fiber, and carried them back to Our Lady. She held each blossom in her hand, replaced them in the tilma, then sent Juan Diego on his way.

After three visits in three days, de Zumarraga's servants were tired of seeing Juan Diego. They tried to ignore him, but he would not leave the waiting room. They could tell he was carrying something inside his tilma, but he would not show them what it was. When they insisted, he opened a corner of his cloak a little so they could get a glimpse of the magnificent roses.

News of the flowers spread throughout the palace until it reached Bishop de Zumarraga. Realizing this must be the sign from Heaven he had asked for, the bishop ordered his servants to admit Juan Diego immediately.

"You asked for a sign," Juan Diego said. "Look." As he unfolded his tilma the roses cascaded onto the floor. But more marvelous than the flowers was the likeness of the Blessed Virgin that appeared inside Juan Diego's cloak. The image depicts the Virgin as the woman who is described in the Book of Revelation, clothed with the sun, with the moon under her feet. But the miraculous image also presents Mary with the dark complexion of an Aztec princess.

Bishop de Zumarraga and everyone else in the room fell to their knees weeping and prayed to Our Lady to forgive them for doubting her. Then the bishop said to Juan Diego, "Well, show us where the Lady from Heaven wants her church to be built."

After he pointed out to the bishop the spot Our Lady had chosen for her church, Juan Diego returned home where he found his uncle healthy and strong as the Virgin had promised. Juan Bernardino said the Blessed Mother appeared to him too, and asked that at Tepeyac she be known as Holy Mary of Guadalupe.

Bishop de Zumarraga built a church at the place the Virgin had indicated and installed the miraculous image over the high altar. Although cactus fiber cloth deteriorates within a few short years, Juan Diego's tilma has survived intact to this day and is venerated by millions of pilgrims every year.

Within ten years of the apparitions some nine million Indians converted to the Catholic faith, drawn by the portrait of the dark-skinned Virgin who had come to one of their own and spoken to him in the native language.

Devotion to La Virgen Morena, "the Dark Virgin," spread throughout Central and South America. In the 17th and 18th centuries it extended to regions that became part of the United States. The Franciscan and Jesuit fathers installed copies of the miraculous image in their mission churches in New Mexico, Texas, Arizona, and California. As devotion to Our Lady of Guadalupe increased, new honors were bestowed upon her. In 1737 she was named patron of Mexico City. Nine year later all of Spain's colonies in the New World were placed under the Dark Virgin's protection. In 1910 Pope St. Pius X declared her the Virgin Patroness of Latin America, and in 1945 Pope Pius XII granted Our Lady of Guadalupe the exalted title, "Empress of the Americas."

Juan Diego moved into a small room attached to the church where the miraculous image was displayed. He lived there until his death on May 30, 1548. When Pope John Paul II visited the modern Basilica of Our Lady of Guadalupe in 1990, he beatified Juan Diego. The Holy Father returned to Guadalupe again in January 1999. On that occasion he entrusted the future of the Americas to the Blessed Mother and elevated the liturgical commemoration of Our Lady of Guadalupe from a memorial to a feast.

The right-to-life movement has adopted Our Lady of Guadalupe as its patron. Just as this image of the Mother of God touched the hearts of millions of Indians and led them away from a religion that demanded human sacrifice, many who actively oppose abortion pray that Our Lady of Guadalupe will convert contemporary society which tolerates the killing of the unborn.

To Prevent Child Abuse

St. Germaine Cousin (c.1579-1601) Feast day: June 15

*Beaten, underfed, denied even the comfort of a mattress
to sleep on, St. Germaine Cousin's father and stepmother
stopped just short of killing the poor disabled child.*

Most pitiable among the saints is Germaine Cousin, a peasant girl from the village of Pribac near Toulouse. Born with a withered right arm and a repulsive skin condition, she later developed tuberculosis which caused hideous swellings on her neck. Her father, Laurent Cousin, hated the sight of her. Germaine's mother Marie Laroche died soon after the child was born. When Laurent remarried, Germaine's stepmother treated the child literally like an unwanted dog, feeding her scraps, making her sleep in the barn or under the stairs, insisting she keep away from her stepbrothers and stepsisters who might become infected by casual contact with Germaine. The Cousins' neighbors in the village followed the family's lead at first, mocking the child and making her life endless misery. None of the little girls of the village would have anything to do with her.

While still a girl Germaine was sent to tend the family's sheep. Alone in the fields she kept up a constant conversation with God. She began to go to Mass each morning and prayed the rosary many times in the course of the day. Germaine's genuine piety coupled with her meekness in the face of cruelty won over the villagers of Pribac, who repented of mistreating the poor girl. But the attitude of Germaine's family did not change.

Then the people of Pribac began to whisper of Germaine's

miracles. To go to Mass she had to leave her sheep untended, but they never wandered off, nor were they attacked by wolves. After a heavy rain the stream that separated Germaine's field from the church flooded, some said she walked across the surface of the water, while others reported that the torrent parted for her just as the Red Sea had parted for Moses.

Finally, to atone for years of neglect, Laurent offered Germaine a real bed and a place at the table. Germaine declined the offer. So many years of abuse may have made her suspicious of this unexpected act of kindness, or perhaps she felt self-conscious about joining a family that had never wanted her. Whatever her reasons, Germaine kept to her routine of watching the sheep and sleeping under the stairs.

One morning she did not get up at her usual time. When Laurent went to wake her he found Germaine dead on her pallet. She was only 22 years old.

A fervent local cult grew around her tomb. Today Pribac welcomes an annual pilgrimage. Visitors must wait in line to enter the Cousin house and pray at the crawlspace where the patron saint of abused children lived and died.

To Prevent Sexual Abuse

St. Maria Goretti (1890-1902) Feast day: July 6

*Twelve-year-old Maria Goretti rejected 20-year-old
Alessandro Serenelli's attempts to seduce her. When he tried
to rape her she fought him off. As she lay dying from the
stab wounds Alessandro inflicted on her, she forgave him.*

*M*aria Goretti was the third child of poor farmers, Luigi
and Assunta Goretti, of the village of Corinaldo near Ancona in
southern Italy. The family was desperately poor; their farm was
too small to support two adults and four children. In 1898 Luigi
and Assunta gave up their few acres and moved the family to Fer-
riere di Conca, where they worked as tenant farmers for Count
Mazzolini. Their neighbors, the Serenelli family, moved with them
and the two clans lived together in a large loft over a barn.

Two years later Luigi died of malaria. To feed her children
Assunta went to work in the fields while Maria stayed at home
to cook, clean, and care for her younger sisters. As her twelfth
birthday approached Maria looked forward to making her First
Communion, but Assunta told her daughter it would have to be
postponed; Maria had had no formal religious training. Undeterred, Maria arranged with a priest in a nearby town to give her
instruction. She made her Communion in May 1902.

Among the Serenellis was 20-year-old Alessandro. Maria
treated him like an older brother, and he appeared to be a decent
young man: he worked hard, went to Mass, and joined in praying the rosary with his family. But in June Alessandro made sexual advances to Maria. When she rebuffed him he threatened to

kill her if she told anyone.

On July 5 Maria was on the verandah outside the barn caring for her baby sister. While everyone else was in the fields, Alessandro suddenly appeared. He grabbed Maria and forced her to go up to the loft where he tried to rape her. Maria fought back so Alessandro pulled out a knife and stabbed her fourteen times. Then he ran off, leaving Maria bleeding to death on the floor.

Maria was still alive when her mother and the Serenellis returned. They rushed her to a hospital where the surgeons tried to save the girl's life, but the internal injuries were too severe. Before she slipped into unconsciousness Maria received the Last Rites and stated that she forgave Alessandro. She died on July 6.

Alessandro Serenelli was arrested, tried, and sentenced to thirty years in prison. In 1910 he released to the public a statement of remorse. Once out of prison he visited Maria's mother to beg her forgiveness. On Christmas morning both Alessandro and Assunta knelt side by side at the altar rail and received Communion together. Assunta said later, "If Maria could forgive him, I can too." Alessandro eventually joined the Capuchin order as a lay brother. He died in 1970.

Many miracles were reported following Maria's funeral. Pope Pius XII beatified her in 1947 and canonized her in 1950 in the presence of her mother and other members of her family. In his canonization sermon the Holy Father addressed St. Maria, "In you...the children and all the young people will find a safe refuge, trusting that they shall be protected from every contamination."

For Racial Justice
St. Peter Claver (1580-1654) Feast day: September 9

The Jesuit missionary, St. Peter Claver, is the patron of racial justice. During an apostolate that lasted forty-four years, he defied the conventions of his time and devoted himself to caring for the physical and spiritual welfare of the hundreds of thousands of Africans brought to the slave market of Cartagena, Colombia.

eter Claver's parents were farmers in the province of Catalonia in northeastern Spain. When he was a boy they sent him to study with the Jesuits in Barcelona. There Peter proved to be intelligent and devout, but also hesitant and indecisive. Life as a Jesuit appealed to Peter, but he was reluctant to commit himself to a religious vocation. After a period of vacillation that lasted for several years, Peter Claver entered the Jesuit novitiate.

His superiors sent him to study philosophy at the College of Montesión in Palma on the island of Majorca. There, once again, Peter was troubled by doubts. Perhaps he was not destined for an active life of preaching and parish work; perhaps he should leave the Jesuits and join a monastic order. Fortunately there was a man on Majorca who would help Peter resolve his misgivings.

The porter at Montesión was a 72-year-old lay brother named Alphonsus Rodriguez. Brother Alphonsus had begun his adult life as a businessman with a wife and children. Following the deaths of his entire family Alphonsus entered the Society of Jesus as a lay brother and was made the college doorkeeper. Visitors to Montesión and passersby who stopped to talk with Brother Alphonsus found him to be a shrewd judge of character and a source of profound religious counsel. Peter Claver began to visit the porter and confide his doubts to him.

Brother Alphonsus insisted that Peter was well-suited to the Jesuits and urged him to go to the Americas as a missionary. The idea stunned Peter at first, but Alphonsus finally was able to convince him that the way to overcome his fears was to embrace a life of heroic sacrifice.

In 1610 Peter's superiors agreed to send him to the Americas, but they suggested that first he should be ordained a priest. Once again Peter hesitated. How could he commit himself to the priesthood when he was not even certain that he was suited to the religious life, let alone fit to be a missionary. The Jesuit superiors, who must have been models of patience, let Peter have his way and sent him to Cartagena, Colombia, unordained. He was thirty years old.

In the 17th century Cartagena's location on the Caribbean Sea made it one of the New World's principal slave markets. Slavery, virtually unknown in Western Europe during the Middle Ages, returned with the Age of Discovery. In 1435 Pope Eugenius IV condemned European colonists who enslaved the local populations of the "new lands." In 1537 Pope Paul III denounced the idea, prevalent among some Europeans, that Native Americans could be enslaved because they were less than human. In 1591 Pope Gregory XIV threatened to excommunicate slave traders and slave owners.

Although these pontiffs denounced slavery, they were nonetheless voices crying in the wilderness. The overwhelming opinion among Catholic theologians of the time, supported by the statements of popes Nicholas V, Calixtus III, Sixtus IV, Alexander VI, and Leo X, upheld the ancient practice of enslaving captives taken in a just war. European colonists exploited this rationale to make slaves of Native Americans, Africans, and Asians.

During Peter Claver's lifetime, a thousand enslaved Africans were unloaded in Cartagena every month. They stumbled out of the dark holds of the slave ships, filthy, covered with sores, weak from hunger and thirst, often sick, some dying, and all of them half-crazed with terror. The only kind white face the Africans saw belonged to a Jesuit priest, Father Alphonsus de Sandoval. When he heard the roar of the harbor cannon signaling the arrival of another slave ship, Father de Sandoval gathered up food, water, and medicine and hurried to the slave pens near the docks. Not long after Peter Claver's arrival in Cartagena, Father de Sandoval started taking the timid newcomer with him.

His experiences among the slaves transformed Peter. At last he had found something to which he could commit himself. He told his superiors in Cartagena he was ready to be ordained a priest. After having bound himself body and soul to Christ, Father Claver took another vow: to devote his life to the service of the Africans.

Once he had a purpose, Peter's anxieties and uncertainties vanished. Every time a new slave ship approached Cartagena, Peter hurried to the docks. He did not wait for the slavers' human cargo to come ashore; he took the pilot's boat out to the ship, then climbed down into the hold to begin his work at once. Usually he worked alone. Even sailors who were accustomed to life on a slave ship could not bear the dreadful sights, sounds and smells below deck.

On shore the captives were herded into slave pens. Once again Peter went with them. Here he was met by his interpreters, men of many different nationalities who spoke the languages of Guinea, the Congo, and Angola, the lands from which most of the captives came. Through his interpreters Peter tried to calm the Africans' fears (the sailors liked to tell the slaves that in Cartagena white men would drain their blood to dye their sails, and use their fat to caulk their ships). On subsequent visits, Peter's interpreters began to help him explain the Catholic faith to the Africans. It is said that during the forty-four years Father Claver served in the slave market of Cartagena, he baptized 300,000 Africans. It is impossible to assess today if that number is accurate.

What we do know, however, is that Peter considered his converts to be his parishioners. There was nothing Peter could do for those converts who were sold to plantations, settlements, or mines far beyond his reach, but he devoted himself to the care of those slaves who lived in Cartagena or were within striking distance of the city.

Father Claver made regular visits to outlying plantations so his converts could hear Mass, receive the sacraments, and continue their religious instruction. He settled disputes among the slaves and reproached brutal slaveowners. He also did all he could to persuade the masters to obey the law which forbade the splitting up of slave families.

Most of the white population of Cartagena despised Peter Claver. Some protested that Father Claver profaned the sacraments by giving them to "animals." Others complained that Father Claver kept the slaves from their work. Certain well born ladies refused to enter a church if Father Claver had said Mass there for a congregation of slaves. Even some of the Jesuits thought Peter was too zealous in his care for the Africans. Yet after years of caution, Father Claver had found his vocation and nothing could deter him.

In the last four years of his life Peter was seriously ill, but he continued to go out to meet each new slave ship. During the final year of his life, he made the trip to the harbor strapped to a horse. One day he collapsed in the slave pen and was carried back to his room in the Jesuit residence. Those Jesuits who had been embarrassed if not offended by Father Claver still avoided him. He was alone through most of his final illness. The only man who tried to nurse Peter regularly as he lay dying was an

African servant. Late in the evening of September 7, 1654, Peter Claver received the Last Sacraments. He fell unconscious and died shortly after midnight. Anxious to see their saint one last time, a crowd of slaves broke down the gates of the Jesuit residence.

On January 15, 1888, Peter Claver was canonized by Pope Leo III. Alphonsus Rodriguez, the porter at Peter's college and his confidant, was canonized on the same day.

For Political Prisoners

St. Maximilian Maria Kolbe (1894-1941) Feast day: August 14

The Nazis imprisoned Maximilian Maria Kolbe, the patron
of political prisoners, in Auschwitz. He was arrested
because he was the founder and leader of a worldwide
religious movement, the Knights of the Immaculate,
and because he had sheltered Jewish refugees.

There is no disputing this simple fact: the Jews were the principal victims of the Third Reich. It was an essential tenet of the Nazi creed that the New Europe could not be born until every Jew on the continent had been exterminated. And the Nazis went about their task with inhuman efficiency.

Nazi hatred, however, was not one-dimensional. It was expansive, even ambitious. It embraced Slavs and Gypsies; pacifists and Communists; Soviet POWs and homosexuals; Catholic priests, monks, nuns, lay brothers and seminarians; Jehovah's Witnesses and Protestant pastors; and anyone with a physical or mental impairment. Nazi hatred knew no limits, and by 1945 at least six million Jews and five million Gentiles had fallen victim to it. On August 22, 1939, one week before the Nazi invasion of Poland, Adolph Hitler gave the Wehrmacht their instructions: "Kill without pity or mercy all men, women, and children of Polish descent or language....Be merciless. Be brutal. It is necessary to proceed with maximum severity. The war is to be a war of annihilation."

Approximately 6,028,000 Poles—22 percent of the country's population—perished in raids, ghettoes, mass executions, prisons, death camps, and epidemics. Reading accounts of those first days of the invasion of Poland is chilling. In Poland's western provinces 531 villages and towns were burned and 16,376 civilians, most of them Christians, were murdered. The first victims in the town of Bydgoszcz were a group of Boy Scouts, aged 12 to 16. They were lined up against a wall in the market square and shot. When a priest rushed forward to give them the Last Rites, he was shot too.

After the initial chaotic violence against Polish Christians and Jews, the Nazis began a well-orchestrated campaign against Poland's political, military, cultural, and intellectual elite. Heinrich Himmler told his SS officers, "You should hear this but also forget it again—shoot thousands of leading Poles."

Through the Nazis' grim efficiency Poland lost 57 percent of its attorneys, 45 percent of its physicians and dentists, 40 percent of its university professors, 30 percent its technicians, 18 percent of its clergy, and 15 percent of its schoolteachers. All scientific, cultural, and literary institutions were shut down. Universities and secondary schools were closed, their libraries and laboratories pillaged.

The Nazis also targeted the Catholic Church in Poland. In 1939, 80 percent of the Catholic clergy and five bishops of the Warthegau region had been deported to concentration camps. In Wroclaw 49.2 percent of the clergy were dead; in Chelmno 47.8 percent; in Lodz 36.8 percent; in Poznan 31.1 percent. In the Warsaw diocese, 212 priests were killed. Of 690 priests in the Polish province of West Prussia, at least 460 were arrested and 214 executed, including the entire cathedral chapter of Pelplin.

In a letter dated December 10, 1939, Cardinal Augustine Hlond, Archbishop of Gniezno-Poznan, described the situation to the Holy See: "The Cathedral has been turned into a garage at Pelplin; the bishop's palace into a restaurant; the chapel into a ballroom. Hundreds of churches have been closed. The whole patrimony of the Church has been confiscated, and the most eminent Catholics executed."

During this nightmare Maximilian Maria Kolbe, a Conventual Franciscan priest and the founder of a religious movement known as the *Militia Immaculatae*, or in English the Knights of the Immaculate, was arrested with 48 of his priests and brothers. After short periods in various labor camps, Kolbe was sent to Auschwitz.

Kolbe came from a profoundly religious family; both of his brothers became priests and his mother Marianna spent the last 33 years of her life as a Felician sister. Marianna Kolbe told this story about her son. When the boy was ten years old, he had a vision of the Blessed Mother. In her hands Our Lady held two crowns, a white one signifying purity and a red one signifying martyrdom. "Which do you want?" Mary asked the boy. "I choose both," Kolbe answered. For the rest of his life Kolbe felt certain that one day he would give his life for love of Christ.

Kolbe was sixteen when he entered the novitiate of the Conventual Franciscans. Noting the young man's intelligence his superiors sent him to Rome, where he received doctorates in philosophy and theology and was ordained a priest. It was in Rome that Kolbe founded his religious movement, the Knights of the Immaculate. Its members consecrate themselves to the Blessed Virgin, use every means available to spread the gospel, and work to bring about a religious conversion of individuals and society as a whole.

When Kolbe returned home to Poland he took his Knights with him. On land west of Warsaw he built a religious complex he named "The City of the Immaculate," Niepokalonow in Polish. He started a radio station and published magazines and daily newspapers to broadcast his message of religious renewal. In 1930 Kolbe opened a Niepokalonow in Japan and then one in India. By 1936 he was the superior of 760 priests and brothers at Niepokalonow in Poland.

Kolbe's advanced degrees, his rank as superior of a large religious community, and his involvement in mass media made him a natural target for the Nazis. To make his case even worse he was sheltering 1500 terrified Jewish refugees at Niepokalonow. On February 17, 1941 Kolbe was arrested by the Nazis. After a period of captivity in Warsaw's Pawiak prison, Kolbe was sent on May 28 to Auschwitz.

At Auschwitz Kolbe and several other Catholic priests were assigned as slave labor to a work detail under the capo the camp's inmates called "Bloody" Krott. A sadist, an ex-criminal, and a virulent priest-hater, Krott had a reputation for working Catholic clerics to death. On one occasion Krott loaded down frail Father Kolbe with a heavy burden of lumber and ordered him to run. the priest barely managed to go a few steps before he tripped and fell. As Kolbe lay sprawled on the ground, Krott kicked him repeatedly in the head and stomach, flogged him with a heavy whip, then tossed his unconscious body into a muddy pit and left him for dead. Incredibly, Father Kolbe survived this brutal beating.

And yet even in Auschwitz Kolbe practiced his vocation. Although it was strictly forbidden he heard confessions in the barracks at night, led his fellow inmates in prayer, and tried to restore the faith of men who, because of the savagery they saw all around them, no longer believed in God.

Near the end of July a man from Kolbe's barracks, Labor Block 14, escaped. In retaliation Karl Fritsch, the camp commandant's adjutant, selected ten men at random and sentenced them to be starved to death in punishment bunker 11. One of the ten, Francis Gajowniczek, a Polish army sergeant, began to weep. "My wife," he cried. "My poor children! I will never see them again."

Before the condemned men could be marched away, Kolbe approached Fritsch. "Please," he said, "I want to take the place of that man." He pointed to Francis Gajowniczek.

"Why?" Fritsch asked. "Who are you."

"I am a Catholic priest," Kolbe answered. "I am sick. I can barely work. This man is young and strong, and he has a family. I would like to die in his place."

Fritsch hesitated a moment, then said, "Accepted."

Father Kolbe and the nine other prisoners were stripped naked and marched to the punishment bunker. All the men were locked in the same cell. They received no food or water. The only time the door opened was when the guards came to drag out the bodies of the dead.

On August 14, 1941, five men were still alive, but only Father Kolbe was conscious. They were taking too long to die and the cell was needed for a new group of prisoners. A guard came in with a syringe and murdered each of the survivors with a lethal injection of phenol. Their bodies were burned in the Auschwitz ovens and their ashes dumped in a pit on the edge of the camp. It is said that when Fritsch related to Auschwitz Commandant Rudolph Hoess the story of Kolbe's sacrifice and the cremation of his body, Hoess, a former Catholic, laughed, "A saint without relics!"

Francis Gajowniczek survived the concentration camp. When he returned home to Warsaw, he found that both of his teenage sons had been killed during the Warsaw Uprising in the final weeks of the war. His wife was alive but emotionally scarred—she never recovered from the death of her children. Gajowniczek tracked down members of Kolbe's Knights of the Immaculate and told them what their founder had done for him. His testimony started the process of canonization for Father Kolbe. Francis Gajowniczek was in Rome in 1971 when Pope Paul VI beatified Maximilian Kolbe, and again in 1982 when Pope John Paul II canonized him. He died in Poland on March 13, 1995.

Today the Knights of the Immaculate are found in Australia, Africa, Asia, Europe, and North and South America. In

Libertyville, Illinois, the Knights have built MaryTown as the headquarters for the thousands of American Catholics who have followed Kolbe in consecrating themselves to Mary. The friars and their lay associates continue the work of St. Maximilian, spreading his message of consecration and conversion using, as Kolbe himself did, the most up-to-date means of communication. Prominent websites such as CatholiCity.com and Catholic-Goldmine.com are run by Kolbe's Knights.

The City of the Immaculate Kolbe founded in Nagasaki, Japan, is also still operating. In August 1945, an atomic bomb all but leveled the city, but the Knights' headquarters emerged unscathed, save for a few broken panes of glass.

For the Peaceful Transition of Power

St. Chad (c.630-672) Feast day: March 2

During the Florida recount of the 2000 U.S. presidential election a reporter recalled the story of St. Chad, who thought he had been appointed bishop of York, then discovered his appointment wasn't legitimate. The story was repeated so often during the month-long ballot recount dispute that St. Chad became the de facto patron of disputed elections and a saint to invoke for a peaceful transition of power.

$\mathcal{S}$t. Chad came from a family of churchmen: two brothers, Cynibill and Caelin, were ordained priests, while Chad and his older brother Cedd became bishops. Chad began his religious vocation at an early age. As a boy he lived and studied with the great St. Aidan at the abbey of Lindisfarne in Northumbria. When he was still in his teens he traveled with his boyhood friend St. Egbert to Ireland's Mellifont Abbey, where he aspired to deepen his religious formation among the Celtic monks. Upon his return to England he was ordained a priest.

By this time Chad's older brother St. Cedd had already established the monastery of Lastingham in Yorkshire as a missionary center to bring Christianity to the pagan East Saxons. Chad joined his brother on his preaching expeditions. In 664, as he lay dying, Cedd bequeathed the rule of his monastery to Chad. But Chad had not even settled in as abbot when King Oswy named him bishop of York.

This appointment was problematic. St. Wilfrid had been already consecrated bishop of York, but he was overseas and he showed no sign of returning. With the understanding that Wilfrid had abandoned his see, Chad accepted the bishopric of York.

Although Chad's consecration was irregular, no one had a bad word to say against him. The author of the *Life of St. Wilfrid*, written about 715, describes Chad as "a most sincerely religious servant of God and an admirable teacher." St. Bede says Chad "devoted himself to maintaining the truth and purity of the Church."

As bishop he made visits to every corner of his diocese, preached tirelessly, and traveled humbly on foot rather than on horseback. Like his teacher St. Aidan and his brother St. Cedd, no village was too small, no cottage too humble for Chad to enter and teach the Christian faith.

Then unexpectedly Wilfrid returned to England. When he found Chad was in residence in York he retired quietly to Ripon Abbey. The uncomfortable situation dragged on for three years until 669 when St. Theodore of Tarsus, the new archbishop of Canterbury, arrived in England. After studying the case Theodore told Chad his consecration was invalid and he must give way to the true bishop of York, Wilfrid. "I gladly resign," Chad said. "I never thought myself worthy of the office and took it only under obedience."

Chad returned to his monastery at Lastingham. But his humility impressed Theodore. When the see of Mercia fell vacant Theodore named Chad bishop and consecrated him personally.

Since Mercia was a large diocese Theodore told Chad he would have to abandon his custom of going everywhere on foot and travel on horseback. The archbishop even presented Chad with a horse for the purpose. When Chad began to protest, Theodore hoisted the reluctant rider up onto the horse.

Chad established his cathedral at Lichfield and built a small monastery beside it as a retreat from the demands of office. Chad had been bishop for about two years when one day a monk named Owini heard mysterious, heavenly voices singing in the monastery chapel where Chad was praying. The invisible choir sang for the bishop for half an hour before returning to Heaven. Then Chad opened the chapel window, clapped his hands to get Owini's attention, and asked him to fetch all the monks. When the community had gathered the bishop told them he would die soon and that he wanted them to live in harmony with each other and follow the monastic rule he had taught them. Last of all he begged for their prayers.

A week later Chad lay on his deathbed. After receiving Holy Communion for the last time he passed away peacefully. In Ireland St. Egbert, Chad's life-long friend, had a vision of St. Cedd and a multitude of angels descending from Heaven to conduct Chad's soul to the Beatific Vision.

During the Middle Ages St. Chad's relics were preserved in a shrine in Lichfield Cathedral. Some of the saint's bones survived the iconoclasts of the Reformation and these relics are enshrined today in Birmingham's Catholic Cathedral of St. Chad.

St. Chad achieved new notoriety from the contested U.S. presidential election of the year 2000. During the dispute over ballot chads in Florida, newspaper reports frequently recalled the story of St. Chad, who had assumed an office that belonged to someone else until his superior directed him to surrender it.

A Healing Touch:
Saints for Good Health

SAINT BLAISE

A Healing Touch:
Saints for Good Health

Most of Christ's miracles when he was physically present on earth were miracles of healing. They revealed his divine power, but they also were a sign of his compassion. Since the earliest years of the Church, Christians have appealed to the saints to use their influence with Christ so he would heal them of their ills.

Saints can be invoked anywhere, yet in ancient times the devout often felt drawn to go to the tomb of the saint. Of course, the impulse to go on pilgrimage certainly continues today, especially to shrines of the Blessed Virgin Mary such as Lourdes, Fatima and Guadalupe, but also to shrines of saints such as St. Anne de Beaupré in Canada's Quebec Province and St. Therese of Lisieux in France.

In the Middle Ages the desire to be in the physical presence of the saint was so strong that the sick tried to be present whenever a saint's relics were being translated, or moved, from the grave to a shrine. The faithful believed that at the moment the saint was being honored, he or she would be especially generous in granting favors. The earliest account of miracles that attended a translation comes to us from St. Ambrose. He tells us

that in 386, when he translated the relics of the martyrs Ss . Gervasius and Protasius from their graves to a basilica in Milan, crowds of the sick surged forward to touch the bier on which the bones were being carried. Many of the sick were healed.

The patron saints who appear in this chapter are among the most popular on the Church's calendar. Their special areas of patronage have been widely recognized for many centuries. St. Lucy for eye trouble. St. Agatha for breast diseases. St. Blaise for throat ailments. St. Apollonia for toothache.

St. Peregrine Laziosi has been the patron saint of cancer sufferers for at least 300 years (although he died in the 14th century, he was not canonized until 1726). Devotion to St. Peregrine became especially strong in the 20th century when it seemed that every family had lost someone dear to some form of cancer.

The most dramatic evolution of a saint's cult is that of St. Aloysius Gonzaga, who in recent years has been invoked as the patron of AIDS sufferers and AIDS caregivers. This may surprise readers who remember when St. Aloysius was held up as the patron of Catholic youth and a model of purity. Nonetheless, Aloysius' selflessness, his compassion, his absolute determination to overcome his own squeamishness, not to mention fear, in the presence of victims of an epidemic make him an ideal patron for victims of AIDS.

For Headaches

St. Acacius (died 303) Feast day: May 8

Headache sufferers invoke St. Acacius, a martyr who was tortured by having thorns bound tightly around his head.

Acacius came from Cappadocia in what is now Turkey. He was a centurion in the Roman army, stationed in Thrace. During Diocletian's persecution of the Church Acacius was arrested for refusing to sacrifice to the gods.

The Tribune Firmus ordered Acacius tortured. Among other agonies he endured was that of having thorn branches twisted tightly around his head.

When Acacius would not apostasize, Firmus sent him to Byzantium—modern Istanbul—for execution. At the place of execution Acacius was scourged and then beheaded.

During the Middle Ages, St. Acacius was listed among the Fourteen Holy Helpers, a group of patron saints invoked for common ailments and troubles. The Fourteen Holy Helpers have their own feast day, August 8.

Today, Christians still turn to St. Acacius for help in obtaining relief from the pain of headaches—and as a model of one who heroically bore intense pain for the love of God.

For Toothaches
St. Apollonia (died 249) Feast day: February 9

Toothache sufferers invoke St. Apollonia. In the course of her martyrdom her executioners knocked out her teeth.

The Roman Empire which Decius inherited in the year 249 showed every sign of deterioration. The once formidable Roman army was now fighting defensive actions against barbarian tribes that assailed the empire on every front. At home, great cities such as Carthage, Ephesus, and Rome itself went into decline as the senators and other members of the upper classes retired to their estates in the countryside, the better to escape political rivalries and murderous plots.

In desperation Emperor Decius looked to the ancient gods of Rome for help. In 249, he published an edict commanding citizens throughout the empire to appear before a local commission and publicly worship the Roman gods. This order Christians could not obey. Over the previous 200 years, persecution had flared up at various times and in various places in the empire. Under Decius, for the first time in the history of the Church, persecution was empire-wide.

Several eyewitness accounts of the Decian persecution have come down to us. One of the most vivid is a letter Dionysius, Bishop of Alexandria, sent to his fellow bishop, Fabius of Antioch, describing what happened to the Church in Alexandria.

A mob, incited by a pagan prophet, rampaged through the city, seizing Christians and torturing them wherever they were found—in the streets, in their places of business, even in their homes—before taking them outside the city walls for execution. Dionysius records that one of their victims was "the wonderful old lady Apollonia." Her attackers beat her so savagely about the head and face that they broke or knocked out all her teeth. Then they dragged her outside the gates where a large bonfire was already burning. The mob gave Apollonia a choice: recite prayers to the pagan gods or be burned alive. Apollonia asked for a little time to compose herself before she made her decision. The moment her captors released her, she leapt into the flames.

Although Bishop Dionysius' account of St. Apollonia's martyrdom states that she was elderly, in art she is invariably depicted as a beautiful young woman holding a tooth in a large pair of pincers. St. Apollonia is also the patron saint of dentists.

For Stomach Ailments
St. Erasmus (died c.303) Feast day: June 2

St. Erasmus is invoked against stomach ailments because he was martyred by having his intestines wound on a windlass.

Both St. Jerome and St. Gregory the Great mention St. Erasmus as a bishop of Formiae and a martyr. Aside from these meager facts we know nothing about him.

Legend says that St. Erasmus endured an especially gruesome martyrdom. The executioners slit open his abdomen and wound his intestines on a windlass or reel. A painting of the martyrdom of St. Erasmus by the 17th-century French master Nicholas Poussin is displayed in the Vatican Museums and a mosaic facsimile of the painting can be found in St. Peter's Basilica.

Because of the windlass, sailors took St. Erasmus as their patron. Over time his name became corrupted to "Elmo," and the blue electrical discharge sometimes seen running along the rigging of a ship or crowning the mast became known as St. Elmo's fire. Sailors interpreted the phenomena as a sign that St. Elmo had their ship under his special protection.

For Throat Ailments
St. Blaise (died c.316) Feast day: February 3

Every year on St. Blaise's day churches are filled with
Catholic faithful who line up to have their throats blessed.
The blessing recalls an event in St. Blaise's life. As he went to
his martyrdom, he saved a child who was choking to death
from a fish bone lodged in his throat.

Most of the stories told about St. Blaise are legendary. Only a handful of facts about this martyr have come down to us. He was bishop of Sebastea in Armenia when he was seized during Diocletian's persecution of the Church and beheaded.

The legend of St. Blaise says that when the persecution began, Blaise went into hiding. He found a cave in the mountains and lived there peacefully among the wild animals. The animals never harmed him, and Blaise, for his part, healed them of any wound or sickness.

One day hunters stumbled upon the bishop's hiding place. They found Blaise sitting at the mouth of the cave surrounded by a throng of wild beasts. The sight astonished and frightened the hunters. They fled from the clearing, then hurried back to the city to report what they had seen to the governor, Agricolas.

Upon hearing the story Agricolas suspected that the hunters had seen a fugitive Christian. He sent a troop of soldiers to arrest Blaise.

As the soldiers marched Blaise back to the city, they encountered a poor woman whose only possession, a pig, had just been carried off by a wolf. At Blaise's command the wolf released the pig and crept back into the woods.

When Blaise arrived at the tribunal Agricolas saluted him. "Greetings, Blaise, friend of the gods."

Blaise answered, "Greetings, my lord, but not in the name of the gods, for they are really demons."

Offended by Blaise's retort, Agricolas ordered him strung up by his wrists and his sides torn with an iron rake. Then he had the jailers drag Blaise off to prison.

Later that day, the woman whose pig Blaise had saved visited him in prison. She brought with her food and two candles to dispel the darkness of the saint's cell. To this day, two crossed candles are used in the St. Blaise blessing.

Agricolas ordered additional tortures for St. Blaise, who bore them all and refused to renounce his faith. Finally Agricolas admitted defeat and condemned Blaise to death. As he was led to the place of execution, St. Blaise was approached by a woman. In her arms she held her little boy. The child had a fish bone stuck in his throat and was choking to death. Blaise made the sign of the cross over the child and said a brief prayer. The fish bone was dislodged. St. Blaise—moments before his own execution—saved the child's life.

For Arthritis and Rheumatism
St. James the Greater (1st. century) Feast day: July 25

Legend says that as St. James was being led outside the walls of Jerusalem to the place of execution, he saw a man crippled with arthritis sitting in the shadow of the gate. Invoking the name of Jesus, James cured the man.

Two apostles bore the name James. The St. James discussed in this chapter is called "the Greater" because he, his brother St. John and St. Peter were members of Our Lord's inner circle. These three apostles were alone with Christ when he raised Jairus' daughter from the dead and when he cured St. Peter's mother-in-law. They were the only apostles to witness the Lord's glorious Transfiguration and the only apostles present during his bitter agony in the garden.

The gospels record that James and John also distinguished themselves by their zeal—and their ambition. When Samaritans refused to let Jesus enter their village, the brothers urged the Lord to let them "bid fire to come down from heaven and consume them." Christ had to remind these "sons of thunder" that the Son of man came not to destroy, but to save.

On another occasion the mother of James and John approached Jesus with the request that her two sons would sit beside him, one on his right hand and the other on his left, when he came into his Kingdom. Although Jesus answered that such honors were not his to give, the other ten apostles resented this attempt by the brothers to win special privileges from the Lord.

St. James and St. John were the sons of Zebedee. Father

275

and sons were fishermen who worked on the Sea of Galilee. Their home village may have been Bethsaida, which was also the home of that other team of fishermen brothers, St. Peter and St. Andrew.

The night Jesus was arrested James fled like all the other Apostles. Later St. Peter found the courage to follow the Lord at a distance to Caiaphas' house, and St. John appeared the next day with the Blessed Mother to keep watch as Jesus hung on the cross, but James never came out of his hiding place.

He was with the other Apostles in the upper room when the Risen Christ appeared to them on that first Easter. A few days after the Resurrection, James, John, Peter and several other apostles encountered Jesus again on the shore of the Sea of Galilee. The Lord granted the fishermen a miraculous catch, served them a meal of roasted fish, and commanded Peter, "Feed my lambs, feed my sheep." Finally, James witnessed Christ's ascension into Heaven and was present in the upper room on Pentecost when the Holy Spirit descended upon the Apostles and upon the Blessed Mother in tongues of flame.

Tradition says that after Pentecost St. James left Jerusalem to preach the gospel in nearby Judea and Samaria. This seems probable since the Acts of the Apostles mentions Peter and John, but not James, preaching in Jerusalem.

Although St. James was not in Jerusalem, he was close enough to fall into Herod Agrippa's grasp when the king began his persecution of the Church. At Herod's command James was beheaded. Thus St. James the Greater became the first of the apostles to be martyred.

A legend records that as St. James was being led to execution with a rope around his neck he passed a man crippled by arthritis or rheumatism who begged the apostle to cure him. St. James stopped and said, "In the name of Jesus Christ, for whom I am being led to execution, stand up and bless your Creator." The man stood up, completely cured, and gave thanks to God.

The most famous and most disputed tradition associated with St. James states that he brought the gospel to Spain and that following his death his body was taken there for burial. The earliest surviving account of St. James' travels in Spain dates from the seventh century, but comes from a source in Asia Minor. St. Julian (died 690), bishop of Toledo, wrote a narrative of all the travels of the apostles, but never alludes to St. James evangelizing Spain.

It is possible that at some early date Christians took the relics of St. James to Spain. The great shrine of St. James at Compostela was built over an ancient Christian cemetery in which there was a *martyrium*, a small shrine to a martyr. Archaeologists have not been able to determine which martyr is buried there; but whether the relics are those of St. James or another unknown martyr, the shrine at Compostela has drawn crowds of pilgrims since the ninth century.

In works of art St. James has been depicted in three distinct ways: as an apostle; as a pilgrim wearing a hat with a cockle shell pinned to its brim (the cockle shell was the emblem of pilgrims who had successfully completed a journey to Compostela); and sometimes as a mounted warrior trampling a Moor. The last depiction dates from Christian Spain's centuries-long warfare to drive out the Moorish invaders. Legend has it that in one desperate battle the Spaniards gained the upper hand after St. James rode down from Heaven to fight beside the Christian knights. This warlike St. James is known as *Santiago Matamoros*, St. James the Moor-slayer.

For Eye Trouble

St. Lucy (died c. 304) Feast day: December 13

Tradition provides three different explanations why St. Lucy is invoked by people with eye ailments. The simplest reason is that Lucy's name is derived from the Latin word, lux, which means light. Another explanation is that during St. Lucy's martyrdom, the executioner tore out the saint's eyes. Finally, another more gruesome tradition says that when a pagan suitor complimented Lucy on the beauty of her eyes, she plucked them out and handed them to him.

The four great virgin martyrs of the early Church are St. Agnes, St. Agatha, St. Cecilia, and St. Lucy. Lucy's name appears in the Roman Canon of the Mass, and there is reason to believe that it was placed there by Pope St. Gregory the Great in the 6th century. Devotion to St. Lucy has remained strong for over 1700 years, not only in her native Sicily but throughout the Christian world. Even the overwhelmingly Protestant countries of Scandinavia celebrate the feast day of "Santa Lucia."

As is the case with so many of the ancient martyrs, very few facts about the life of St. Lucy have come down to us. She was martyred during the persecution of Diocletian, probably in Syracuse, the city that has always been the center of devotion to Lucy.

By the fifth century a legendary life of St. Lucy had been written to fill in the details. The author tells us she came from a Christian family in Syracuse. By the time Lucy was about twenty years old her father was already dead. Her mother, Eutychia, was very ill, having suffered for four years from a hemorrhage. In hope of a cure, mother and daughter traveled to the tomb of St.

278

Agatha in Catania. The women spent the night beside the martyr's tomb and while they slept, Agatha appeared to Lucy in a dream. Calling Lucy "sister" Agatha assured her that her mother had been healed. Then Agatha said that just as she was famous and revered in her native Catania, Lucy would be famous and revered in her home, Syracuse.

The next morning Eutychia was overjoyed to find that she had been cured. Lucy took this opportunity to ask her mother to let her break off her betrothal to a young pagan and consecrate her virginity to Christ. Eutychia agreed, and mother and daughter returned home to Syracuse where they distributed Lucy's dowry to the poor.

Lucy's fiancé, however, was not happy about being jilted. He denounced her as a Christian to the consul Paschius.

Seeing how highly Lucy prized her consecrated virginity, Paschius ordered the cruelest punishment he could think of: he sentenced the virginal Lucy to life in a brothel. When the guard tried to lead her away, however, Lucy did not move. She was supernaturally rooted to the ground. No amount of pulling or pushing, not even a team of oxen, could dislodge her from the spot.

Believing that Lucy was using witchcraft, Paschius called a band of sorcerers to break Lucy's spell. When they failed Paschius commanded his servants to pile wood around Lucy and burn her where she stood. But the flames never touched her. Finally one of the consul's friends plunged a dagger into Lucy's throat. Even then she lingered until a priest came. After she had received Holy Communion for the last time, Lucy closed her eyes and died.

Although much of the account of St. Lucy's martyrdom seems legendary, Lucy and Eutychia's pilgrimage to the tomb of St. Agatha rings true. It is possible that it is an actual detail from St. Lucy's life that Christians told each other down through the years.

For Cancer

St. Peregrine Laziosi (1260-1335) Feast day: May 1

St. Peregrine, the patron of all those who suffer from cancer,
was himself miraculously cured of cancer of the foot.

*I*n the 13th century the Pope and the Holy Roman Emperor were fierce rivals. Each claimed to be the ultimate political power in Europe. The rivalry was especially intense in Italy where two factions sprang up. The Ghibellines, the supporters of the emperor, were led by the old aristocracy whose wealth, power, and privileges depended on the strength of the Holy Roman Empire. The pope's supporters, the Guelphs, came largely from the city-states of Italy where the people resented the emperor's attempts to crush their ancient independence and make them vassals of the empire.

The city of Forli had allied itself with the emperor. So violent was Forli's rejection of the pope that the entire town had been placed under interdict, the harshest penalty the Church could impose. The churches were closed, no Masses could be said, all the sacraments were suspended, and the dead could not receive burial in consecrated ground.

In 1283 Pope Martin IV sent St. Philip Benizi, Prior General of a new order, the Servites, to Forli to convince the people to reconcile with the Holy Father. Benizi failed miserably. The interdict had intensified the anti-papal feelings of the citizens of Forli. Benizi's calls for repentance served only to enrage the Forlians. A riot broke out in which an 18-year-old boy, Peregrine Laziosi, slapped Benizi across the face.

When St. Philip Benizi patiently turned the other cheek and waited for a second blow, Laziosi felt the rage drain out of him. St. Philip's Christ-like meekness filled Laziosi with shame; he begged the saint's forgiveness, then embarked upon a life of prayer and penance.

In 1292 Peregrine left his home for Siena, where he joined the Servites. He proved to be a model priest—reverent at Mass, patient in the confessional, generous to the poor and the help-less. After thirty years Peregrine's superiors sent him home to Forli to found a Servite house there.

It was in Forli that Peregrine learned that he had cancer. The disease had begun in his right foot and was progressing up his leg. A repulsive open wound appeared at Peregrine's knee. A physician, Paolo Salazio, proscribed amputation to save Father Peregrine's life.

The night before his surgery Peregrine dragged himself to the large crucifix in the chapter room. There he prayed until he drifted off to sleep. In a dream Peregrine saw Christ come down from his cross and touch the cancerous leg. In the morning, when Dr. Salazio arrived for surgery, there was no sign of the can-cer. There was not even a trace of the loathsome wound at Pere-grine's knee.

Peregrine continued in his ministry for many years, final-ly dying of a fever when he was nearly eighty years old. Today, his incorrupt body rests in the Servite Church at Forli. Many pil-grims still come to honor him and to ask his intercession. In the United States, the Servites have established a national shrine to St. Peregrine in Chicago. The shrine publishes a newsletter, *Celebrate Life*, especially for those who are dealing with cancer.

For Breast Cancer

St. Agatha (date unknown, perhaps c.250) Feast day: February 5

*The grisly legend of St. Agatha records that one of the tortures
she endured was having her breasts cut off. She has always
been invoked against all illnesses that afflict the breast. Today
St. Agatha is invoked especially against breast cancer.*

*D*evotion to St. Agatha is ancient, particularly in Sicily, but historical facts about her are few. She was martyred in Catania —more than that no one can say. We are not even certain when she died since some early sources say she was a victim of persecution by the emperor Decius in the third century. Others say she was martyred under Emperor Diocletian in the first years of the fourth century. We know that by 350 her cult was well established since both St. Ambrose and Pope St. Damasus I wrote in praise of St. Agatha.

The legend of St. Agatha, which dates from the early fifth century, says that she was a wealthy noblewoman of Catania in Sicily. The pagan consul Quintianus lusted after her, but she rejected him. He sent her to a brothel where he gave the madam, a woman named Aphrodisias, thirty days to corrupt Agatha. At the end of the month Aphrodisias admitted defeat. She told Quintianus it was "easier to split rocks" than to shake Agatha's Christian faith or overcome her resolve to remain a virgin.

Once again Agatha appeared before the consul. His lust now turned to hate. Quintianus had Agatha stretched on the rack, but the pain to her torn limbs did not move her. Enraged, Quintianus ordered his torturers to cut off Agatha's breasts.

The jailers carried Agatha, mutilated and unconscious, back to her cell. Quintianus forbade anyone to bring her food or water or any medical treatment, but St. Peter appeared in Agatha's cell and restored her breasts.

When Quintianus was informed that Agatha was healed and whole again, he had her rolled over burning coals until she was nearly dead. Once again he ordered her carried back to her cell where she died of her wounds.

While Christians buried Agatha, Quintianus rode to her house to loot it of all its riches. On the way, as he passed beside a river, his horse threw him and Quintianus landed in the river where he drowned. His body was never recovered.

For AIDS Sufferers
St. Aloysius Gonzaga (1568-1591) Feast day: June 21

When an epidemic struck Rome, St. Aloysius Gonzaga overcame his fear of catching the plague himself and volunteered to work at the Jesuit hospital. In recent years, St. Aloysius' compassion for incurables has caused him to become patron of AIDS sufferers and AIDS caregivers.

*M*anufacturers of mass-produced statues, prints, and holy cards of St. Aloysius Gonzaga have done the young man no favor. Their sentimental, doe-eyed, often effeminate images distort the true character of Aloysius. He was the headstrong, combative, eldest son of a warlike family. St. Aloysius' best biographer, Father C.C. Martindale, SJ, described him as "by nature a hard man; uncompromising; going through life with his teeth clenched." And in a famous letter written to his brother, Aloysius described himself as "a piece of twisted iron" who had entered the religious life to get twisted straight.

Aloysius inherited his contentious spirit from his father, Ferrante Gonzaga, the marquis of Castaglione. In order to pursue a military career, Ferrante left his home in northern Italy to offer his services to Philip II, King of Spain. Philip sent Ferrante to North Africa to fight against the Moors and then to Spain's northern border to fight against the French. In Madrid Ferrante met a fellow Italian, Marta Tana Santena, a baron's daughter who was serving as a lady-in-waiting to the Queen of Spain. In rank they were well matched. Ferrante was related to the Duke of Mantua, Marta to the delle Roveres, a clan which had produced two popes.

They were married in Spain, and after the wedding Ferrante and Marta returned to Italy to take up residence in the dark, squat tower that was the ancient residence of the marquises of Castaglione. There, on March 9, 1568, Aloysius Gonzaga was born.

It was a difficult birth. The doctors feared both Marta and the unborn child would die. Ferrante, helpless and panicky, ordered the doctors to baptize the child while he was still in the womb and do whatever was necessary to save Marta's life—even if that meant destroying the child. The doctors balked. To kill an unborn child was a capital crime, but there was no telling what Ferrante would do to them if his wife died.

Now Marta appealed to the Blessed Virgin for help. Instantly the delivery became much easier. Marta gave birth to a boy, but the child appeared more dead than alive. The doctors baptized him; Marta made the sign of the cross over him, at which the baby stirred and cried.

The following day Ferrante celebrated the birth of his heir with artillery salutes fired from the castle walls, a *Te Deum* sung in the parish church, and a festival in the town with games, music, dancing, and free bread and wine for all.

Europeans in 1568 lived in a perilous world. Plague threatened their lives; heresy threatened their souls; the Turks threatened their freedom. Aloysius was three years old in 1571 when a Christian fleet routed the Turkish navy at the Battle of Lepanto. Yet the Turks still menaced Christians in southern and eastern Europe. Ferrante was often called to war, and in 1572 he took four year old Aloysius with him to a military camp on the Po River.

From 1572 until 1576 Ferrante was away from home fighting the Turks. When he returned to Castiglione he was pleased to find that Aloysius had grown to be a quiet, serious, determined boy. Ferrante imagined that with such qualities Aloysius might have a career as a statesman ahead of him.

But Aloysius was thinking of becoming a priest, although

he had never mentioned it to his father. His mother's angry response when he had told her—"Let's have no more of that"—had indicated to the boy that it was best to keep his aspirations to the priesthood to himself.

When Aloysius was nine years old Ferrante sent him along with his younger brother, Rodolfo, to Florence, to the splendid court of the Gonzagas' cousin, the Grand Duke Francis de Medici. Almost all of Aloysius' biographers mention that as he approached adolescence he became a solemn boy who did not join the games and amusements of other young people his age. Aloysius might sound like a prig, but his reaction becomes more understandable once we know what amusements young people pursued in 16th century Italy.

Marriage among the nobility in Renaissance Europe was a way to consolidate wealth, power, and influence. Consequently young people looked for love elsewhere. It was common to see pairs or small groups of young men strolling about a church during Mass, plainly surveying the women in the congregation. Intimate parties in a fashionable lady's private garden were another likely place to meet a lover. As a devout, serious boy, Aloysius would not tolerate companions whom he considered to be morally loose.

Nonetheless, Aloysius did go out in society. He attended horse races, banquets and elaborate parties in palace gardens. He appears to have enjoyed these occasions—as long as the fun remained lighthearted. If it took a turn toward the lascivious he left.

Much has also been made about Aloysius' preference for black or dark colored clothing. It is true that darker clothes appealed to Aloysius' sense of austerity, but even these solemn outfits were made of silk and velvet, embellished with heavy gold or silver lace, gold buttons, and black plumes. Compared to his contemporaries who wore garishly colored doublets and white satin leggings, Aloysius' fashion sense was severe, but still opulent by our standards.

One final point should be made about the social circles in which Aloysius moved. The Italian nobility was hungry for power, land, and grand titles, and this hunger drove many nobles to commit murder. Aloysius' own family was caught up in plots and blood feuds. Two of his brothers were murdered, his mother Marta nearly died at the hands of a knife-wielding assailant, and Rodolfo, Aloysius' brother, helped plot the death of their uncle. Is it any wonder that Aloysius shunned a world that was conceited, frivolous and bloody?

During his stay in Florence Aloysius met a Jesuit priest who gave him a book on how to contemplate the mysteries of the rosary. Interior prayer was new to Aloysius, who had always prayed aloud. Combined with his negative reaction to so much of Florentine society, the new spiritual discipline made a powerful impression on Aloysius. In the Church of the Santissima Annunziata he knelt before the famous fresco of the Annunciation and promised Our Lady to do all he could to keep himself free from the vices that surrounded him. He was about 12 years old at the time and, like so many adolescents, he took his resolution to an extreme. Aloysius began to keep his eyes downcast lest he should see something sinful. It is said that he refused to look a female in the face, including his own mother. If this is true, it is the prime example of that relentless streak St. Robert Bellarmine would contend with years later as Aloysius' spiritual director.

In 1579 Ferrante moved his sons to the palace of their uncle the Duke of Mantua. The palace was a magnificent place, so large that it was nearly a city in itself. It was the site of even more dissolute activity than the palaces of Florence.

In Mantua Aloysius was stricken with a kidney disease. The doctors prescribed a very limited diet. If only they had known what type of patient they were dealing with. Aloysius, who was growing more and more literal minded, followed the regimen so strictly that after a year on this restricted diet his digestion was ruined. For the rest of his life he found it hard to keep down most types of food.

In spite of his poor health Aloysius began to practice severe penances. He beat himself with a leather dog leash until he felt blood running down his back. He refused to have a fire in his room even on the harshest days of winter. He rose at midnight to pray on the bare, cold stone floor. And he fasted three days a week. Given the state of his stomach, fasting was probably more of a relief than a penance.

Bear in mind Aloysius was only twelve at the time. Not only was he risking harm to his body, he was also putting his soul in jeopardy. In spiritual matters Aloysius was immature. He had not made his First Communion. He had no spiritual director. To advance in holiness he was relying on his own intractable will. To a boy, the ability to kneel in prayer for an hour on a bare stone floor may seem like a triumph of the spirit over the flesh. Yet it also served as a temptation to the sin of pride. It could even have led to the heretical notion that one can achieve salvation by one's own efforts, without God's grace.

In 1580 Ferrante called his boys back to Castiglione. After an absence of three years, Marta insisted that it was time they came home. Aloysius brought with him the devotional habits he had developed in Florence and Mantua. As a novice at meditation, however, he did not know how to focus his thoughts. By chance he located a copy of St. Peter Canisius' summary of Christian doctrine. At the end of the book was a list of recommended subjects for contemplation. Now at least Aloysius had a rough guide. He spent many hours in his room practicing mental prayer.

That same year, 1580, St. Charles Borromeo, the Cardinal Archbishop of Milan, visited Castiglione. Marta offered to lodge him at one of the family's castles, but St. Charles preferred to stay at the residence of the parish priest. It was there that Aloysius visited him. Borromeo was charmed by the boy, and they had long conversations together about the religious life. When Borromeo learned that Aloysius had not made his First Holy Communion, the cardinal asked the parish priest for permission to give the Sacrament to Aloysius himself.

For the following three years Aloysius straddled two worlds. Obedient to his father, he took dancing and fencing lessons and acquired other refinements a future marquis would need. When he had leisure to follow his own inclinations, he prayed, meditated, and performed acts of penance. By 1583 Aloysius was convinced he had a religious vocation. He put his mother in an impossible position when he asked her to break the news to Ferrante.

When Marta told Ferrante that Aloysius wanted to become a Jesuit, the old soldier exploded in rage. Ferrante threatened to have Aloysius flogged. He turned on Marta, saying she had coerced Aloysius into a religious vocation so her favorite, Rodolfo, could inherit. He summoned Father Paterno, Aloysius' confessor, and accused him of abusing his authority by filling a 15-year-old boy's head with pious nonsense. The family squabble ended in a stalemate. For the next two years, neither Ferrante nor Aloysius would back down. Finally Ferrante threw Aloysius out of the house.

With one servant, Aloysius moved to a country house the Gonzagas owned about a mile outside of town. A few days later Ferrante sent the governor of Castiglione to the house to look in on his son. Aloysius's servant refused to let the governor in, so the man drilled a peep hole through the door. Peering inside he saw Aloysius on his knees before a crucifix, stripped to the waist, beating himself with a leather whip.

Ferrante would not believe the governor's report. The following day he went to the house himself, looked through the peep hole, and was stunned by the sight of Aloysius, on his knees, half naked, his back and shoulders raw and bleeding. Ferrante ordered his son to come out and return home. Aloysius obeyed, but every day now he asked his father's permission to join the Jesuits. Ferrante procrastinated for several weeks, but at last gave his consent.

Thus Aloysius, with a large retinue of servants as well as a chaplain, a doctor, and his old tutor, set out for the Jesuit novitiate in Rome. Once he arrived, Aloysius was obliged to make formal visits to the palaces of cardinals whose families were as distinguished as his own. Then he had a private audience with Pope Sixtus V who had just been elected. The pope asked, "Do you realize how wearisome the religious life can be?" The Holy Father's question surprised Aloysius, but it did not put him off. With the pope's blessing, he returned to the novitiate of Sant' Andrea al Quirinale.

Aloysius was not in Sant' Andrea long before he realized that for all his scruples, he still had a misguided notion of what constituted poverty. He had come with two cassocks, both of finer cloth than those of the other novices, two caps, a felt hat, a red vest, two jackets, an overcoat, a housecoat, two pairs of breeches, four pairs of stockings, twelve shirts, twelve handkerchiefs, nine towels, and twelve pairs of shoes. In fairness, Aloysius realized his wardrobe was ludicrous. Now, in a manner that was typical of Aloysius, he became so strict with himself regarding possessions that he owned only two books, a Bible and a copy of St. Thomas Aquinas' *Summa Theologica*. When he discovered that his roommate also possessed a copy of Aquinas, Aloysius gave his to a novice who did not have one.

The spiritual director of the Roman College was St. Robert Bellarmine. For twelve years he had been the college's finest professor of theology. Now he was retired from the classroom so he could write his great compendium of Catholic doctrine. Bellarmine recognized Aloysius' religious practices for what they were—undisciplined. He ordered the young novice to give up his extreme mortifications. Furthermore he was to stop spending hours in private prayer and to restrict himself to praying at the times appointed by the Jesuit rule. Aloysius obeyed, but not perfectly. In spare moments he made brief visits to the Blessed Sacrament.

Of all the classes required of the novices Aloysius found theology particularly difficult. Literal minded as he was he had no head for speculation. Nonetheless, he applied himself to his theological studies with his usual grit and he succeeded. His superiors chose him to be among the novices who took part in public theological disputes.

There was one trial, however, Aloysius never learned to tolerate. On the streets people were forever pointing him out— a Gonzaga heir who gave up his title to be a poor Jesuit. Much worse was the attention he received from his relatives and other high churchmen. Whenever he was scheduled to participate in a public debate, his uncle, Cardinal Scipio Gonzaga, would come with several other cardinals and their retinues. The audience would be teeming with prelates and their courtiers, all there expressly to see Aloysius. It was humiliating. On one occasion Aloysius' opponent even began the dispute with an oration in praise of the Gonzaga family. The novice had meant it as a compliment, yet the speech irritated Aloysius. Throughout the debate he could not manage to keep the anger out of his voice.

To his dismay, each afternoon Aloysius and a fellow novice were sent to work either at a prison or at a hospital. Aloysius hated the hospital work. He was squeamish, and 16th-century hospitals were anything but tidy and antiseptic. Once again he relied on sheer force of will to clean repulsive sores and change fouled sheets and bloody bandages.

In January 1591 the plague struck Rome and the surrounding countryside. The city's hospitals were so crowded many of the sick and the dying had to be laid on pallets and mats on the ward floors. The Jesuits opened a hospital, and the need for nurses was so great that even the Father General worked in the wards. Initially Aloysius was assigned the task of begging for the hospital's support but later, at his request, Aloysius' superiors permitted him to work in the hospital.

Many novices had themselves become ill with the disease, yet Aloysius remained undeterred. He did what needed to be done in the wards, no matter how distasteful. He went into the streets and carried the ill and the dying to the hospital on his back. He undressed them, washed them, put fresh clothes on them, found them a bed or at least a pallet, and fed them. One of his fellow novices, a young man named Tiberio Bondi, testified later that after working with Aloysius he felt ashamed for holding back from the sick when Aloysius was giving his all.

On March 3, 1591, Aloysius contracted the plague. At first it seemed that he would recover, but no treatment broke his recurrent fevers or cured his persistent cough. He lingered for three months, dying on June 21, 1591. Aloysius Gonzaga was 23 years old.

It was the custom among the Jesuits to wrap their dead in a shroud and lay the body in the bare earth. St. Robert Bellarmine, who was certain that Aloysius was a saint, persuaded his superiors to place Aloysius' body in a coffin and entomb it in the vault beneath the Church of the Annunziata next door to the Roman College. He argued the coffin would make it easier to identify Aloysius' body when the cause for his canonization had begun. Today the relics of St. Aloysius Gonzaga and St. Robert Bellarmine are enshrined in neighboring altars in Rome's magnificent Church of San Ignazio.

For the Mentally Ill
St. Dymphna (7th century) Feast day: May 15

Two reasons account for St. Dymphna being patron of the mentally ill. First, her own father was deranged; second, when the relics of St. Dymphna were transferred from her grave to a shrine, many mentally ill persons present at the ceremony were healed.

Some 25 miles east of Antwerp in Belgium, in the town of Gheel, there is a hospital for the treatment of the mentally ill. It was founded in the 9th century near the shrine of St. Dymphna, a martyr whose relics had been discovered in the vicinity. In the Middle Ages the translation of the bones of a saint from an ordinary grave to a shrine always attracted a large crowd of the faithful. The sick turned out in large numbers, hoping that as the relics of the saint passed by they would be cured. On the day St. Dymphna's relics were enshrined the mentally ill in the crowd were healed. This was taken as a clear sign that Dymphna was their patron.

The hospital that opened near the shrine adopted an unusual approach to treating mental illness. Rather than being locked up, the patients were placed in private homes. There they lived and worked with families who supervised them. Integrating the mentally ill into the larger community is commonplace today, but it was a pioneering treatment in the 9th-century. The hospital at Gheel still treats the mentally ill.

Although St. Dymphna died in the 7th century, her story was not recorded until sometime before 1247, by Pierre, a canon of the Church of St. Aubert in Cambrai. He said he based his account on oral tradition; more likely what Father Pierre heard was local folklore.

According to Pierre, Dymphna was the daughter of Damon, a pagan Irish chieftain. Not long after Dymphna converted to Christianity, her mother died. The loss of his wife unhinged Damon. In his madness he declared that he would marry Dymphna, the only woman in the world who bore a resemblance to his lost love.

To escape her father, Dymphna, accompanied by her confessor, a priest named Gerebernus, set sail for the Continent. The fugitives landed at Antwerp and traveled inland to Gheel. Believing they were safe at last, Dymphna and Gerebernus built two separate cells for themselves beside a chapel dedicated to St. Martin of Tours. There they settled down to a contemplative life.

But the mad Irish chieftain had followed his daughter. He traced her route by the Irish coins she had used. When Damon caught up to Dymphna at Gheel, he commanded the terrified girl to marry him. Still she refused, so Damon beheaded his own child, while his attendants murdered the priest Gerebernus.

The local people placed the bodies of Dymphna and Gerebernus in simple stone sarcophagi and buried them in a cave. Fragments of the sarcophagi are extant in Gheel. There exists also a brick inscribed with the name DYMPNA which is said to have been found inside her sarcophagus. St. Dymphna's relics are enshrined at Gheel, St. Gerebernus's at Xanten.

To Protect and Guide:
Saints to Keep You Safe

SAINT CHRISTOPHER

To Protect and Guide:
Saints to Keep You Safe

In the years after Emperor Constantine brought Christianity out of the catacombs, Christians regarded as special protectors saints who had been either a native of their town or had been martyred there. In Catania the "local hero" was the virgin martyr, St. Agatha; on the island of Corfu it was the shepherd-who-became-a-bishop, St. Spiridon; in Thessalonica it was the soldier-martyr, St. Demetrius.

Residents of these towns rejoiced that they had a saint in Heaven who would intercede with God to keep his or her own townsfolk safe from drought, famine, plague, invasion, and a host of other perils. Towns that were not fortunate enough to have their own saint were pitied. The only remedy their residents had was to go on a long and arduous pilgrimage to someone else's saint.

Some of the patrons who appear in this chapter are still very much hometown saints. Naples has perhaps fifty patron saints, but St. Januarius, or San Gennaro as he is more commonly known, ranks first. The diocese of Ascoli Piceno also has more than one heavenly protector, but St. Emidius takes pride of place. On the other hand, the Anglican diocese of Winchester has had a stormy relationship with it's patron, St. Swithun. In 1538, after 600 years of veneration, St. Swithun's shrine was dismantled and his bones scattered by Henry VIII's agents, zealous Protestants determined to sever Swithun's connection with the city where he had spent his entire life. Then, in 1962, the cathedral authorities decided to reverse some of the iconoclastic damage wrought by the Reformation. They commissioned the construction of a new memorial to St. Swithun, built on the site of his long gone medieval shrine.

For Safe Travel

St. Christopher (died c.250) Feast day: July 25

The most popular of all the patron saints, St. Christopher, whose name means Christ-bearer, is the patron of travelers because one night he carried the Christ Child safely across a raging river.

Two misconceptions about St. Christopher have been current since 1969: first, that the Vatican demoted him so he is no longer a saint; second, that the Vatican removed his name from the calendar because he never existed. Both are false. Not only has St. Christopher remained a saint in good standing, but there is no doubt that there was an early martyr named Christopher.

How did these rumors start? In 1969, when Pope Paul VI authorized a complete revision of the Church's liturgical calendar, the feast days of popular saints such as St. Barbara and St. Catherine of Alexandria were eliminated because the Vatican hagiographers, a group of scholars known as the Bollandists, believed these individuals were purely mythical figures. At the same time other saints, such as St. Christopher, had their feast days downgraded from the General Calendar, which applies to the entire Church, to an optional memorial, which permits local churches to decide if they will commemorate the saint or not. Catholics in general and the media who reported the story were confused by the shake-up of the saints. It didn't help that most bishops and parish priests didn't bother to explain to the people in the pews what was happening. As a result, the misapprehension about the status of St. Christopher, one of the most popular saints of all time, has lasted for over thirty years.

The Roman Martyrology, the ancient compendium of the faithful who were martyred during those first centuries of the Church, says that Christopher died in Lycia during the persecution of the emperor Decius. His executioners tried to burn him alive, but the flames did not touch him. Next they shot Christopher full of arrows and then beheaded him. Devotion to St. Christopher is ancient in both the East and the West; churches were being dedicated to him as early as 452.

The best legends are told about the most popular saints. The legend of Christopher says he was tall and strong. He was vain about his physique, and searched the world to find a king who was worthy of his strength. When he found a powerful king in Canaan, Christopher offered to serve him. The king was delighted to win the loyalty of as fine a man as Christopher. He made him a member of his court.

One day the king's fool was singing a tune that made frequent mention of the devil. Every time Satan's name was sung, the king, who was a Christian, made the sign of the cross. "Why do you do that?" Christopher asked the king. "I make this sign," the king answered, "to ward off the devil so he will do me no harm."

"If you are afraid of the devil," Christopher said, "Then I will go serve him, because I will serve no one except the most powerful lord in the world."

Out in the desert Christopher encountered a band of men on horseback. "What are you doing in this wasteland?" the leader asked.

"I am looking for the devil," was Christopher's reply. "I hear that he is the greatest lord in the world."

"You've come to the right place," the leader responded. "I am the devil."

So Christopher joined the devil's band. One day as the devil and his men were riding along, a roadside cross came into view. Trembling, the devil reined in his horse, and led his men on

300

a long detour around the shrine, through rough and rocky country, before he returned again to the road.

"What was that all about?" Christopher asked.

"There was a man named Christ who was nailed to a cross," the devil answered. "Every time I see a cross, I think of Christ and am afraid."

"Then Christ must be stronger than you," Christopher said. "I will go serve him."

After long searching, Christopher met a hermit who told him the kind of service Christ required.

"You will have to fast in penance for your sinful life," the hermit said.

"I cannot do that," Christopher said. "My appetite is too great. Let the Lord Christ require something else from me."

"Then spend your days in prayer," the hermit said.

"I don't know any prayers," Christopher answered. "Give me some other task to perform."

The hermit thought for a moment before he spoke again. "There is a river nearby. The water is deep and the current is strong. Many travelers have drowned there. Go live beside the river and carry on your shoulders anyone who wants to cross."

"This I can do for Christ," Christopher said. So the hermit baptized Christopher and sent him off to the river. Christopher built himself a hut near the riverbank, and found a stout staff to steady himself when he carried travelers.

One day, while he was resting in his hut, he heard a child's voice crying, "Christopher, come out and carry me across."

Outside the hut Christopher saw a little boy. He grabbed his staff, put the child on his shoulder, and stepped into the water. But the farther he went, the rougher the current and the heavier the little boy became. With each step, the waves grew higher and the weight of the child increased. Christopher was afraid he would lose his step, that both he and the little boy would be swept away and drowned. At last, exhausted and gasping for breath, he crawled up the bank on the opposite shore.

"Boy," Christopher said, "with your weight you nearly killed us both. Who are you?"

The little boy answered, "I am he who created the whole world. I am Christ your king." Then the Christ Child vanished.

Not long after this the emperor Decius published an edict outlawing Christianity. Christopher went to the city of Samos in Lycia to try to help imprisoned Christians, but was arrested himself.

The governor of Samos had Christopher bound to an iron chair and a fire lit beneath it, but the flames never harmed him. Then he ordered Christopher bound to a column and shot with arrows. When the executioners found that Christopher was still breathing, they cut him down from the pillar and beheaded him.

In the Middle Ages it was customary to place a large statue or painting of St. Christopher near the church door. It was believed that whoever saw an image of the saint would be safe from harm all day long. In more recent times it has become popular among many Catholics to place a medallion or pin honoring St. Christopher in automobiles, as a way of invoking the saint's protection on the road. But whatever the manner of our comings and goings, St. Christopher stands ready to offer his guidance—and to show us how we too can become "Christ bearers" in our lives.

For Safeguard Against Thieves
St. Dismas (1st century) Feast day: March 25

To avoid pickpockets, con artists, and thieves of all kinds, invoke
St. Dismas, a convicted thief who was crucified with Jesus
and repented of his crimes as he hung on his cross.

All that we know for certain of St. Dismas, the Good
Thief, is found in St. Luke and St. John's accounts of the Passion
of Jesus Christ. The twenty-third chapter of St. Luke's gospel
provides the most details. It records that two convicted thieves
had been sentenced to be crucified with Christ. As the thief on
Christ's left hung on his cross (tradition says his name was Gestas),
he cursed God and mocked Jesus. "Are you not the Christ? Save
yourself and us!"

His partner in crime (tradition says his name was Dismas)
rebuked him. "Do you not fear God, since you are under the
same sentence of condemnation? And we indeed justly; for we
are receiving the due reward of our deeds; but this man has done
nothing wrong."

Then the repentant thief said to Christ, "Jesus, remember
me when you come in your kingly power."

Jesus answered, "Truly, I say to you, today you will be with
me in Paradise."

St. John's gospel adds some further information. The nine-
teenth chapter records that the Jews did not want the corpses of
the condemned men profaning the Sabbath. So as sundown approached, the Roman governor of Judea, Pontius Pilate, sent soldiers to Calvary to hasten the deaths of Jesus and the two thieves

by breaking their legs. When the soldiers arrived, Jesus appeared to be dead. To make sure, one of the soldiers pierced Christ's side with his lance. The two thieves were still alive, however, so the soldiers smashed their leg bones. No longer able to support their hanging bodies, Dismas and Gestas suffocated.

By the fourth century many legends had grown up around the two thieves. A collection of religious fables called *The Arabic Gospel of the Infancy of the Savior* tells how the Holy Family, as they fled into Egypt to escape King Herod, discovered that they would have to pass through country infested with robbers. Mary and Joseph decided to travel by night, hoping they would avoid being seen. But two thieves—Dismas and Gestas—stopped them on the road. Gestas would have robbed Mary and Joseph, but something moved Dismas to stop him. He offered Gestas a bribe to let the Holy Family go free.

Mary, deeply touched by Dismas' compassion and generosity, told him, "The Lord God will sustain you with his right hand, and will grant you remission of your sins." Then the Christ Child spoke up: "Thirty years from now, Mother, I will be crucified at Jerusalem, and these two robbers will be raised on crosses along with me, Dismas on my right hand and Gestas on my left. And after that day Dismas shall enter into Paradise."

In more recent times devotion to St. Dismas took a practical turn. In 1959 Father Charles Dismas Clark, SJ, and Morris Shenker, an attorney, founded Dismas House, a half-way house which offers ex-convicts a temporary home, counseling, and help finding a job. Father Clark's story was dramatized in the 1961 movie *The Hoodlum Priest.* Today, there are many Dismas Houses throughout the United States

Since St. Dismas shares March 25 with the greater feast of the Annunciation, in prison chapels all over the United States St. Dismas' day is kept on the second Sunday of October.

To Avoid or End Drought

St. Swithun (died 862) Feast day: July 2

On his deathbed St. Swithun asked to be buried in the common cemetery of Winchester Cathedral, but in 971 the bishop had St. Swithun's body translated to a splendid shrine inside the cathedral. The ceremony was marred by heavy storms, which witnesses took as a sign of the saint's displeasure. Ever since, St. Swithun has been invoked when rain is needed.

The Norman Conquest of 1066 gave England a new royal family, aristocracy, language, a system of laws, and even a new assembly of saints. Under Norman bishops and abbots, devotion to the old Anglo-Saxon saints faded away, replaced by devotion to saints who hailed from the Continent. St. Swithun, the Anglo-Saxon bishop of Winchester, was one of the few old English saints who maintained his following. By the time Henry VIII broke with Rome, some 60 churches were dedicated to St. Swithun, making him the second most popular native-born saint (Thomas Becket ranked first) in England. Even after the Reformation St. Swithun endured as a part of rural folklore; country people said if it rained on St. Swithun's Day, July 15, the rain would not stop for forty days.

Swithun (or Swithin) was born in Winchester about the year 800 when the city, already the seat of the Saxon kings of Wessex, was poised for greatness. In 829 King Egbert of Wessex became the king of all England and made Winchester the capital of the nation. For the next 400 years, Winchester would vie with London to be the most important city of the realm.

Christianity came to Winchester in 634 when Bishop Birinus

evangelized the region. Cenwalh, King of Wessex, converted and in 643 began building a church dedicated to the Holy Trinity and to Saints Peter and Paul; it became known as the Old Minster (Anglo-Saxon for mission church). Sometime around 805 Swithun's parents enrolled him in the school attached to the Old Minster.

In time Swithun was ordained a priest. About 825 King Egbert named Swithun to be his personal chaplain and appointed him tutor to his son, Ethelwulf. When Bishop Helmstan passed away in 852, Ethelwulf, now King of England, named Swithun successor to the see of Winchester.

During the ten years that Swithun was bishop he involved himself in local matters and also in national affairs. He was a prodigious restorer of tumbledown churches in his dioceses, and an enthusiastic builder of new churches in parts of the country that had never had a resident priest. He made Winchester more accessible to trade by building a bridge across the River Itchen. And he supported the new law of tithes which set aside a tenth of all lands in the kingdom for the support of the Church and its work.

There's a story of St. Swithun sitting on his River Itchen bridge, watching workmen completing the job. Along came a poor woman carrying a basket of eggs to market. As she moved carefully among the builders, one of them, as a cruel joke, jostled her. Down the woman went, smashing all her eggs. An angry Swithun rebuked the workman. Then he knelt beside the weeping woman and made the sign of the cross over her shattered eggs. At once they were whole again.

As he lay dying Swithun forbade the priests of the cathedral to bury him inside the Old Minster. He wished to be buried in the cemetery on the north side of the church "where his grave might be trodden on by passersby and the rain from the eaves drip upon it." St. Swithun died on July 2, 862, and was buried as he wished.

For more than 100 years he lay in peace. Then, in 964, a

new bishop, St. Ethelwold, decided to expand the Old Minster. The heart of his renovated cathedral would be the shrine of St. Swithun. On July 15, 971, an impressive procession of churchmen and members of the royal court braved a downpour to escort St. Swithun's bones from his grave to the new shrine inside the Cathedral. Commoners said that the day's heavy rains were the heavens weeping for Swithun whose last wish was being disregarded.

A new cathedral, built by the Normans, was consecrated in 1093, but St. Swithun's gold and silver shrine remained the centerpiece of the church. It stood behind the High Altar until 1538 when Henry VIII's commissioners destroyed it. Thomas Wroithesley, John Williams, and Richard Pollard (who had just come from Canterbury where he had despoiled the shrine of St. Thomas Becket) slunk into the cathedral at three o'clock in the morning to dismantle St. Swithun's shrine. They packed up the gold, silver, and jewels, smashed the stone carvings, and scattered the saint's bones. In 1962 a new shrine of St. Swithun was erected on the same spot where the medieval one stood. It is a memorial only since it contains not even a fragment of the saint's body.

In 1125, Reinald, monk of Winchester, was named bishop of the diocese of Stavanger, Norway. To his new home he took missals, vestments, church vessels—and the arm of St. Swithun. The relic established devotion to the English saint among the Norwegians. The relic of St. Swithun's arm disappeared during the Reformation, but St. Swithun has not been forgotten in Stavanger where both the Catholic church and the Lutheran cathedral bear his name.

Traditionally, St. Swithun's feast day was kept on July 15, the day his relics were translated from the graveyard to the cathedral shrine. The Anglican Church still observes St. Swithun's feast on that day. In 1969, Pope Paul VI approved a revised calendar for the Roman Catholic Church that shifted many feast days of the saints. Under this new calendar, St. Swithun's commemoration was transferred to July 2, the anniversary of his death.

Against Lightning
St. Thomas Aquinas (1224/5-1274) Feast day: January 28

Though St. Thomas, the Church's preeminent theologian,
is best known as the patron of Catholic schools, he is also
invoked for protection against lightning. St. Thomas himself
had a terror of violent storms. When he was a young boy,
his baby sister was killed by a bolt of lightning.

St. Thomas Aquinas was born in Roccasecca, Italy into a prominent family with noble blood. The family had at least nine children, five daughters and four sons. Thomas was the youngest boy. Before he was five years old, lightning struck the tower in which Thomas slept with his younger sister. The bolt killed the baby girl, and several horses that were in the stable on the first floor of the tower, but Thomas and the children's nurse were not harmed. For the rest of his life, Thomas dreaded violent storms, electrical storms especially.

When Thomas was five years old his parents offered him to the great Benedictine Abbey of Monte Cassino, hoping that someday he would be named abbot of this wealthy monastery. Within five years, however, the glorious Benedictine career the Aquinos had planned for Thomas was destroyed by political upheavals in Italy.

The long-term quarrel between the pope and the emperor over who had supreme political power in Western Europe took an especially ugly turn in the first half of the 13th century. The emperor at this time, Frederick II, was perhaps the most intelligent, cultured man ever to occupy the throne of the Holy Roman Empire.

But intelligence and good taste were not Frederick's only qualities. He was ambitious and ruthless. His goal was to make the office of the Holy Roman Emperor hereditary rather than a title granted by the pope, and he planned to absorb all of Italy, including Rome and the Papal States, into his empire.

Both objectives were anathema to Pope Gregory IX. He denounced Frederick as a liar, a heretic, and a hedonist who had adopted the Muslim custom of keeping a harem. (It is true that Frederick kept a Saracen-style harem, complete with eunuchs as guards). Frederick answered in kind, saying Gregory was an extortionist, an Antichrist, and that he was irrationally opposed to all secular rule.

The name-calling ended with the pope excommunicating the emperor. As part of his retaliation, Frederick occupied Monte Cassino and expelled all monks who had not been born in the abbey's territory—a decree which left only eight monks in the monastery and sent Thomas back home to Roccasecca.

In 1239, the Aquinos sent Thomas to the University of Naples. There he studied the complete works of Aristotle—a rare opportunity for which Thomas, ironically, had Frederick II to thank. The emperor's court at Palermo was an ongoing symposium of Christian, Jewish, and Muslim scholars. The Muslims had brought with them many Greek texts unavailable in Christian Europe, among them the works of Aristotle, all of which were soon translated from Arabic into Latin.

Aside from Aristotle there was another influence present in Naples at the time that would shape Thomas' life: the Dominicans. This new order of friars had been founded in 1215 by St. Dominic to teach the truths of the faith and combat errors through energetic preaching. The learning, piety, and poverty of the Dominican friars attracted Thomas. In 1244, when he was 20 years old, Thomas entered the Dominican order.

His now widowed mother, Theodora, and Thomas' brothers were angry with his choice. They still hoped Thomas would join the Benedictines, the most respected of the religious orders, and in time become abbot of Monte Cassino. Instead he had joined an order whose members supported themselves by begging in the streets.

Theodora was so angry she sent her son Reginald to bring Thomas home, by force if necessary. When Reginald and some armed friends found Thomas they tore his Dominican habit, but Thomas fought them off. Then they forced him to mount a horse, and led him to a family-owned castle in the neighborhood, Montesangiovanni, where Theodora was waiting. She pleaded and argued with Thomas to leave the Dominicans, but he refused. In frustration, his mother had Thomas locked in his room overnight. The next day the family set out for Roccasecca.

Although Thomas was confined to the castle, he had freedom of movement within the house. He spent part of his time disputing with his sister Marotta, who insisted that Thomas should obey their mother. Marotta never persuaded Thomas to submit to the family, but he did convince her to become a nun. Wisely, Marotta elected to join a Benedictine convent.

As time dragged on and Thomas showed no signs of giving in, the Aquino brothers resorted to crude tactics: they sent a prostitute to Thomas' room to seduce him. For the first time since he had been kidnapped by his family, Thomas vented his anger He grabbed a burning stick from the fireplace and chased the woman out of his room.

For a year the Aquinos kept Thomas at home. But in the summer of 1245, Theodora finally relented and gave Thomas permission to return to the Dominican house in Naples. He had barely arrived when his superiors sent him to study theology at the University of Paris. There he met his fellow Dominican, St. Albert the Great, one of the great polymaths of the Middle Ages. When the Dominicans commanded Albert to go to Cologne to teach at the university there, he took Thomas with him.

Today St. Thomas is heralded as perhaps the finest intel-lect the Church has ever produced. His genius was not immedi-ately grasped by his fellow students in Cologne, who nicknamed him "the Dumb Ox" for his girth and his silence in the lecture hall. One day Albert named two students to debate a difficult theological question; one of the students he chose was Thomas. The first student spoke, confident that his explication of the problem was definitive. When Thomas responded, his classmates were astonished: his analysis of the problem was a model of clar-ity. "You can call him the Dumb Ox," Albert said to the class. "The bellowing of that ox will be heard throughout the world."

In a very short time Thomas' bellowing was indeed heard. Two years after his ordination to the priesthood at age 25, the Dominicans sent Thomas to teach theology at the University of Paris. By 1257 Thomas had so distinguished himself that he was ap-pointed master of the University's school of Theology. In the years that followed Thomas was recognized as perhaps the greatest mind in Christendom through publication of such works as the *Summa Contra Gentiles,* a book written for non-believers to show them the reasonableness of the faith, and the *Summa Theologica,* an awe-inspiring work that undertakes to reconcile all of Catholic doctrine with natural philosophy.

In addition to being a world-class scholar, Thomas was also a man of deep prayer. His celebrated hymns in praise of the Bless-ed Sacrament—*Pange Lingua* and *Tantum Ergo*—are known and loved by Catholics to this day.

There is a story that on one occasion at Naples, while Thomas was praying before a crucifix, he heard Christ say, "You have written well of me, Thomas. What do you want as your re-ward?" Thomas answered, "Nothing but you, Lord."

Thomas' routine was to rise early every morning, confess to his secretary Reginald of Piperno, and then say Mass. Afterwards he would make his thanksgiving by hearing the Mass Reginald offered. Then he would start teaching. On the feast of St. Nicholas, December 6, 1273, Thomas was saying Mass in the Dominican church's chapel of St. Nicholas. As usual, Reginald was acting as his server. During the Mass Thomas had an epiphany that changed him utterly. That day he abandoned his work on the *Summa Theologica* and refused to start any new project. Reginald tried to get Thomas to write again, at least at a slower pace. The more Reginald cajoled him, the more impatient Thomas became. Finally he blurted out, "Everything I have written seems to me like straw."

Reginald didn't understand how Thomas could say such a thing. But he did have the sense to realize the great man was physically and mentally incapable of writing.

A few weeks later Thomas said he would like to visit his sister, Countess Theodora of San Severino. When Thomas and Reginald arrived at the castle, Theodora came out to greet her brother, but Thomas could hardly utter a word in response. For the three days he stayed with his family, Thomas seemed confused. He walked with a limp. His hands had lost their dexterity. Her brother's pathetic condition dismayed Theodora. When he left, she grieved as if he were already dead.

Some of Thomas' biographers have said that he had a revelation at the altar on St. Nicholas' day, that God showed him how human reason paled before the glory of the Beatific Vision. This may be the case, but it is also possible that Thomas suffered a stroke. A third possibility is the power of Thomas' mystical experience left him a physical wreck.

Back in the Dominican house of Naples, Thomas received an order to attend the Second Council of Lyons, called by Pope Gregory X to reconcile the Latin and Greek Churches. Thomas obeyed. Thomas had not traveled far when he had an accident. He struck his head against a low hanging tree branch and was knocked off his mule. His worried traveling companions asked if he was hurt; Thomas answered, "A little."

The band continued on their way for a few more hours until Thomas could go no further. They were near Maenza, the castle of his niece, Countess Francesca. He wanted to stop there.

Initially it seemed that he might recover from his accident. He ate a little fish. He was able to say Mass. He received a few visitors, Franciscan friars and Cistercian monks, who had heard the great theologian was in the neighborhood. But his condition began to worsen, and Thomas asked to be moved to the Abbey of St. Mary at Fossanova, six miles away. He explained to his niece and friends that if the Lord was coming for him, as a priest he would "rather be found in a religious house than in a castle."

Thomas was moved to Fossanova, where the monks gave him an upper room in the guest house. As word spread that Thomas was dying, Dominicans from the nearby towns of Anagni and Gaeta, and Franciscans from Terracina joined the one hundred Cistercian monks and lay brothers of Fossanova in praying and keeping vigil. On March 4, Thomas made a general confession to Reginald and received Holy Communion for the last time from Theobald, the abbot of Fossanova. Early in the morning of March 7, 1274, Thomas Aquinas passed peacefully to eternity.

Against Earthquakes
St. Emidius (died 304) Feast day: August 5

*The people of the diocese of Ascoli Piceno assert that the
intercession of St. Emidius has saved them many times from the
ravages of earthquake. Holy cards from the region traditionally
show the saint holding up the wall of a crumbling building.*

St. Emidius, the bishop of Ascoli Piceno, was martyred during the emperor Diocletian's persecution of the Church.

A legendary account of his life says that he came from Trier in Germany. After his baptism he traveled to Rome. In his zeal for his new faith he entered a temple of Aesculapius and smashed the statue of the god. Pope Marcellus I hid Emidius in Rome, then sent him to eastern Italy as bishop of Ascoli Piceno. Emidius preached boldly in public and made many converts—a course of action which attracted the attention of the Roman authorities. He was arrested with three companions, Saints Valentinus, Germanus and Eupolus, and all four were beheaded.

Devotion to St. Emidius came to the United States in the 19th century. In 1869 Joseph Alemany, the first archbishop of San Francisco, petitioned Blessed Pope Pius IX to establish the feast of St. Emidius as a special day of prayer in California for protection against earthquakes. Since then St. Emidius has been invoked in dioceses throughout the state.

Against Volcanic Eruptions
St. Januarius (died c.305) Feast day: September 19

In 1631 an eruption of Mount Vesuvius threatened Naples. The people of the city prayed to their primary patron, St. Januarius, to spare them. In answer to their prayers the flow of lava abated and Naples was saved. Ever since, St. Januarius has been invoked against volcanic eruptions.

An ongoing point of dispute is whether St. Januarius — perhaps more commonly known by his Italian name, San Gennaro —was bishop of Benevento or Naples. But leave that to the partisans of each city. What is certain is that he was a bishop who was martyred during the persecution of Diocletian.

Captured while on his way to visit some imprisoned Christians, Januarius was at first thrown into a fiery furnace, but emerged unscathed. Then he was taken to the arena and thrown to the lions. But the beasts refused to touch him. Finally, the saint was beheaded. Christian women collected his blood in a glass vial and placed it in his tomb.

Seventeen centuries later, this vial of blood continues to astound the world by mysteriously liquefying several times each year. The first such liquefaction was recorded in 1389, and since that time countless pilgrims have witnessed this unexplained event. No "miracle" has been more thoroughly investigated than this one. Although there is no agreement about exactly what occurs—and no official Church declaration that the liquefaction is indeed a supernatural event—even skeptics admit that something happens.

The phenomenon occurs three times a year: on September 19, St. Januarius' principal feast day; on the feast day commemorating the translation of St. Januarius' relics to Naples, celebrated in early May; and on December 16, the anniversary of the day Naples was saved from an eruption of Mount Vessuvius through the intercession of St. Januarius.

On these occasions, the priest brings out the relic. It is a dark red, solid mass, which half fills a small glass vial four inches in height and about two and a quarter inches in diameter, set in a metal reliquary. As the assembled clergy and people pray, the officiating priest holds the reliquary near a silver bust of the saint, which is believed to contain the saint's skull. In anything from two minutes to an hour, the solid mass becomes liquid and increases in volume. The priest declares, "The miracle has happened!" at which point the congregation chants the *Te Deum*. Then everyone in the church surges forward to kiss the relic.

The liquefaction continues to defy scientific explanation. The speed of liquefaction seems unrelated to the prevailing temperature. The blood has liquefied in a matter of minutes when the temperature was as low as 60°F while on other occasions it has taken as long as 45 minutes to liquefy although the temperature in the church was measured at nearly 80°F. Nor has anyone been able to explain why the volume of the relic increases after liquefaction, or why it sometimes appears to boil while on other occasions it looks like thick mud.

Sometimes the blood does not liquefy at all, and this is taken as a warning from the saint or a sign of his displeasure; such a failure to liquefy occurred the year the voters of Naples elected a Communist mayor. On other occasions the blood has liquefied spontaneously, as when the late Cardinal Terence Cooke—Archbishop of New York, and now a candidate himself for sainthood—visited the cathedral in 1978.

Against Snakebite

St. Paul (died c.67) Feast days: June 29 and January 25

*Psychologists tell us that fear of snakes is one of our primal
phobias. To ward off serpents, pray to the great apostle, St. Paul.
The Acts of the Apostles records that when Paul was shipwrecked
on the island of Malta, he was bitten by a poisonous snake.
By God's grace he survived unharmed.*

The great apostle Paul was born in Tarsus in Cilicia, in
what is now Turkey. In his letter to the Philippians he tells us he
was "of the people of Israel, of the tribe of Benjamin, a Hebrew
born of Hebrews; as to the law a Pharisee." At his circumcision
he was named Saul.

Many Christians assume that at his baptism Saul took the
name Paul. This is not the case. Like most Jews of the time he had
both a Hebrew name used by his fellow Jews and a Greco-Roman
name that he used in the larger Gentile society. Greek was the
dominant language in the Roman Empire in the first century of
our era, which made the necessity of using a different name even
more pressing for Saul. *Saulos* in classical Greek means conceited, affected, effeminate. *Paulos*, on the other hand, comes from
the classical Greek word for rest or calm.

From his father Saul inherited the title "citizen of Rome."
This is not as strange as it may at first appear. From the earliest
days of the empire the Romans had extended citizenship to the
people they conquered. It was an ingenious strategy designed to
foster loyalty to Rome. Citizenship brought a host of rights. In
criminal matters especially citizenship conferred certain privi-

317

leges which Paul would invoke more than once. A Roman citizen could not be tortured. A Roman citizen had the right to have his case tried by Caesar. If sentenced to death a Roman citizen could be beheaded, but he could not be executed by such gruesome methods as crucifixion or being thrown to the wild beasts.

Saul's father was a tentmaker and he taught his son the trade. When he was an adolescent, Saul was sent to Jerusalem to study with Rabbi Gamaliel. After finishing his studies at Gamaliel's school, Saul stayed on in Jerusalem and appears to have become an official at the Temple. He witnessed the stoning of St. Stephen and, "consenting to his death," guarded the coats of the men who stoned Christianity's first martyr.

After the death of Stephen, Saul joined a general persecution of Christians in Jerusalem. The Acts of the Apostles tells us that in his zeal, Saul "laid waste the church, and entering house after house, he dragged off men and women and committed them to prison." Many Christians fled the city, so Saul appealed to the high priest to give him letters to the leaders of the synagogues in Damascus, authorizing him to arrest any Christians he found there and bring them back to Jerusalem for trial. Saul departed for Damascus, "breathing threats and murder against the disciples of the Lord."

On the road to Damascus Saul had an experience that changed his life, changed the Church, and, we can say without hyberbole, changed the world. He was not far from his destination when a blinding light from Heaven flashed all around him. Saul's horse reared up, throwing him to the ground. Then Saul saw Christ and heard him cry out, "Saul, Saul, why do you persecute me?" Saul, trembling in the dust of the highway, asked, "Who are you, Lord?"

The Lord answered, "I am Jesus whom you are persecuting." Then he commanded Saul to continue to Damascus and wait; he would be told what to do.

The men who had accompanied Saul were perhaps more terrified than he was. They had heard Christ's voice but had seen no one. Now as Saul got up from the ground, he told his men that he was blind. They led him into Damascus, to the house of a Jew named Judas. For three days Saul sat in Judas' house on Straight Street, enduring his blindness, pondering what had happened to him, refusing to eat or drink.

After three days Christ commanded a Christian named Ananias to visit Saul. But Ananias did not want to help a man who had done so much evil to the Church in Jerusalem and who had authority from the High Priest to persecute the Christians of Damascus. The Lord reassured Ananias that Saul had changed; he had become "a chosen instrument of mine to carry my name before the Gentiles." So Ananias overcame his reluctance and went to Judas' house. There he laid his hands on Saul, restoring his sight. Then he baptized him.

Both the Christians and the Jews of Damascus were astonished by Saul's transformation. Overnight the man who had come to lead Christians to prison was boldly preaching the gospel in synagogues.

In the eyes of the Jews Saul was a traitor; some felt he deserved to die for defecting to the Christians. When word leaked out that there was a plot to assassinate Saul, the Christians of Damascus considered how to smuggle him out of the city. Since the killers watched the city gates even at night, some Christians took Saul to a house that had a window cut into the city walls. From there they lowered him to safety in a basket.

Saul returned to Jerusalem, eager to join the disciples, but "they were all afraid of him, for they did not believe that he was a disciple." St. Barnabas, the first to believe that Saul's conversion was sincere, took it upon himself to introduce Saul to the apostles. Saul told them of his experience on the Damascus road and what he had done in Damascus after his baptism. Once the apostles had expressed confidence in Saul, he mixed easily with the Christians of Jerusalem.

In Jerusalem Saul made his first attempt to bring the Greeks to the faith. It was a dismal failure, which actually gave rise to a Gentile plot to kill him. For Saul's own sake and the peace of the Church in Jerusalem, the apostles sent Saul back to Tarsus.

For five or six years Saul remained in his home town. If he preached Christianity there we have no record of it. Then one day Barnabas came to visit him. The Church was growing, especially in Antioch, Syria. Barnabas invited Saul to work with him in that great city. In one year Barnabas and Saul made a multitude of converts. The Acts of the Apostles says that it was during the stay of Barnabas and Saul in Antioch that the followers of Christ were first called "Christians."

Inspired by the Holy Spirit, the leaders of the Church in Antioch sent Barnabas and Paul—for that was what he was now called—on a missionary journey that began in Cyprus, Barnabas' home. The most striking event in their travels occurred at the city of Lystra, where Paul healed a man who had been crippled from birth. The pagans of the city were convinced that Paul and Barnabas were gods, identifying Barnabas as Jupiter and Paul as Mercury. In their joy at receiving heavenly visitors, the Lystrians prepared to sacrifice an ox to Barnabas and Paul. Nothing the two disciples did or said could stop them.

This first missionary journey of St. Paul took place about the years 46 to 48. The conflict between St. Paul and St. Peter probably occurred toward the end of this mission, about the year 48, in Antioch.

Most Jews who had converted to Christianity still followed the Law of Moses, particularly the kosher laws and the obligation to circumcise male children. Although Peter was comfortable eating non-kosher meals with Gentiles, and did not require Gentile male converts to be circumcised, he pretended to believe the exact opposite whenever Jewish Christians were present so as not to scandalize them. Paul, who by this time recognized that his mission was primarily to the Gentiles, saw that requiring non-Jews to observe Jewish religious customs—particularly insisting that adult Gentiles submit to circumcision—would be a formidable and unnecessary obstacle to conversion. At Antioch Paul denounced Peter as a hypocrite. Certainly the accusation of hypocrisy stung St. Peter. We do not know if he and St. Paul were ever able to heal the breach caused by this quarrel.

Since some issues were not resolved in Antioch, all the apostles met in Jerusalem for the first council of the Church. There the more conservative party, led by St. James, waived the requirement that Gentile converts undergo circumcision, but insisted that Gentiles refrain from eating meat sacrificed to idols, food that contained blood, and meat from animals who had been strangled rather than butchered—three requirements that came directly from the kosher laws. Paul and the other apostles agreed to the compromise.

Just after the council of Jerusalem, Paul suggested to Barnabas that they retrace the steps of their first mission together. Barnabas agreed, but wanted to bring his nephew, John Mark along. This young man had been a companion of Paul and Barnabas for a brief time during the first mission, but went home unexpectedly. Paul refused to travel with John Mark. Barnabas took it as an insult and refused to travel with Paul. In the end, Barnabas and his troublesome nephew went in one direction and Paul with two disciples, Timothy and Silas, went in another.

Paul and his companions traveled through Asia Minor, then across the Bosphorus to Philippi and Thessalonica in Macedonia, down to Athens and Corinth in Greece, on to Ephesus on the coast of modern Turkey, and back to Palestine, to Caesarea.

At Thessalonica Paul left Silas and Timothy and went on to Athens alone. In the Agora, the central marketplace of the city, he met some of the city's philosophers. The ancient writers tell us that Athenians craved novelties. The ideas Paul espoused intrigued them, so they escorted him to the Areopagus, a high hill where the Athenian legislature met. There they sat down to hear what he had to say.

"Men of Athens," Paul began, "I perceive that in every way you are very religious. For as I passed along and observed the objects of your worship, I found also an altar with this inscription, 'To an unknown god.' What therefore you worship as unknown, this I proclaim to you."

It was a shrewd beginning since it flattered the Athenians, suggesting that the true God had to some degree made Himself known to them in preparation for the full revelation that arrived now with Paul. Tailoring his sermon to his audience, Paul departed from his usual survey of the history of salvation from Abraham to Jesus. Instead he adopted an abstract, philosophical approach he hoped would appeal to the learned men of Athens. The doctrine of the resurrection of the dead, however, proved to be a stumbling block to the Greeks. Many members of the audience went away openly mocking Paul, but a few believed—among them, St. Dionysius, the first bishop of Athens and the city's patron saint.

From Athens Paul went to Corinth and took up residence with a Jewish Christian couple, Aquila and Priscilla, who had recently settled in Corinth after Emperor Claudius banished all the Jews from Rome. During the eighteen months Paul was in Corinth, he had predictable confrontations with members of the local synagogue. Although Crispus, the leader of the synagogue, converted to Christianity, most of the congregation remained openly hostile to Paul and his message. They tried to persuade Gallio, the Roman proconsul of the region, to act against Paul, but Gallio refused to get involved in what he perceived to be a religious squabble. Before his enemies could bring any charge against him, Paul traveled with Aquila and Priscilla to Ephesus which was the greatest city of the eastern Roman Empire. It was home to over 300,000 people in St. Paul's day, the seat of Rome's proconsul of Asia, and site of the most popular shrine of the Greco-Roman world—the Temple of Diana of the Ephesians.

Like Paul, Aquila and Priscilla were tentmakers, and the apostle spent many hours every day working with them at his trade to support himself. When he was not making tents, Paul preached to and disputed with the Jews and Gentiles of the city. After two years, Paul's congregation in Ephesus was so large the craftsmen who sold figurines of the goddess Diana saw a serious drop in their business. In the wake of an anti-Christian riot, Paul decided to leave Ephesus for Macedonia.

One night on his way to Macedonia, Paul was preaching in a third floor room of a house in Troas. Sitting in a window was a young man named Eutychus. Lulled by the sound of Paul's voice, Euthychus became drowsy and fell from his perch on the window-sill. In the street below a crowd of people gathered around the boy; when they realized he had died in the fall they began to wail. Paul hurried downstairs, picked up the body and held it in a tight embrace. Then he said to the crowd, "Do not be alarmed, for his life is in him." And Eutychus came back to life.

At the end of his third mission, Paul returned to Jerusalem. His presence rankled the Jews of the city. They charged him with sacrilege and disturbing the peace by bringing Gentiles into the Temple. A mob seized Paul, dragged him outside the Temple, and began to beat him. They might have killed the apostle there in the street if a Roman guard had not rushed in to give him safe escort to the Fortress Antonia, where Christ had been tried by Pontius Pilate twenty years earlier.

The tribune Lysias mistook Paul for an Egyptian sorcerer, so Paul asked permission to explain who he was and what he was doing in Jerusalem. His defense was a thinly-veiled summary of the Christian faith, a ruse which enraged the mob and irritated

Lysias who could not understand what Paul was talking about. He was going to have Paul flogged to get straight answers out of him, but Paul claimed immunity from torture as a Roman citizen. So instead Lysias sent Paul to prison.

Meanwhile a band of Jewish men swore to each other not to eat or drink anything until they had killed Paul. When Paul's nephew heard of the plot he came to the prison to inform his uncle that his life was in danger. Paul called one of the prison guards to escort the young man to the tribune. Lysias was informed of the plot and had Paul taken in the middle of the night, under heavy guard, to Caesarea to be placed in the custody of the Roman governor, Felix.

This prisoner intrigued Felix since Felix's wife Drusilla was Jewish. Paul had been in the governor's custody only a few days when Felix asked him to preach to him and Drusilla. Paul chose a topic that fit his situation, preaching to Felix about justice and the judgment that is to come. By the time Paul had finished Felix had not converted, but he felt uneasy.

For two years Paul remained in prison in Caesarea. At this time a new governor, Festus, came from Rome. Festus wanted to resolve Paul's case and suggested that he be returned to Jerusalem for trial. Paul, fearing death there, once again claimed his privilege as a Roman citizen to appeal to Caesar to be his judge. So Festus sent Paul off to Rome.

Soon after leaving port the ship which carried Paul met contrary winds. A battering storm drove the ship off course, and the violent sea broke the vessel into two parts. The rear half sank, but the front half ran aground on the island of Malta. Those aboard the ship—all of whom survived—struggled ashore, where some sympathetic Maltese built them a fire.

Paul was carrying a bundle of sticks to the fire when a viper emerged from the wood and sank its fangs into his hand. Paul shook his hand vigorously over the fire until the snake dropped into the flames. The Maltese waited for Paul's arm to swell up from the poison, a sign that he was about to die. But by God's grace he showed no ill effects at all from the snakebite.

After three months on Malta waiting for good sailing weather, Paul departed for Rome. Although we have no record of his trial, he must have been acquitted for we do know that he rented a house in the city and went about freely, "preaching the kingdom of God and teaching about the Lord Jesus Christ quite openly and unhindered," as is described in the final words of the Acts of the Apostles.

When the emperor Nero initiated his cruel persecution of the Christians of Rome, Paul was among those arrested. Christians who were not Roman citizens died gruesome deaths. Some were burned alive to light Nero's garden. Others were torn apart by wild beasts. St. Peter was nailed to a cross, although he made it worse by asking to be crucified upside down because he considered himself unworthy to die as the Lord had died. St. Paul, as a Roman citizen, was simply beheaded.

Ancient tradition says Paul was martyred at the site of the Abbey of Tre Fontane near the Ostian Way. He was buried in a cemetery where the Basilica of St. Paul Outside the Walls now stands. An old tradition says that Peter and Paul were martyred on the same day, June 29, but this is unlikely. Since the possible dates of their martyrdoms range from 64 to 67, it is even conceivable that the two great apostles died in different years.

In 1823 the 1500-year-old Basilica of St. Paul Outside the Walls burned. From around the world contributions poured into Rome to finance the reconstruction. During construction, workmen found a tomb. The inscription on the slab read "PAULO APOST. MART." (Paul, Apostle and Martyr). That tomb can still be seen under the high altar of the reconstructed basilica.

Against Temptations of the Devil

St. Benedict (c.480-550) Feast day: July 11

*On one occasion the devil reminded St. Benedict of a woman he
had known before he became a monk. The feelings of lust were
so strong that Benedict nearly abandoned the religious life,
but he overcame the temptation and remained faithful to his
calling. For this reason Christians invoke St. Benedict
whenever the devil tries to lure them into sin.*

*I*t is impossible to overestimate the importance of St.
Benedict in the life of the Church in the West. His Rule has been
the model for virtually every religious order founded over the last
1500 years. His monks and nuns brought England, Germany, and
Austria to the faith. In the *scriptoria* of his monasteries Benedictine monks copied and preserved the literary heritage of ancient
Greece and Rome. Armed with these texts, the Benedictines were
able to rebuild classical culture in the heart of barbarian Europe.

Benedict was born in a Christian household in Nursia near
the town of Spoleto in central Italy. His parents sent him to Rome
to study, but the young Benedict was so appalled by the licen-
tiousness of the Romans that he quit school and headed south
into the mountains to live as a hermit. Along the way Benedict
met a monk named Romanus who said he knew a place where
Benedict could hide from the world. Romanus took the young
man to a cave at Subiaco. It was high on a crag with a spectacu-
lar view of a mountain gorge. Benedict lived in this remote spot
for three years. Romanus, whose monastery was higher up on the
mountain, brought Benedict food every day, lowering it in a bas-

ket from the edge of a cliff down to Benedict's cave. A little bell, tied to the rope, alerted Benedict that his meal had arrived.

One Easter a priest who lived in the region had a vision of Christ. "How can you feast," the Lord said, "when my servant is starving in the wilderness?"

Wrapping up his Easter dinner, the priest left for the mountains to find the servant of the Lord. He found Benedict in his cave and offered to share his meal with him. "You know this is Easter," the priest said.

"Your kind visit makes this a great feast," Benedict replied.

"No, truly," the priest said. "Today really is Easter." Poor Benedict had lived in isolation for such a long time he had lost track of the calendar.

Soon after the priest's visit several shepherds stumbled on Benedict's cave. At first they were frightened, since Benedict, who was dressed in animal skins, looked more like a wild man than a monk. Upon speaking with him, however, they realized that they had found a saint. So began a reciprocal relationship between Benedict and the shepherds. They brought him food, he taught them the faith.

One day the devil tempted Benedict by reminding him of a woman he had known before he began the religious life. The sexual temptation was so strong that Benedict was on the verge of leaving his hermitage and going back to the world. Instead he pulled off his clothes and threw himself into a patch of thorn bushes. He rolled in the thorns until the pain to his torn skin drove away the feelings of lust.

By now Benedict's reputation for sanctity had spread throughout the region. An entire community of monks called on him, begging him to become their abbot. Benedict demurred; he told the monks they would chaff under his spiritual direction. When they insisted, Benedict yielded. He left his cave for the monastery, which tradition says was the Monastery of Vicovaro, about twenty miles from Subiaco.

Benedict's term as the abbot of these lax, undisciplined monks played out exactly as he had predicted. They rebelled against Benedict's strict regime. When they realized he would not modify his views of the religious life, the monks decided to do away with him by poisoning his wine. At dinner, the monk who served at the abbot's table presented the wine pitcher to Benedict for the customary blessing. As Benedict made the sign of the cross over it, the pitcher shattered.

Realizing that his monks had tried to kill him, Benedict said, "God have mercy on you. How could you have conspired to do this? Didn't I warn you that my way of life would not harmonize with yours? Go and find an abbot who is more to your liking. I cannot stay here any longer."

Benedict returned to Subiaco. His reputation was such that men who wanted to pursue the religious life flocked to him. He founded twelve communities, with an abbot and twelve monks in each. Then Roman nobles began to send their sons to Benedict to be educated. Among the first were Ss. Maurus and Placid, who came as young boys and stayed on to become two of Benedict's most faithful disciples.

The Rule Benedict wrote for his monks was in part a reaction against the extremes practiced by some monks, particularly those who lived in the deserts of the East. Left to their own devices, these monks, almost all of whom lived as hermits, literally tortured their bodies. They deprived themselves of sleep, of food, of water. They stood naked for hours in the hot sun or up to their chins in icy water. Some went mad. Others starved to death.

Benedict's response was to develop a method that was practical, made no irrational demands on the body, and could be flexible without compromising its spiritual principles. The great 20th century Benedictine historian Dom David Knowles wrote that Benedict offered his followers a monastery that was "neither a penitentiary nor a school of ascetic mountaineering, but a family, a home [for] those seeking God."

The success of Benedict's community aroused the resentment of a local priest, Florentius. He spread lies about Benedict. No one believed him. So he tried to keep men from joining Benedict's monastery. New recruits came anyway. Finally Florentius poisoned a loaf of bread and delivered it to Benedict, begging him to accept it as a token of remorse. By God's grace, Benedict knew the bread was poisoned. He gave the loaf to a raven, commanding it to take the bread where no one would find it. In a final effort to ruin Benedict's reputation, Florentius hired prostitutes in the vain hope that they would seduce the monks.

Realizing that Florentius would never stop his attacks on the community, Benedict moved with his monks to Monte Cassino. They built a new monastery on the summit, converting an old temple of Apollo into a chapel dedicated to St. Martin.

Benedict's sister, St. Scholastica, also came to Monte Cassino to found a convent. The story of her life on the mountain and the last time she and her brother Benedict saw each other is told elsewhere in this book.

Benedict was about 70 years old when he had a premonition that he was about to die. The day he told his monks to prepare his tomb he came down with a violent fever. He lingered for six days. On the final day, the monks carried Benedict into the chapel to receive Holy Communion for the last time. He asked several of his monks to support him so he could die standing up with his hands raised in prayer.

Pope St. Gregory the Great, who began his religious life as a Benedictine, tells us that on the day St. Benedict died two monks had a vision. They saw a fine road covered with gorgeous carpets and illuminated on either side by thousands of lights. It traveled in a straight line eastward and up to Heaven. A man of splendid appearance asked the monks, "Do you know who passed this way?" "No, sir," they answered. "It was the blessed Bene-dict," he said, "the Lord's beloved. He traveled this road when he went to Heaven."

Since at least the 15th century, many devout Christians have worn the St. Benedict Medal as a sign that they trust in the intercession of St. Benedict to protect them from the snares of the devil. On one side of the medal is an image of St. Benedict holding a cross in one hand and his Rule in the other. A cup and a raven flank the saint, symbols of the two occasions when ene-mies tried to poison him. Above the cup and the raven is the inscription, "*Crux Sancti Patris Benedicti*" (Cross of the Holy Father Benedict). Around the rim of the medal is the inscription, "*Ejus in obitu nro praesentia muniamus*" (May we at our death be fortified by his presence).

The opposite side of the medal bears a cross with the let-ters CSSML, initials for "*Crux Sacra Sit Mihi Lux*" (The Holy Cross be my light), and the letters NDSMD, initials for "*Non Draco Sit Mihi Dux*" (Let not the dragon be my guide). In the corners of the cross, set in circles, are the letters CSPB for "*Crux Sancti Patris Benedicti.*" Circling the outer edge of the medal are the letters VRSNSMV—SMQLIVB, initials for "*Vade Retro Satana, Nunquam Suade Mihi Vana—Sunt Mala Quae Libas, Ipse Venena Bibas*" (Begone, Satan, do not suggest your vani-ties to me—evil are the things you offer, drink your own poison). Finally, at the top of the cross is either the word "*Pax*" (peace), or the monogram IHS (Jesus).

Comforters and Consolers:
Saints for Various Needs

SAINT MARTIN DE PORRES

Comforters and Consolers:
Saints for Various Needs

One of the ironies of the cult of the saints is that St. Anne, whom Tradition (but not the Bible) tells us is the Mother of Mary, had a feast day and churches dedicated to her memory centuries before such signs of esteem were given to St. Joseph. Hard as it may be to believe, there actually was a reason for slighting the husband of Mary, the foster-father of Jesus. In the early Church so many heretical groups denied the divinity of Christ that it seemed best to downplay Joseph's role in the Holy Family. St. Joseph was finally assigned a feast day on the universal liturgical calendar in the late 15th century, and since then the popes and the faithful have been making up for lost time. Devotion to him is intense throughout the Catholic world. He is venerated as patron of the dying, protector of families, and patron of the Universal Church. In recent years in the United States a new devotion to St. Joseph has emerged: he is invoked by people looking to buy or sell a house.

Another modern, predominately American, phenomenon is devotion to St. Jude. No one knows why St. Jude is the patron of impossible cases. Even the Bollandists, an association of Church scholars who for over 300 years have been the leaders in the study of the lives and cult of the saints, have not been able to track down the origins of St. Jude's patronage. One thing is certain, however; in 1929, at the outset of the Great Depression, a Claretian priest, Father James Tort, the pastor of Our Lady of Guadalupe Church on the south side of Chicago, began conducting novena devotions to St. Jude for his largely unemployed congregation. The novena in Chicago established St. Jude's reputation as a wonder-worker. Devotion to him spread quickly to every part of the country, and Our Lady of Guadalupe Church was designated the National Shrine of St. Jude. An essential part of the St. Jude devotion is to make his name known. In America anyone who has received a favor from the saint publicizes it by placing a small ad in the classified section of a newspaper. Usually the ad just reads, "Thank you St. Jude!"

Even more contemporary than the cult of St. Jude is devotion to St. Faustina Kowalska and the Divine Mercy. The movement has its basis in the revelations which St. Faustina, a young Polish nun, received from Christ between 1931 and 1938. In a very short time the Divine Mercy movement has spread around the globe—perhaps because it's greatest promoter is Pope John Paul II. As archbishop of Cracow he was an advocate for the cause to make Sister Faustina a saint. As pope he beatified her, canonized her, established the Sunday after Easter as Divine Mercy Sunday, even blessed an altar in St. Faustina's honor at the Church of Santo Spirito in Sassia, just one block away from the Vatican.

For the Lovelorn

Legend says that Valentine, a priest imprisoned and then beheaded for his faith, befriended his jailer's daughter. As he headed off to death he left her a farewell note signed "from your Valentine." The modern practice of sending Valentine's Day cards pays tribute to a great lover of God.

Valentine is a saint about whom so much confusion exists that some have concluded he could not have existed at all. This is far from the case. There was a Roman priest named Valentine who was beaten and beheaded during the reign of Emperor Claudius II about the year 270. He was buried on the Flaminian Way outside Rome. By 350 a basilica had been built over his grave. About 820 Pope St. Paschal I transferred the martyr's relics to a chapel he built in the Church of St. Praxedes as a shrine to St. Valentine and another martyr, St. Zeno.

The source of the confusion is that the old martyrologies, or lists of saints, name yet a second St. Valentine on February 14. This Valentine is said to have been a bishop who was beheaded at Terni sixty miles from Rome during the reign of the emperor Claudius II. It's certainly possible that there were two Valentines, but it is more probable that they are both the same man with two cities claiming the honor of being the location of the martyrdom and in possession of the relics (the basilica in Terni still claims to have the bones of St. Valentine).

Legend has it that while he was a prisoner, Valentine became friends with his jailer's daughter, who was impressed by his

335

faithfulness and Christian charity. On the day of his death the soon-to-be-martyr wrote a farewell note to his friend, signing it "from your Valentine." Today, tens of millions of people exchange "Valentines" with friends and loved ones on February 14.

The specifically romantic element of St. Valentine's Day stems most likely an ancient pagan holiday. February 15th was celebrated in imperial Rome as the Feast of Lupercal, in honor of the god of fertility. On the eve of Lupercalia, young men would draw lots bearing the names of different girls; the two would then be sweethearts for the whole year. The belief that lovers were destined to be paired in mid-February extended even to the animal kingdom—in the late 14th century the poet Geoffrey Chaucer wrote in *The Parliament of Fowls* that on Valentine's Day "every fowl comes...to choose his mate."

Since Valentine's feast was celebrated on the eve of Lupercalia, pastors often looked to the saint to ensure that any romantic adventures embarked upon by the faithful were rooted in and informed by authentic Christian love. Today St. Valentine is still petitioned for the grace of a pure and noble love, both by those who are already betrothed or married and by those still looking for a mate.

For the Infertile

St. Anne (1st century) Feast day: July 26

*Couples experiencing difficulty conceiving a child have
always prayed to St. Anne. She was an elderly woman who had
despaired of ever having children when at long last God heard
her prayers and she became pregnant. The daughter who
was born to her was the Blessed Virgin Mary.*

None of the gospels make mention of the Blessed Virgin
Mary's parents, but the *Protoevangelium of James*, an apocryphal
work written about 150 A.D., presents the complete story of Ss.
Anne and Joachim.

Their home was in Jerusalem, and though they had lived
long and happily together Anne and Joachim grieved that they
had no children. One day when he brought an offering to the
Temple a fellow worshipper mocked Joachim, saying anyone who
had not added to the number of the people of Israel had no business making sacrifices. Anguished and humiliated, Joachim went
out to the desert where he fasted and prayed for forty days, begging God to bless him and Anne with a child. Suddenly an angel
came down from Heaven and said, "Joachim! The Lord has heard
your prayer. Go home for your wife Anne shall conceive."

Meanwhile Anne was venting her grief in her garden
when an angel appeared to her. "Anne, Anne, you shall conceive,"
he said, "and your seed shall be spoken of in all the world."

In her eagerness to share this news with Joachim, Anne
left her garden and stood at the city gate waiting for her husband. When she saw him in the distance she hurried out to meet

him. "Now I know the Lord God has blessed me exceedingly," she said. "I, the childless, shall conceive."

Nine months later Anne gave birth to an infant girl whom she named Mary. When their daughter was three years old Anne and Joachim led her to the Temple and offered her to the Lord. Mary remained in the Temple until she was betrothed to Joseph.

The cult of St. Anne first took root in the East. It was already well established by 550 when the emperor Justinian built a church in Anne's honor in Constantinople. The earliest reference to devotion to St. Anne in the West dates from the 8th century. The Feast of the Immaculate Conception, which celebrates the day Our Lady was conceived in the womb of her mother, was originally known as the Feast of the Conception of St. Anne.

In Europe St. Anne's primary shrine, which claims to possess her relics, is at Auray in Brittany. In the New World, the great center of devotion to Our Lord's grandmother is the Shrine of Saint Anne-de-Beaupre in Canada's Quebec Province. St. Anne has always been invoked by infertile couples, and she is also the patron of expectant mothers and women in labor.

To Overcome Religious Doubts
St. Thomas the Apostle (1st century) Feast day: July 3

*Doubters, skeptics, and cynics—anyone who finds it
hard to believe—should turn to St. Thomas, the apostle
whose doubts were put to rest by Christ himself.*

Thomas the Apostle speaks up three times in St. John's
gospel. When Jesus announces that he will travel to Bethany to
see Lazarus, a journey the apostles believe to be dangerous,
Thomas says to his fellow disciples, "Let us also go, that we may
die with him." At the Last Supper Thomas articulates the confusion of the Twelve when he responds to the Lord's promise to
one day take his disciples to be with him, by saying, "Lord we do
not know where you are going; how can we know the way?"

But the most famous episode in the life of St. Thomas occurs after the Resurrection. Thomas was not in the upper room
on the night of the first Easter when the Risen Christ appeared
to the apostles. When the others told him they had seen the
Lord Thomas was skeptical. In his unbelief he laid down a challenge, "Unless I see in his hands the print of the nails, and place
my finger in the mark of the nails, and place my hand in his side,
I will not believe."

Just eight days later Christ appeared again suddenly in the
midst of the apostles. Turning to Thomas he said, "Put your finger here, and see my hands; and put out your hand, and place it
in my side; do not be faithless, but believing."

Thomas, doubting no longer, exclaimed, "My Lord and
my God!" Catholics still pray this exclamation silently at Mass at

the elevation of the Host.

Then Christ said, "Have you believed because you have seen me? Blessed are those who have not seen and yet believe."

A tradition that goes back at least to the early third century claims that St. Thomas preached the gospel in India and was martyred at Mylapore by four soldiers who ran him through with spears. It is true that a Bishop John from India attended the Council of Nicaea in 325, but there is no way of knowing if the Christians he represented were descended from the church St. Thomas founded.

"Doubting Thomas" also plays a part in the story of the Assumption of the Blessed Virgin. All the apostles had returned to Jerusalem to be with Mary when she died except Thomas, whose long journey from India delayed him. When he arrived at last he found the apostles standing around a tomb filled with roses and lilies, but no body. They tried to tell Thomas that Mary had been taken up to Heaven body and soul, but Thomas, for whom apparently old habits died hard, refused to believe them. Suddenly the sash Our Lady had been wearing around her waist fluttered down from the sky and landed at Thomas' feet. Once again, confronted with physical evidence, Thomas believed.

For Confidence in Divine Mercy
St. Faustina Kowalska (1905-1938) Feast day: October 5

*The visions St. Faustina Kowalska received of the Lord
have given rise to a world-wide renewal of confidence
in the mercy of Christ. Pope John Paul II named
St. Faustina the Apostle of Divine Mercy.*

The village of Glogowiec, Poland, where St. Faustina Kowalska was born in 1905 no longer exists: it was swallowed up by the sprawling neighboring town of Swinicie Warckie. But the two room stone and brick cottage where the Kowalski family lived still stands, and the little church of St. Casimir where Faustina was baptized and where she made her First Holy Communion is still a thriving parish.

Faustina's parents, Stanislaus and Marianna, were farmers. They had a handful of dairy cows and a few acres where they planted rye—scarcely enough to support the Kowalskis and their ten children. In order to supplement the family income Stanislaus did carpentry work.

The Kowalskis were devout Catholics. Each morning Stanislaus recited the Little Office of the Immaculate Conception. During Lent he substituted the Lamentations of the Lord's Passion. Faustina showed signs of piety at an early age. Sometimes Marianna found her seven-year-old daughter sitting up in bed in the middle of the night praying when she should have been sleeping.

At age fifteen Faustina went to work as a housemaid. She was conscientious about her work and her employers liked her, but Faustina felt drawn to a religious vocation. Marianna did not want Faustina to become a nun, and her father said he did not have the money for the dowry, the customary gift a family made to the convent when a young woman entered a religious order.

The crisis came when Faustina was nineteen. She went to a dance in Lodz with her older sister Josephine. On the dance floor she believed she saw Jesus covered with the wounds of his Passion. "How long will you keep putting me off?" he asked. Faustina left the dance and went to the Cathedral of St. Stanislaus Kostka where she prostrated herself before the tabernacle. An interior voice told her to go to Warsaw and enter a convent there. The next day Faustina took a train to Poland's capital.

The convents of Warsaw were unwilling to accept a semi-literate girl with no skills other than housekeeping. One religious order after another turned Faustina away until at last the Sisters of Our Lady of Mercy agreed to take her on as a postulant. They put the newcomer to work in the kitchen. In time she took the name Maria Faustina of the Blessed Sacrament.

There was nothing extraordinary about Faustina's life in the convent until the evening of February 22, 1931. She was in her cell when Christ appeared before her, his right hand raised in blessing, his left hand touching the side of his chest from which issued two rays of light, one red, the other colorless. Christ commanded Faustina, "Paint an image according to the pattern you see, with the signature: Jesus, I trust in you."

The Lord gave her other instructions as well. She was to urge sinners to approach Christ with confidence. She was to do all she could to have the Church establish the first Sunday after Easter as the Feast of Mercy. And she was to publicize Christ's promise to protect whoever venerated his image under the title Divine Mercy. "I have opened my heart as a living fountain of mercy," Christ told Faustina. "Let all souls draw life from it."

For seven years Christ visited Faustina. In obedience to her superior and her spiritual director, Faustina kept a diary of everything she saw and everything Christ said to her. The finished book runs to over 600 pages and is likely to be recognized as one of the great mystical texts of the 20th century.

In 1936 Faustina was diagnosed with tuberculosis. For the next two years the disease drained all her strength. On the night of October 5 the sisters gathered around Faustina's bed to pray. When the prayers for the dying were concluded Faustina did not appear to be *in extremis*, so the nuns dispersed. Only one, Sister Amelia, stayed behind. At 10:45 it became clear to Sister Amelia that Faustina was in her final moments. She ran to fetch the Mother Superior, but when they returned Faustina was dead.

Devotion to the Divine Mercy increased steadily in Poland after World War II. Faustina's supporters, hoping to see her canonized, sent a copy of her diary to Rome. Since Sister Faustina had very little formal education, her diary was filled with misspellings, bad punctuation, and confused sentence structure. Vatican theologians had a difficult time making much sense of Faustina's diary, and what they could make out sounded heretical. In 1958 the Vatican suppressed the cult of Divine Mercy.

In 1965 Karol Wojtyla, archbishop of Cracow, gave his blessing to the preparation of a new, corrected edition of Faustina's diary. This led to Faustina's case being accepted by the Congregation for the Causes of Saints. In 1983 Karol Wojtyla, now Pope John Paul II, beatified Faustina. In 2000 he declared her a saint. And five days later the Holy Father formally established the first Sunday after Easter as Divine Mercy Sunday.

For Those Suffering Discrimination
St. Martin de Porres (1575-1639) Feast day: November 3

Illegitimate and of mixed race, Martin de Porres
suffered discrimination all his life, not only from the
civil authorities but even from his brother Dominicans.

*I*n Lima, Peru, on December 9, 1575, Ana Velazquez, a freed slave, gave birth to an infant boy. The child's father was Don Juan de Porres, a Spanish gentleman, but because the boy was born with the features and dark complexion of his African mother, Don Juan refused to acknowledge him. The register of Martin's baptism records that he was the "son of an unknown father." When Ana gave birth to Don Juan's daughter Juana two years later, the Don rejected the dark-skinned little girl, too.

Don Juan's conscience troubled him, however, and after several years of neglect he began to take responsibility for his children. Martin was eight and Juana six when their father sent them to school, arranged for Martin to learn a trade, and gave Ana enough money so the family would no longer live in poverty.

Martin was apprenticed to a barber surgeon, a peculiar pairing of professions that combined cutting hair and trimming beards with treating wounds and setting broken bones. For four years he worked at his craft. At age sixteen Martin asked the Dominicans of Holy Rosary Friary to accept him as a *donado,* a layman who performed menial work in return for the privilege of wearing the habit and living with the religious community. This position ranked near the bottom of the hierarchy of religious vocations but it was the best to which Martin could aspire. By law descendants of Indians and Africans were barred from becoming full members of religious orders.

At the time Martin entered Holy Rosary his father was the governor of Panama. It offended Don Juan's pride to see his son reduced to servant status. The prior of Holy Rosary, Juan de Lorenzana, offered to turn a blind eye to the law and let Martin take his vows as a lay brother, but Martin declined. Having such a glaring exception made in his favor may have made the sixteen-year-old boy self-conscious. By the time he was 24, however, Martin had overcome his misgivings. He took Father de Lorenzana up on his offer and made his vows as a Dominican brother.

Holy Rosary was home to 300 men, not all of whom were as open-minded as Father de Lorenzana. One novice who didn't like the way Martin had trimmed his hair called him a "mulatto dog." A priest mocked Martin for being illegitimate and descended from slaves.

Eventually Martin was put to work in the infirmary where he became every patient's favorite nurse. Not only did he treat the friars' illnesses, he also cheered them with cool drinks, fresh fruit, and clean sheets. In time the friars began to tell stories of miraculous cures which Martin had performed. He restored the severed nerves in the hand of a novice who had been slashed by a knife. He healed the gangrenous leg of a priest who was preparing for its imminent amputation. He miraculously and immediately brought back to perfect health a priest who had received the Last Rites and was awaiting death.

There were other marvelous stories the Dominicans told about Martin—that he levitated when he contemplated a crucifix or adored the Blessed Sacrament, and that on a moonless night the Blessed Virgin had sent two angels with candles to light Martin's way to the chapel for Matins. The stories of miracles garnered Martin attention, but it was his compassion for those who were suffering that won him love and respect.

After 48 years serving the community of Holy Rosary Martin himself fell mortally ill with a high fever. As he lay dying all the priests and brothers came to his sickroom. Those who could not wedge themselves into the room crowded together outside the door. The Dominicans had sung the *Salve Regina* around the deathbed and were chanting the Creed when Martin closed his eyes and let the crucifix he was holding in his hand drop to his chest. The saint was dead.

Distinctions of class and race were forgotten at Martin's funeral. After the Requiem Mass had been said, the viceroy of Peru, the archbishop of Mexico, the bishop of Cuzco, and the judge of the Royal Court confounded the prejudices of their time. They humbly carried the body of a poor, illegitimate man of mixed race to its grave, paying him the honor that belongs to those who are great in the Kingdom of God.

For the Falsely Accused
Bl. Miguel Agustin Pro (1891-1927) Feast day: November 23

*The police who charged Miguel Agustin Pro with conspiring to
assassinate a general of the Mexican army knew the charge
had no basis in fact. Father Pro was not executed because
he was a terrorist, but because he was a Catholic priest.*

On the morning of July 31, 1926, for the first time in the
400 year history of Catholic Mexico, no priest mounted the steps
of an altar to offer the Holy Sacrifice of the Mass. By order of the
Mexican bishops, and with the approval of Pope Pius XI, the celebration of Mass, the administration of the sacraments, and the
day-to-day cycle of devotional exercises were suspended in every
cathedral, church, chapel, and shrine throughout the country. It
was not an interdict; it was a church strike.

For eleven years the Church in Mexico had tried to reach
some type of reasonable accord with Mexico's aggressively anti-
Catholic government, but without any success. The federal government refused to discuss amending the Constitution which
stripped the Church of its rights, its property, and its freedom.

The president of Mexico, Plutarco Elías Calles, had encouraged the state governors to enact the most stringent laws against
the Church in their own districts. In Tabasco, Governor Tomás
Garrido Canabal sponsored new legislation ordering all Catholic
priests to marry, outlawing any priest who remained celibate, and
setting the minimum age for priestly ordination at 40. By 1926
only two or three priests were still ministering to the faithful in
Tabasco. The rest had fled, were in prison, or had been shot. In

other parts of the country priests who said Mass and administered the sacraments, nuns who kept their vows, and laity who sheltered priests and concealed the Blessed Sacrament in their homes did so at the risk of their lives.

At this critical moment in the life of the faith, Father Miguel Agustin Pro, SJ, came home to Mexico from his studies in Belgium. One of ten children of a well-to-do family (his father was an engineer), he had been preparing since 1911 for a vocation as a Jesuit priest. The anti-Catholic atmosphere in Mexico had forced him to break off his studies several times in the fourteen years between Pro's entrance into the Jesuit novitiate at El Llano in the state of Michoacan and his ordination in 1925 in Enghien, Belgium. In July 1926 Father Pro began to practice a clandestine ministry in Mexico City.

With the churches closed Father Pro established Communion Stations in private homes throughout the city. "In this way," he wrote in a letter, "I daily distributed some three hundred Communions. On the First Fridays there was a considerable increase; the last First Friday I distributed 1200 Communions."

Disguised as a mechanic, or a student, or a man taking his dog for a walk, Father Pro went from house to house, hearing confessions, baptizing infants, blessing marriages, and giving the Last Rites to the dying. He even effected a few conversions. He went to see a sick woman who had abandoned the faith. The first time Father Pro visited her, she "let loose a torrent of curses and blasphemies against what we hold most holy and sacred. A mouth truly hellish," he said. "But in six days she has completely changed. Very likely she will die tomorrow as the result of an operation, but I will bring her Holy Communion early."

When Father Pro was arrested it was through a most unexpected set of circumstances. A militant young Catholic, Luis Segura Vilchis, decided to assassinate General Álvaro Obregón to draw international attention to the terror that was being inflicted on

Catholics by the Mexican government. Two young men, Juan Tirado and Lamberto Ruiz, agreed to join Segura in the assassination.

On Sunday, November 13, 1927, as General Obregón was being driven through Mexico City's Chapultepec Park, Segura drove his own car along side the general's car and into it tossed a dynamite bomb. The general escaped unharmed, but Segura lost control of his car and crashed into another automobile. Segura and his accomplices escaped into the crowd of bystanders, but Tirado and Ruiz were captured.

At the police station both Tirado and Ruiz were tortured. One of them disclosed Segura's identity. He was arrested immediately. When the police learned that just a few days before Segura had bought the car from Humberto Pro, Father Pro's brother, a warrant was issued for Humberto's arrest.

At the Pro family's home the police arrested Humberto and took his brother Roberto and Father Pro along for good measure. Segura appealed to the chief of police General Roberto Cruz, insisting that the Pros were completely innocent of the assassination attempt, but Cruz did not care. Humberto and Roberto were active in Catholic organizations, and Miguel was an underground Catholic priest. Cruz would make an example of the priest and his activist brothers. There was no trial, just summary executions ordered by Cruz and approved by President Calles.

Father Pro was the first to die. In the courtyard of the police station he knelt, prayed, and kissed a small crucifix he always carried with him. Then he stood and walked to the wall where he made the Sign of the Cross over his executioners and over the spectators. "May God have mercy on you," he said. "May God bless you."

Finally Father Pro extended his arms like Christ on the cross and as the command to fire was given Father Pro cried out, "Viva Cristo Rey!" Long live Christ the King!

Then came the executions of Humberto Pro, Luis Segura

Vilchis and Juan Tirado. Roberto Pro was released, but expelled from Mexico.

The bodies of Father Pro and Humberto were returned to the Pro family. The two brothers were given a joint funeral and together were carried through the streets of Mexico City to the Dolores Cemetery. People threw flowers from balconies as the coffins passed, and thousands joined the procession. Many in the crowd surged forward to touch Father Pro's coffin. At a time when martyrdoms were almost a daily occurrence in Mexico, the spontaneous outpouring of religious devotion at the death of Father Pro was extraordinary.

When the committal prayers were finished and the coffins had been lowered into their graves, Miguel Pro, the martyrs' father, approached the two priests who had conducted the funeral and asked them to intone the *Te Deum*. And so the funeral of the martyrs concluded with a hymn of triumph.

For Prisoners

St. Leonard of Noblac (6th century) Feast day: November 6

Legend says that Clovis, the first Christian king of the Franks,
promised to release any prisoner St. Leonard visited. This
story became the basis of devotion to St. Leonard of
Noblac as the patron of prisoners.

There is no doubt that a holy hermit named Leonard
lived in the 6th century near the French town of Limoges. But
since the earliest surviving history of St. Leonard dates from about
1025, it is difficult to say what, if anything, in his biography is fac-
tual. According to an 11th century biography, St. Leonard was related to Clovis, king of the Franks. Like Clovis, Leonard was a
pagan. The bishop of Paris, St. Remy, who converted Clovis to
Christianity also converted Leonard. After his baptism Leonard
spent some time in a monastery but felt called to live as a hermit.
He ventured deep into the forest near Limoges where he built a
hut for himself and lived happily in perfect solitude.

One day Clovis, his wife St. Clothilde, and several other
members of the royal court were hunting in the Limoges woods
when unexpectedly the queen went into labor. The only help for
miles around was Leonard, who hurried from his cell and by a
combination of practical medicine and profound prayer helped
Clothilde deliver a strong, healthy child. In gratitude Clovis
promised Leonard as much land as he could travel by donkey in
one night.

Leonard accepted the gift, and he managed on his donkey
to cover a considerable piece of real estate. He called the place

Noblac, built a chapel there in honor of the Blessed Virgin Mary, and made it a center of missionary activity to bring the pagan Franks of the surrounding region to the faith.

Another story involving Clovis and Leonard explains how the saint came to be venerated as the patron of prisoners. At the end of a war with a hostile neighbor, Clovis made his cousin an offer: he would free every prisoner Leonard visited.

During the First Crusade Bohemund, prince of Antioch, was captured by the Muslims. During his two years of captivity he prayed to St. Leonard for deliverance. When at last Bohemund was freed, he returned home to France and went on pilgrimage to Noblac to the tomb of Leonard. At the shrine the grateful crusader left a valuable votive offering, a heavy silver chain modeled on the chains he had worn during his imprisonment.

Devotion to St. Leonard as the patron of prisoners continues to this day. In 1962 Thomas Neil Libby, an Anglican priest, opened St. Leonard's House in Windsor, Ontario, as a halfway house or residence for ex-convicts to help them reintegrate into society. By 2001 St. Leonard's Society was operating twenty such houses in Canada.

For Impossible Cases

St. Jude (1st century) Feast day: October 28

Although no one can say how St Jude came to be associated with impossible cases, we do know when devotion to him as the saint of the desperate first became popular. During the Great Depression, the pastor of a church on Chicago's south side invited his unemployed parishioners to join him in a novena to St. Jude.

Open the classified section of almost any newspaper in the United States and you'll see small ads that read "Thank you, St. Jude!" The "forgotten saint," as Jude is often called, enjoys one of the largest and most devoted followings in America. Why? Because he has a reputation for providing help when all other help has vanished.

In St. John's account of the Last Supper St. Jude asked Christ, "Lord, how is it that you will manifest yourself to us and not to the world?" This is the only time in the gospels that Jude speaks and the only time the evangelists mention him outside of their lists of the twelve apostles. From St. Luke's catalog of the apostles we learn that Jude was the brother of another apostle, St. James the Less, and was related to Our Lord. The historian Eusebius (263-339) records that about the year 90 Emperor Domitian, fearing a rebellion against Roman authority in Judea, tracked down all who claimed to be of the House of David. Two of Jude's grandsons were arraigned before the emperor, but when he saw that these two frightened men were only common laborers who waited for a kingdom that was not of this world, he sent them home unharmed.

A legend, already old when Eusebius wrote it down early in the fourth century, tells how Abgar, king of Edessa, was dying of leprosy. He sent a letter to Jesus asking him to come and heal him. Our Lord answered that he himself could not come but that he would send one of his apostles. To console the king Jesus took a cloth and pressed it to his face. When he took it away a perfect portrait of Christ was imprinted on the fabric. After the Ascension St. Jude took this portrait of Christ, called the Mandylion, to Edessa and healed Abgar. (Most statues and pictures of St. Jude show him holding a portrait medallion—a clear reference to the Mandylion.)

His work done in Edessa Jude returned home, teamed up with the apostle Simon, and then traveled to Persia where both apostles were martyred. Tradition says Jude was beaten to death with a club.

Although no one knows how St. Jude came to be associated with impossible cases, we do have a record of how devotion to him grew in the United States. The Claretian Fathers staffed Our Lady of Guadalupe parish on the south side of Chicago in a neighborhood surrounded by steel mills. The Depression of 1929 hit the steelworkers especially hard; many lost their jobs and had no way to support their families. To counteract his parishioners' desperation and despair, Father James Tort started a novena to St. Jude. The devotion was repeated week after week throughout the Depression, then through World War II, and again through the war in Vietnam. With each new crisis St. Jude's popularity increased, and in time Our Lady of Guadalupe Church was named the National Shrine of St. Jude. Today the shrine receives hundreds of thousands of petitions every year, and the Claretians publish *The Voice of St. Jude*, a newsletter that reports uplifting stories of answers to prayer.

For the Dying
St. Joseph (1st century) Feast days: March 19 and May 1

On his deathbed St. Joseph was comforted by Jesus and Mary.
Christians ask St. Joseph, patron of the dying, to likewise win us
the assistance of Jesus and Mary at the hour of our death.

The fear of heresy delayed devotion to St. Joseph for nearly fourteen hundred years. So many heretical splinter groups had denied the divinity of Christ that Church authorities felt it was more important to emphasize that God was Christ's father than to venerate the man who was the husband of Mary and the foster-father of Jesus.

If St. Luke's gospel tells the story of the infancy of Christ from Mary's viewpoint, St. Matthew's gospel gives us the story from St. Joseph's perspective. He is introduced as a just man, a descendant of King David, a native of Bethlehem, and a carpenter living in Nazareth, engaged to Mary. After the Annunciation, when Mary told Joseph that she was pregnant, he resolved to break off the engagement privately. Under the law of Moses given in the book of Deuteronomy, if Joseph had made a public charge of infidelity against Mary she would have been stoned to death. Before Joseph could do anything, however, God granted him his own annunciation. An angel of the Lord visited Joseph in a dream, urging him to take Mary as his wife and assuring him that the child she carried had been conceived by the Holy Spirit.

Joseph must have died before Christ began his public ministry. If he were still alive he would have stood with Mary at the foot of the Cross, and there would have been no need for Jesus to entrust his mother to St. John.

Although there are isolated examples of Joseph receiving early veneration in Egypt, in England, and in Germany, the Church did not grant him official recognition until 1479, when Pope Sixtus IV established March 19 as the feast of St. Joseph. From that point devotion to St. Joseph increased dramatically. The Franciscans, the Carmelites, and the Jesuits all promoted St. Joseph. St. Teresa of Avila (1515-1582) who was particularly attached to him, said of St. Joseph in her *Autobiography,* "With other saints it seems the Lord has given them grace to be of help in one need, whereas with this glorious saint I have experienced that he helps in all our needs."

As if to make up for centuries of lost time, the hierarchy and the faithful rushed to heap new honors on St. Joseph. In 1555 he was named patron of Mexico; in 1678 he was named Protector of the Missions in China; in 1726 his name was added to the Litany of the Saints; and in 1870 Blessed Pope Pius IX named him patron of the Universal Church. Pope Pius XII called upon St. Joseph to join in the struggle against Communism by making May Day, May 1, the feast of St. Joseph the Worker. In 1962 Blessed Pope John XXIII inserted Joseph's name into the Roman Canon of the Mass. And in Italy the feast of St. Joseph is celebrated as Father's Day.

Followers of the Little Way:
Saints for Children

SAINT ANTHONY

Followers of the Little Way:
Saints for Children

An entire book could be devoted to the patrons of children. More saints have been assigned to watch over infants, little boys and girls, and adolescents than any other single segment of society perhaps because they are the most vulnerable members of the human family.

In this chapter the saint with the longest history as patron of children is St. Nicholas, the 4th-century bishop of Myra and one of the most popular saints of all time. The number of churches, chapels, and altars dedicated to him throughout the Christian world defies counting. His cult is still strong in the Eastern Rites of the Catholic Church and in the Orthodox Church, but in the West St. Nicholas has suffered a setback.

Beginning in the mid-19th century, most particularly in the United States, St. Nicholas became tangled up with Santa Claus. As a result, devotion to Nicholas has diminished. It's hard to pray seriously to someone described as "a right jolly old elf." It would take too long to explain how St. Nicholas came to be associated with Santa, but interested readers will find the story laid out in two fine books, Charles W. Jones' *Saint Nicholas of Myra,*

Bari, and Manhattan: Biography of Legend, and Stephen Nissenbaum's *The Battle for Christmas*.

In addition to patrons specifically of children, this chapter presents saints whose patronage extends to areas that are of special concern to children and their parents. Here are saints who can help ward off nightmares, locate lost objects, make good and lasting friendships, and find television programs and websites which are friendly to children.

It bears repeating that most patron saints are not formally appointed by the Vatican but are rather the result of popular devotion. The latest example of a grass roots devotion to a new patron saint is St. Isidore of Seville. In 1999, Catholic web surfers began lobbying Rome to name this 6th-century bishop patron of the internet. At this writing the Vatican has made no declaration regarding St. Isidore but by popular acclamation he has already become the patron saint of internet users.

For Children

St. Nicholas (died c.350) Feast day: December 6

Since the Middle Ages St. Nicholas has been venerated as the patron of children. He restored to life three little boys who had been murdered by an innkeeper.

The Christian world is filled with churches, chapels and altars dedicated to St. Nicholas. Russia, Greece, Sicily, the province of Lorraine in France, the province of Apulia in Italy, as well as many cities and dioceses all claim him as their patron. In the East, fishermen and sailors invoke St. Nicholas before setting sail. Austrians, Germans, Swiss, Belgians, Dutch, and their relatives who emigrated to the United States and other parts of the world celebrate Nicholas' feast day as a prelude to Christmas. For 1700 years he has remained one of the most popular saints of the Christian world.

Nicholas was born to a Christian family in Patara in what is now Turkey. He became a priest and eventually was named bishop of Myra. Nicholas was imprisoned during Diocletian's persecution of the Church, but was released when Constantine published the Edict of Milan which legalized Christianity. Although his name does not appear on the oldest lists of bishops who attended the Council of Nicaea, a strong tradition among the Greeks insists he was there and that he even slapped Arius across the face for asserting that God the Son is inferior to God the Father. For the rest of his life Nicholas was a tireless opponent of the Arians. When he died he was buried in his cathedral at Myra.

Many legends attached themselves to the great bishop and are still well-known, the most famous being the story of his compassion for three poor young women. Their father had lost his fortune, and with it all hope of providing dowries for his daughters. In the first stage of their poverty the family survived by selling whatever was of value in their home. Once that money was spent and there were no more valuables to pawn, it appeared certain the women would have to support themselves as prostitutes.

Nicholas heard of their plight, and one night walked to the house and tossed a bag of gold coins through an open window. These coins were enough for the eldest daughter to make a good marriage. The second night Nicholas walked to the house again and threw a second bag of coins through the window. Now two of the daughters had dowries. On the third night Nicholas repeated his act of charity, but as he tossed the bag filled with gold coins through the open window, the door of the house flew open and the father rushed out. He embraced Nicholas, kissed his hands, and tearfully thanked him for his goodness.

Another story of the saint was well-known in the Middle Ages and Renaissance but has been forgotten in our more squeamish age. Once while traveling Nicholas stopped at an inn for the night. The innkeeper boasted that he had fresh meat and would prepare a fine meal for the bishop. Nicholas pushed the man aside and walked into the kitchen. On the floor was a large wooden tub filled to the brim with freshly slaughtered meat. Nicholas made the sign of the cross over the tub. Immediately the meat came together and three young boys stood up, alive and whole.

A third legend tells of Nicholas' powerful intercession after his death. A ship was caught in a violent storm at sea and the terrified passengers and crew prayed to St. Nicholas to help them. Suddenly the bishop appeared on deck saying, "You asked for help, here I am." Nicholas put his hand on the tiller and at that moment the storm abated.

In the 11th century the Seljuk Turks began encroaching on the territory of the Byzantine Empire. By 1084 Myra, the site of the tomb of St. Nicholas, was controlled by Muslims. The Turks had not defiled the shrine but many Christians, especially in the West, thought it scandalous that the relics of St. Nicholas should be in enemy hands. The Venetians planned to "rescue" the relics from Myra, but merchants from Bari got there first. In 1087 the ship bearing the bones of St. Nicholas arrived in the harbor of Bari. A flotilla of boats sailed out to meet it and a throng assembled on the wharf. Today the relics of St. Nicholas lie in the crypt of the grand Romanesque basilica the people of Bari built for him, and pilgrims—both Catholic and Orthodox—continue to visit the shrine.

It is commonly held that St. Nicholas has evolved into Santa Claus. It is true that giving gifts and candy to children on St. Nicholas Day is an old custom in certain parts of central and northern Europe, but the similarity between St. Nicholas and Santa Claus ends there. Eight tiny reindeer, the sleigh, the sliding down the chimney—none of this has any connection with St. Nicholas. It is derived from the famous Christmas poem, "'Twas the Night before Christmas," attributed to a New York Episcopalian minister, Clement Clark Moore.

Nonetheless at Kale, Turkey, the site of ancient Myra, the Turkish government has erected a statue of Santa Claus outside the basilica that once held the relics of St. Nicholas.

For Adopted Children
St. William of Rochester (died 1201) Feast day: May 23

St. William, the patron of adopted children, had no wife or children. When he discovered an abandoned infant, William took the child into his house and raised him as his own son.

St. William was not a native of Rochester. He was not even English. St. William was a baker and a bachelor from the town of Perth in Scotland. From the time he was a young man William practiced his faith fervently, attending Mass every day and giving generously to the poor.

Very early one morning he discovered a baby boy lying abandoned at the church door. William was filled with compassion and affection for the unwanted infant. He took the baby home, hired a wet nurse to feed him and had him baptized, giving him the name David.

When David was fifteen years old, William announced that they were going on pilgrimage to the Holy Land. They had gotten as far as Rochester in England when, for some unknown reason, David lured his father into the forest outside of town, killed him, and ran off.

David was never seen again, and William's body might have remained in the forest undiscovered if it were not for a madwoman. While wandering in the woods she found William's body. The woman amused herself by making a garland of honeysuckle. She placed it on William's head, then ran away. Several days later the madwoman returned to the body. This time she took the garland off William's head and placed it on her own. She was miraculously and immediately healed of her mental illness.

The woman ran back to Rochester to show everyone that she had been cured and to tell them about the body of the murdered saint who had wrought the miracle. The townspeople carried William's corpse from the woods to the cathedral of Rochester, where they buried him.

Very quickly a popular cult sprang up around the murdered pilgrim whom everyone called "St. William." In 1256 Lawrence of St. Martin, the bishop of Rochester, traveled to Rome to petition for William's formal canonization. If such a decree was granted it has been lost. Nonetheless, William is part of the throng of saints whose "canonization" came through popular acclaim rather than a formal process.

For Youth
St. John Bosco (1815–1888) Feast day: January 31

*St. John Bosco is the patron of youth. He spent virtually
his entire life as a priest reclaiming boys and teenagers
from lives of poverty and crime, and helping them
become productive, virtuous young men.*

John Bosco's life was shaped by the Industrial Revolution. The old rural world, which had hardly changed since the Middle Ages, was slipping away. A new, urban society was taking its place. Peasants who had left their farms to work in factories often found life in a slum much worse than life on the land. When, under the strain of poverty and despair, a family fell apart, it was the children who suffered most. John Bosco dedicated himself to rescuing homeless, abandoned boys from the streets.

John Bosco was born in the village of Becchi in the Piedmont region of northern Italy. His mother could neither read nor write. His father died when John was two years old. The Bosco family was so poor that when John entered the seminary, he was wearing clothes and shoes given to him by a charitable institution.

As a child John was charismatic, athletic and devout. Whenever a circus or a carnival was in the area, John made friends with the acrobats and magicians. They taught him their routines and sleight of hand tricks. Afterwards John would go home and perform for the children in his village, alternating tricks with lessons from the catechism.

John was nine when he had a strange dream. He saw a field full of coarse, misbehaving children. In the dream John leapt into the middle of the children and tried to subdue them by shouting and fighting. Then a man appeared who said, "You'll never change them by fighting. Be gentle and make them your friends." When John told the dream to his family, one of his brothers said, "Maybe it means you'll grow up to be the leader of a gang!"

John was sixteen when he left home for the seminary. His mother warned him if he became one of those grasping, money-hungry priests, she would never set foot in his house. For a while it seemed that John might have a brilliant career ahead of him in the Church. After ordination John's superiors sent him to Turin for further studies in theology at the St. Francis House of Priests, which had a reputation for turning out the best-educated clergy, or "dons" (a respectful title for priests) in Italy.

In Don Bosco's day Turin was being transformed from a provincial town into an economic powerhouse. Thousands of peasants from the countryside crowded into the city in search of jobs. The desperately poor lived in squalid slums. In their frustration and despair some of them turned to crime. When he visited prisons, Don Bosco met boys as young as 12 who were incarcerated with hardened criminals. The needs of such boys were staggering, but Don Bosco did not know where to begin to help.

At this time he met two tireless priests—St. Joseph Cafasso, who worked in the prisons of Turin, and St. Joseph Cottolengo, who had opened hospitals, orphanages, schools, and workshops for the city's poor. Don Bosco joined them.

To the social and political activists, these priests appeared hopelessly backward. Rather than debate the reasons for poverty, ignorance and misery, they worked to meet the immediate needs of the poor. They offered food, shelter, medical care, an education, and job training. "Denunciation and political action we leave to others," Don Bosco said. "We go straight to the poor."

Don Bosco devoted himself to reclaiming the rough teenage boys of the slums, many of whom had lived abandoned on the streets for years. To help them he opened what he called his Oratory. In the evenings he held classes, preached a brief sermon, and led the boys in prayer. On Sundays he led outings which followed a regular routine: Mass, games, a picnic, hikes, music, and Vespers.

What troubled Don Bosco were living conditions for his boys when they weren't at the Oratory or on a Sunday picnic. The ones who did not live in filthy, disease ridden slums were homeless, living under bridges or in alleys. In 1847 Don Bosco convinced his mother to come to Turin and help him open a house in the Valdocco section, a run-down neighborhood on the outskirts of town. Six homeless boys moved in. By 1852, Don Bosco and his mother were caring for 35 boys; 115 in 1854; 400 in 1860; and 600 by 1864. The numbers just kept growing.

Don Bosco followed the example of St. Joseph Cottolengo by providing his boys with an education and job training. The youngsters could choose to be shoemakers, tailors, or blacksmiths; they could work in cabinetry, book binding, or printing shops. Conservatives grumbled that Don Bosco was wasting time and resources on the dregs of society. Progressives denounced Don Bosco for undermining liberalism by teaching bourgeois values to the masses. None of these complaints troubled him.

In 1854 Turin was struck by a cholera epidemic. Within a few weeks 500 people had died. In the panic that attended the epidemic, the sick, the dying, and the dead were left untended. Don Bosco organized his hundreds of boys into teams. Some collected the sick and brought them to hospitals. Others picked up the corpses of the dead and carried them to mortuaries. Don Bosco promised the boys that if they put their confidence in God and committed no mortal sin they would be protected from contracting cholera themselves. Nonetheless, he also gave each boy a bottle of vinegar with which to wash his hands after touching a victim. Some 1400 people would die before the epidemic receded, but none of Don Bosco's boys became sick.

By now ten priests worked with Don Bosco. They were the core of his new congregation, the Salesians, named for Don Bosco's favorite saint, Francis de Sales. Under Don Bosco's leadership the Salesians worked hard to make learning, virtue, and religious practice attractive to the rough crowd of street kids who were their students.

Don Bosco urged his teachers to do everything in their power to convince the boys that they cared about them. Furthermore, he instructed the teachers to praise any boy who took even a small step toward self-improvement. Don Bosco refused to give up on any boy who came to him—even one who stole from him.

At a time when many teachers were aloof and some were brutal, the Salesians' rejection of punishment in favor of persuasion was a radical notion. Don Bosco reminded his priests, "Not with blows but with charity and gentleness must you draw these friends to the path of virtue." Don Bosco always referred to the boys as his friends.

By 1854 Don Bosco opened a preparatory seminary for training adolescent boys for the priesthood. One of the students was St. Dominic Savio. Don Bosco said of of 12-year-old Dominic, "I marvelled at the work of divine grace in one so young." Dominic was truly a religious prodigy. By the time he was 14 he was experiencing periods of mystical ecstasy that on one occasion lasted for six hours. But Dominic was still a boy and he needed Don Bosco's guidance to keep him on the path of sainthood and away from fanaticism.

Dominic wanted to imitate the medieval saints who had practiced penance by torturing their bodies. Don Bosco would not give the boy permission to inflict even the slightest mortification on himself. "We have enough to contend with in heat, cold, sickness, and tedious people," Don Bosco told the boy.

Don Bosco's express instructions did not deter Dominic from performing acts of penance in secret. One bitterly cold night Don Bosco found Dominic shivering in bed covered with nothing but a sheet. As he pulled the blankets up over the boy, Don Bosco said, "Don't be crazy. You'll catch pneumonia." "Why should I?" Dominic answered. "Our Lord didn't catch pneumonia in the stable in Bethlehem."

At the age of fifteen, Dominic developed an inflammation of the lungs. His doctor prescribed bleeding, the usual treatment, which weakened the boy further. On March 9, 1857 he died. Don Bosco wrote the first biography of this teenage saint.

There was one significant stumbling block to the foundation of the Salesians. It did not come from the Vatican—Blessed Pope Pius IX gave provisional approval to the order in 1869 and final approval in 1874. The Salesians' problems came from the state. The new Kingdom of Italy had banned religious orders and closed religious houses.

Don Bosco had as a friend Urbano Rattazzi, the Minister of the Interior who had written the legislation to abolish religious orders in Italy. Rattazzi hated priests, but he liked and admired Don Bosco. With Rattazzi's help, Don Bosco wrote a constitution for the Salesians which described them as, "An association of free citizens living together for the purpose of doing good." Thanks to this carefully worded document, the Salesians were able to operate their schools, homes for boys, and other institutions without government interference.

In 1872 Don Bosco and St. Maria Mazzarello combined to found the Daughters of Mary Help of Christians. This was to be a companion order to the Salesians, with sisters dedicated to teaching poor girls. The Daughters grew nearly as fast as the Salesians, establishing foundations in Europe and in the Americas.

Years of ceaseless activity finally caught up with Don Bosco. As Christmas of 1887 approached, he became so weak he could not leave his room. One day, 30 boys lined up outside his door for confession. Don Bosco's assistants wanted to send them away. "Let them come in," Don Bosco said. "This will be the last time."

On January 31, 1888 Don Bosco died. Forty thousand people came to the church where his body was laid out. On the day of Don Bosco's Requiem Mass, nearly the entire population of Turin jammed the streets to see his funeral procession pass.

Pope Pius XI, who had visited Don Bosco fifty years earlier, canonized him on Easter Sunday 1934. The Italian government declared the next day a national holiday.

The work of Don Bosco continues throughout the world. Today, the Salesians and the Daughters of Mary Help of Christians rescue teenage boys from prostitution in Sri Lanka, combat teen suicide in Italy, and shelter abandoned children in Colombia and the Congo.

For Preventing Nightmares
St. Raphael the Archangel   Feast day: September 29

*St. Raphael, who drove off the evil demon Asmodeus
that terrorized Sarah in the night, is also invoked
to protect us against nightmares.*

Only three archangels are mentioned in Sacred Scripture: St. Michael, St. Gabriel, and St. Raphael. Raphael is mentioned by name as the hero of the Old Testament story of Tobit, but because Raphael's name means "God heals," tradition holds that he was the unnamed angel who stirred the healing waters of the pool at Bethsaida (John 5:1-7).

Raphael appears for the first time in chapter 5 of the Book of Tobit. Tobit, elderly and blind, was unable to travel to the country of the Medes to collect money he had loaned to a man named Gabael. He commanded his son, Tobias, to go in his place, but the youth Tobias was nervous about making such a journey alone. "Find a man to go with you" the father said. Outside his father's house Tobias met a sturdy, handsome fellow who said he knew the way to the country of the Medes and knew Gabael the debtor personally. It was the archangel Raphael in human form.

Young Tobias brought Raphael to meet his father and the elderly man gave his blessing to the trip. And so Raphael and Tobias set out, accompanied by Tobias' dog.

Beside the Tigris River Tobias was resting on the riverbank, washing his aching feet, when a monstrous fish reared up out of the water. Tobias panicked, but Raphael told him, "Catch the fish." Tobias did as he was told and that night the giant fish was supper for Tobias and Raphael. At Raphael's repeated insistence, Tobias kept the heart, gall, and liver of the fish.

Back on the road, Raphael suggested they stop at the city of Rages to visit Tobias' relative Raguel, his wife Edna and his daughter Sarah. Raguel's family was plagued by a demon named Asmodeus. Seven times Sarah had married, and each time Asmodeus had killed the groom on the wedding night. When Raphael suggested that Tobias marry Sarah, the boy balked. "Now I am the only son my father has, and I am afraid that if I go in I will die as those before me did," Tobias said. Then he added, in case Raphael had forgotten, that his parents "have no other son to bury them." But Raphael reassured Tobias that if he and Sarah postponed consummating their marriage for three nights, spending those nights in prayer, the demon's power over them would be broken.

Raguel had barely finished making his guests comfortable in his home when Tobias asked for Sarah's hand. Although Raguel and his wife gave their consent at once, poor Sarah burst into tears at the thought of becoming a widow for the eighth time.

Raguel and Edna wrote out a marriage contract and set their seals to it. Sarah was officially the wife of Tobias according to the law of Moses. As they left for their bridal chamber Tobias explained to Sarah Raphael's plan for vanquishing Asmodeus. So instead of making love the couple spent their wedding night praying earnestly and fervently to God to grant them a long and happy life together.

Raguel rose at dawn. He was so certain that Tobias had become the eighth victim of Asmodeus that he went and dug a grave for him. Meanwhile, Edna sent one of her servants to Sarah's room. When the servant found the couple alive and sleeping side by side, the entire household rejoiced. To celebrate the lifting of the curse on his daughter, Raguel planned a two week long feast. Since Tobias could not leave his own wedding reception, he sent Raphael to the land of the Medes to collect the loan from Gabael.

Two weeks later Tobias was ready to take his wife home. The curse on Sarah had been lifted, Raphael was back, and Gabael had repaid the loan. At this point Rapahel counseled Tobias that upon returning home he was to enter his father's house, give thanks and praise to the Lord God and immediately anoint the eyes of his blind father with fish gall.

Meanwhile Anna, Tobias' mother, spent each day atop a high hill waiting for a glimpse of her son. When at last she saw him coming, she hurried to the house to tell her husband. A servant led the old man outside to greet his son. The family embraced and wept and then gave thanks to God. Young Tobias rubbed the fish gall on his father's blind eyes. Half an hour later the elderly man could see again.

Now father and son wondered how to suitably reward Raphael who had done them so much good. But Raphael would not accept anything. Instead he revealed himself at last: "I am Raphael, one of the seven holy angels who present the prayers of the saints and enter into the presence of the glory of the Holy One." (Tobit 12:15)

In terror, the whole household fell face down on the ground. "Do not be afraid," Raphael said, "you will be safe. But praise God forever." Then the archangel disappeared from their presence.

Devotion to St. Raphael dates back to the early centuries of the Church. In addition to being invoked against nightmares, he is the patron of happy meetings, of young people, of pilgrims, and of all travelers.

Recently a site for Catholic singles opened on the web (www.straphael.net). It is dedicated to St. Raphael because of the part the archangel played in bringing Tobias and Sarah together.

To Find Lost Objects
St. Anthony of Padua (1195-1231) Feast day: June 13

*St. Anthony is invoked to find lost objects because he himself
once lost something valuable. He thought he had misplaced
an expensive book of the psalms which had in fact, been
stolen from him. He prayed to God for its recovery,
and the thief returned the book to Anthony intact.*

As anyone from Portugal will tell you, St. Anthony of Padua was not Italian. He was born in Lisbon in a house that stood just a few steps from the city's austere Romanesque cathedral. The house is gone now; a church stands on the site, but in the crypt below pilgrims are shown a small dark room which is said to be the place where Anthony was born. Pope John Paul II prayed there on his visit to Lisbon.

Not only was Anthony not Italian, Anthony was not his given name. His parents, Martin and Maria Bulhom, had him christened Ferdinand. The Bulhoms must have been comfortable financially since they sent Ferdinand to the cathedral school. Had they been poor they would have apprenticed him to a tradesman so he could help support the family.

Ferdinand, early in his teens, realized that he had a vocation to the religious life. At about age fifteen or sixteen he joined the Augustinians at the monastery of St. Vincent just outside the city walls. The monastery was a bit of a walk from the neighborhood where Ferdinand had grown up, but it was not far enough. His prayers and studies were constantly interrupted by visits from well-meaning relatives, neighbors, and friends. To escape their attention he asked his superiors to transfer him to the Augustinian priory of the Holy Cross at Coimbra, a city far to the north of Lisbon. There, free from distractions, Ferdinand devoted himself for the next eight years to study, particularly of the Bible and the Fathers of the Church.

In 1220 Portugal's King Pedro brought to Coimbra the remains of five Franciscans who had been executed in Morocco by order of the sultan. They had been sent on this dangerous mission by St. Francis himself. The saint of Assisi had become convinced of the futility of the crusades that cost so much in human suffering and accomplished so little. He believed more would be achieved by sending missionaries to convert the Muslims to Christianity than by sending armies to conquer them.

For his first band of missionaries Francis had selected three priests, Bernard, Peter, and Odo, and two lay brothers, Accursio and Adjutus. They traveled from Italy to Spain, then crossed to Morocco. The Franciscans presented themselves to the sultan as chaplains for the Christian mercenaries serving in the Moorish army. The sultan gave them permission to remain in his territory, but commanded them never to preach Christianity to Muslims. The five Franciscans disobeyed almost immediately. They were arrested, taken to the place of execution, and beheaded.

The arrival of the relics of five contemporary martyrs infused Ferdinand with religious exaltation. He felt an irresistible desire to join a mission to the Muslims and perhaps suffer martyrdom too. Since this was not possible for him as an Augustinian, Ferdinand applied for permission to leave the Augustinians and join the Franciscans.

When he entered the Franciscan order Ferdinand took a new name, Anthony. His Franciscan superiors did send him to Morocco, but Anthony never had an opportunity to preach. He came down with a severe fever that kept him confined to his bed for months. Since missionaries cannot be invalids, Anthony was sent home. He never reached Portugal. A storm blew his ship off course and Anthony came ashore at Messina, Sicily.

At the local Franciscan house he learned that a general meeting, or chapter, of all Franciscans was about to take place at Assisi. This gathering, which is known to us as the Great Chapter of 1221, was the last assembly open to all members of the order. St. Francis was still alive, but he did not preside over the meeting. Brother Elias, his vicar general, officiated while Francis sat quietly off to one side. The humility of the order's founder impressed Anthony; he resolved to cultivate the virtue of humility, too.

None of the Franciscan superiors in Italy knew anything about Anthony or his background. For his part, Anthony never mentioned his education or his gifts as a speaker. He was sent to the Franciscan house at Forli in northern Italy where he was put to work as a housekeeper.

Soon after Anthony arrived in Forli, there was to be an ordination at the Franciscan church. By some oversight, no one had been scheduled to preach the ordination sermon. In desperation the Franciscan superior commanded Anthony to climb into the pulpit and trust in divine inspiration. We can imagine the scene—the bishop and all the assembled clergy expecting a lackluster homily from an untrained, unprepared priest. Instead, Anthony opened his mouth and out poured a sermon of remarkable beauty, eloquence, and learning.

Now that the Franciscans had discovered Anthony's gifts they sent him on preaching missions. He is said to have had a fine, resounding voice, and a genius for making difficult theological concepts understandable even to people who had no education at all. When Anthony was scheduled to preach, tradesmen closed their shops, laborers came in from the fields, some people even spent all night in the church where Anthony would speak, just to be certain they had a seat. When even the largest churches could not accommodate the crowds, Anthony preached in the piazzas to audiences that numbered in the thousands.

Anthony's superiors sent him to southern France and areas of northern Italy where the Cathar heretics were especially strong. Rather than attack headon the errors of the Cathars, Anthony preached on the glories of the Catholic faith—and drew thousands of souls back to the Church.

At Padua Anthony delivered a series of sermons on the various ways hatred can poison the soul. As a result of his preaching some long-standing rivals were reconciled, men who had locked away enemies in private prisons released them, and extortionists returned money they had wrung from their victims. One of the most astonishing outcomes of Anthony's preaching was the passage of a new law which spared debtors the suffering of jail if they agreed to sell their possessions to meet obligations to their creditors. Thus, Anthony's preaching inspired the first bankruptcy legislation.

The number of miracles attributed to St. Anthony is extraordinary. Once when preaching in the open air Anthony preserved his audience from a rain storm. The downpour drenched the entire town, but the piazza where Anthony was preaching remained perfectly dry.

On another occasion Anthony tried to convert an especially obstinate crowd. When they ignored him, he went to the river where he preached to the fish. The fish raised their heads above the current to hear the man of God—a miracle which got the attention of even the most hardened sinners.

On a journey in Provence, Anthony and a companion stopped at the home of a poor woman. She served them bread and wine, but in her haste forgot to close the tap of her wine barrel. To make matters worse, Anthony's companion broke his wine glass. With the sign of the cross, Anthony restored the broken glass and refilled the wine barrel.

At Padua a young man who in a violent rage had kicked his mother, repented by cutting off the foot that had done the evil deed. Anthony took pity on the boy and restored the severed foot to his leg.

St. Anthony's reputation as a great wonder-working saint has endured for nearly 800 years, but he is especially invoked to help find lost objects. It is said that a Franciscan novice ran off with a valuable copy of the Psalms which Anthony had been using (some versions of the story say that Anthony had copied out this book himself). As the novice was about to cross a river, he saw a terrifying apparition which commanded him to return what he had stolen. He ran back and handed the book to Anthony personally.

At the age of 36 Anthony, worn out from his labors, died. Crowds of children ran through the streets of Padua weeping and crying out, "Our father Anthony is dead! St. Anthony is dead!"

The number of miracles reported at Anthony's tomb was so great that a year after his death Pope Gregory IX canonized him. It is the shortest official canonization on record.

For Wholesome Television

St. Clare of Assisi (1193-1253) Feast day: August 11

One Christmas St. Clare was so ill she could not leave her bed to attend Midnight Mass. By God's grace she had a vision in which she could see and hear the entire liturgy. In 1958 Pope Pius XII, recalling this miracle, made St. Clare patron of television.

*P*ope Innocent IV was in Assisi with several of his cardinals when Clare died. Her body was taken from her convent, San Damiano, to the Church of St. George for the funeral. As the Franciscan friars began chanting the opening prayers of the Requiem Mass, the pope stopped them and told them to sing the Mass for a Virgin Saint instead. The friars hesitated. To say that Mass over the body of Clare was to publicly declare her a saint.

By 1253 the Church had established a formal process for canonizations, yet in the emotion of the moment—Innocent IV had known Clare personally—the Holy Father was ready to override the normal procedure and proclaim Clare a saint by virtue of his authority. Rainaldo, Cardinal of Ostia, a member of the pope's entourage and the Franciscans' patron, whispered into the pope's ear that it would be prudent to sing the customary Requiem now and afterward let the Curia investigate the merits of Clare's life in the usual way. Innocent IV relented, and the Requiem Mass for Clare proceeded.

Clare was born into one of the leading families of Assisi in 1193. Her father, Favarone Offreduccio, was a knight. Her mother, Ortolana, also came from a noble family. Their family home was situated in the ancient heart of the town, next to the Cathedral of San Rufino, in a neighborhood where all the aristocratic families of Assisi lived. Further down the hill, around the Piazza del Commune, lived the merchant families of Assisi who wanted to strip the nobles of their privilege and make Assisi a republic. One of these anti-aristocratic families was the Bernadones, the family of St. Francis.

Tension between the nobility and the middle classes increased significantly during Clare's childhood. In 1202 civil war broke out. Clare, nine years old at the time, fled with her family and other nobles of Assisi to Perugia, the city that had allied itself with Assisi's aristocrats against the Assisi republicans. The republicans lost, and 21-year-old Francis Bernadone, who had fought against families like Clare's, was thrown into a Perugia dungeon.

Four years later both Clare and Francis were back in Assisi. Clare lived a more or less sequestered life among the women of the household, rarely venturing outside except to go to church. Francis, on the other hand, was much in the public eye. His stint in the Perugian dungeon had sparked a religious awakening that culminated in a dramatic act—the public renunciation of his family and fortune. This was effected when Francis stood in the piazza outside of Assisi's cathedral and, in front of the bishop, stripped off his clothes and handed them back to his father. "Up till now I have called you my father on earth," said Francis. "From now on I desire only to say 'Our Father who art in heaven.'"

Clare was intensely attracted to Francis' heroic embrace of radical poverty for the sake of the Gospel. At her canonization proceedings Clare's lifelong friend, Bona di Guelfuccio, testified that Clare secretly supported the Franciscans with large donations, helping Francis and his followers rebuild the Portiuncula chapel which became their headquarters.

By Lent 1212 Clare, now 18 years old, had decided to join the Franciscans. Her uncle Monaldo had been looking for a suitable young nobleman for her to marry, but Clare kept him at bay without ever hinting that she planned to become a nun. Clare and Francis had set Palm Sunday as the day of her entrance into the religious life. Francis instructed her to put on her finest clothes and go to Mass as usual; after nightfall she should change into simpler garb and sneak out of the house. Francis and the other friars would be waiting for her at the Portiuncula. That night, as Clare hurried to the chapel, the brothers held burning torches to light her way.

Inside the chapel St. Francis cut off Clare's hair and gave her sackcloth to wear. The consecration of women to the religious life was the privilege of a bishop; Francis was not even a priest, yet he took it upon himself to accept Clare as the first nun of the Franciscan order. Since there was not yet a Franciscan convent, Francis and the other friars escorted Clare to the Benedictine convent of St. Paul near Bastia. That is where her family came the next day to fetch her home. Alternating between violent threats and enticing promises, the Offreduccios tried to persuade Clare to rethink what they characterized as a "worthless act." At one point in the quarrel, some of Clare's relatives tried to carry her physically out of the convent. As they grabbed her, she pulled off her veil, exposing her shorn head. The shock of seeing her coarse stubble did the trick. Clare's family left her in peace in the convent.

Clare was in an odd position at St. Paul. This convent was the wealthiest in the diocese of Assisi. The nuns were women from families as noble as Clare's. Each of them had brought a substantial donation, or dowry, for the convent when they entered. The Benedictines lived dignified, almost comfortable lives according the sensible Rule St. Benedict had written 700 years earlier. Clare, in contrast, arrived penniless and desired to leave the genteel piety of St. Paul's to pursue a life of extreme poverty.

Perhaps to thwart any repeat visits from her family, Francis moved Clare to another convent, Sant' Angelo in Panzo, farther away from Assisi. Sixteen days after Clare left home, her 15-year-old sister Agnes joined her. This provoked another outburst from the Offreduccio family. Once again the family's attempts to bring the young women home were frustrated, and once again Francis moved Clare and Agnes, this time to the little Church of San Damiano, a short walk outside the walls of Assisi. The place was and remains an especially holy site for Franciscans: it was in San Damiano that St. Francis heard the voice of Christ urging him to "rebuild my Church which is in ruins."

At San Damiano Clare and Agnes developed a radical form of spirituality that would come to be shared by many women including, eventually, their mother Ortolana. Their commitment to extreme poverty was unknown in convents of their time. Critics said it was degrading for Clare and her nuns to go about barefoot in all weather, to sleep on the floor, to refuse to own any income-producing property that would ensure their support. But Clare desired to practice the absolute poverty embraced by St. Francis and his friars minor. She would fight for many years for the right to do so.

When St. Francis established Clare's community of nuns, he did not give them a formal rule but a rough guideline for the religious life. The first official rule for Clare's nuns was drawn up by that great supporter of the Franciscans, Cardinal Ugolino. This rule tried to bring the Poor Ladies, as they became known, into the mainstream of religious life.

Clare rejected the cardinal's rule because it omitted absolute poverty and made provisions for the nuns to own property. In 1228 Ugolino—now Pope Gregory IX—came to Assisi for the canonization of St. Francis and called on Clare at San Damiano. He pressed Clare to end her resistance to having an income. Clare refused, and was so persuasive in her defense of total poverty that when Gregory returned to Rome he drew up the *Privilegium Paupertatis*, a document which granted Clare's nuns the "privilege of poverty," meaning they could live entirely on alms. It was an important step forward, but it was still a privilege, a concession, not the unqualified approval of the rule Clare wanted.

In 1247 the new Pope Innocent IV submitted his own rule for the Poor Ladies. Like Cardinal Ugolino's rule, it did not confirm Clare's commitment to absolute poverty. Clare rejected it. The stalemate between pope and saint lasted six years. Finally, as Clare lay on her deathbed, Innocent IV came to San Damiano personally and handed Clare a papal document, *Solet Annuere,* approving Clare's own rule for her community. Clare kissed the document again and again. After 42 years, hew way of life had been sanctioned by the Church.

St. Clare is often depicted holding a monstrance. The image refers to an event which occurred in 1244. Frederick II, the Holy Roman Emperor, was at war with the pope. Frederick had marched an army into Umbria to lay waste to the province. Among the soldiers was a large detachment of Saracens brought to Italy purposely to terrorize Christians.

Frederick's army laid siege to Assisi while the Saracens headed for San Damiano. Clare carried the Blessed Sacrament in either a monstrance or a pyx (the sources vary) to the wall of the convent and set it over the main gate. Then she prostrated herself before the Host, begging God to "defend those I cannot protect." She heard a voice answer, "I shall always protect them." When Clare stood up, she saw the Saracens riding away from the convent as if pursued by some Fury. Then Clare instructed her nuns to pray that Assisi would be spared. After a day and a night of solemn prayer, Frederick's entire army abandoned the siege.

This was not the only miraculous occurrence in Clare's life. Clare's canonization proceedings tell of one Christmas Eve in which Clare, unable to attend Mass because of illness, miraculously witnessed the liturgy from her sick bed:

The Lady Clare also narrated how on the most recent night of the Lord's Nativity because of her serious illness she could not get up from her bed to go to the chapel. All the sisters went as usual to Matins and left her alone. The Lady then said with a sigh: Lord God, look, I have been left here all alone with You. She immediately began to hear the organ, responsories and the entire office of the brothers in the Church of St. Francis as if she were present there.

In 1958 Pope Pius XII was likely thinking of this miracle when he proclaimed St. Clare patroness of television.

In the summer of 1253 Clare knew she was dying. Bishops and cardinals came to see her. Her sister Agnes remained a constant presence at her side. Three of St. Francis' closest companions, Leo, Angelo, and Juniper, sat beside her bed reading aloud the Passion of Our Lord from the gospel of St. John—just as they had at St. Francis' deathbed 27 years earlier. Clare died holding in her hands her papally approved rule. After her death, the nuns made a copy of the rule and sewed the original into Clare's habit. It was buried with her, only to be rediscovered in the 19th century when St. Clare's tomb was opened.

Pope Innocent IV did not live to canonize Clare. That honor fell to his successor, Pope Alexander IV in 1255. In 1260, her relics were transferred to the Basilica of St. Clare, a short walk from the place where she was born.

For Wholesome Web Surfing
St. Isidore of Seville (560-636) Feast day: April 4

St. Isidore of Seville's 20-volume encyclopedia, like the internet, is an all-encompassing source of information. For this reason web surfers have chosen him as their patron saint.

By the time Isidore was born, classical Roman civilization had nearly died out in Spain. A century of successive barbarian invasions had driven out the Roman legions, scattered the administrators who had kept roads and aqueducts in good repair, left cities nearly abandoned and libraries and schools in ruins. Isidore's own family, who were descended from Roman senators, survived by collaborating with the Visigoths.

St. Isidore's parents, Severianus and Theodora, produced four children who became saints: St. Leander, bishop of Seville, St. Fulgentius, bishop of Ecija, St. Florentina, an abbess said to have ruled forty convents, and Isidore himself, who succeeded his elder brother to the bishopric of Seville.

When Isidore was five years old his parents enrolled him in the school which was attached to the cathedral in Seville. The boy proved to be a prodigy who mastered Latin, Greek, and Hebrew in a very short time and, under his brother's supervision, began reading the ancient classics and the Hebrew Bible. It was the beginning of Isidore's life-long passion for learning.

Isidore was about 18 years old when his brother Leander was named bishop of Seville. One of Leander's first successes as bishop was to bring the Visigoth prince, St. Hermenegild, from the Arian heresy back to the Catholic faith. This conversion in-

furiated Hermenegild's father, King Leovigild. The king commanded his son to return to the capital city, Toledo. Instead, Hermenegild led a revolt against his father, using Seville as his base of
operations. Leovigild retaliated by launching a persecution of
Catholics—particularly bishops. Then he gathered his army and
laid siege to Seville. The city held out against the king for two
years before it was forced to surrender. To everyone's surprise,
Leovigild was generous; he spared Hermenegild's life, but exiled
him from Spain. Instead of leaving the country, Hermenegild
raised another army and once again made war on his father.

This time Leovigild was merciless. He crushed the rebellion, imprisoned his son, and condemned him to death. At the last
moment the king offered Hermenegild one last chance to save
himself. If he returned to Arianism and took Communion from an
Arian bishop, Leovigild would set him free. Hermenegild refused,
so the king had his son beheaded. Isidore witnessed all this up-
heaval. Certainly it must have confirmed his belief that he was living in a barbarous age.

When Leovigild died in 586 his surviving son, Reccared, inherited the throne. Reccared returned to Catholicism and worked
with Leander to bring Arians in Spain back to the faith. Since
Isidore was a priest by this time, it is likely that he worked closely
with his brother to convert the Arians. Their collaboration paved
the way for Isidore to become bishop of Seville after Leander's
death about the year 600.

We do not have much information about Isidore as a bishop, but we know a great deal about him as a scholar and teacher.
He urged his people to pray often and read often. "When we
pray," he said, "we talk to God; when we read, God talks to us."
The preservation and transmission of knowledge, especially the
wisdom of ancient Greece and Rome, was of paramount importance to him. He knew that the old civilization was passing away,
and he was determined to conserve as much of it as he could for

future generations.

During the nearly forty years he was bishop Isidore wrote dozens of books. His greatest achievement was the *Etymologiae,* a 20-volume encyclopedia of all extant knowledge. In concise, clear, orderly fashion he discussed the essentials of law, medicine, and government; zoology, botany, and geography; metallurgy, agriculture, and architecture; Church history and theology; even how to construct roads and build furniture. It was an incredible, breathtaking achievement.

In March 636 Isidore knew he was dying. He prepared for death in a systematic fashion, first giving away all his possessions to the poor, then publicly asking forgiveness for any harm he had ever done to anyone in his diocese. His attendants carried him inside his cathedral where an auxiliary bishop dressed him in sackcloth while another covered his head with ashes. After he had received Holy Communion for the last time he was taken back to his room. He died on April 4.

Shortly after his death, a council of Spanish bishops who were meeting in Toledo declared him a Doctor of the Church, a title which was confirmed by Pope Innocent XIII in 1722. In 1999, in recognition of his wide ranging intellect, Catholic web surfers began a grass roots movement to have the Vatican formally declare St. Isidore patron saint of the internet.

For Good Friendships
St. John the Evangelist (died c.100) Feast day: December 27

*St. John, the Beloved Disciple, is the patron of good
friendships. While Christ was on earth, John was
Our Lord's closest friend.*

St. Augustine reminds us, perhaps with a touch of envy,
that at the Last Supper, when St. John leaned his head against
Jesus' chest, he heard the beating of the Lord's sacred heart.

Certainly Christ cherished each of his apostles, but John
he loved best of all. He gave the message of the gospel to all his
disciples, he granted authority to St. Peter, but to St. John Jesus
entrusted his Blessed Mother.

John was the son of Zebedee, younger brother of St. James
the Greater. He grew up on the shore of the Sea of Galilee where
he learned the fisherman's trade from his father. John and James
were sitting in their boat with Zebedee mending nets when Jesus
called them to be his disciples.

John, his brother James and Peter, were all part of Our
Lord's inner circle. John was privy to miracles, signs, and intimate moments in the life of the Lord that were kept from the rest
of the apostles. John was in the room when Christ raised Jairus'
daughter from the dead. He saw the Son of God in glory at the
Transfiguration. He was a witness to the terrible agony in the garden, when the Lord sweated blood.

At Jesus' arrest, John was more than likely "the other disciple" who went with Peter to the house of Caiaphas. St. John's
Gospel tells us that John, who was known to the high priest, en-

tered Caiaphas' courtyard without any trouble, but Peter was barred from entering. It was only after John spoke with the woman who kept the gate that Peter was let in. John should have spared himself the trouble. Peter had barely begun to warm himself at the fire blazing in the courtyard when three times he denied he even knew Jesus.

Now that Peter's courage had failed him, only John was left to follow Jesus to Calvary. Together with the Virgin Mary, Mary Magdalene, and the other faithful women, John stood at the foot of the cross as Jesus died. Before he breathed his last, Jesus gave John to Mary as her second son ("Woman, behold your son!"), and entrusted Mary to John's care ("Behold, your mother!").

No doubt John helped Joseph of Arimathea and Nicodemus take Christ's body down from the cross and lay it in the tomb. On the first Easter Mary Magdalene told John and Peter that the Lord's tomb was empty. They raced to the sepulcher, but John, being younger and faster, arrived first. He stood at the entrance, peering in at the rumpled linen cloth in which Jesus had been wrapped. Only when Peter had arrived and had gone into the tomb did John enter. "He saw," the gospel says, "and believed."

That night John was with the other disciples locked in the room they had used for the Last Supper when the Risen Christ appeared to them. Eight days later John witnessed doubting St. Thomas' confession of faith in the risen Lord. At the Sea of Tiberias, after Christ commanded Peter, "Feed my lambs...Feed my sheep" and foretold his eventual martyrdom, Peter pointed to John and asked, "Lord, what about this man?"

Christ's cryptic answer—"If it is my will that he remain until I come, what is that to you? Follow me!"—led to a belief among some of the first Christians that St. John would not die until the Second Coming.

After Christ's Ascension and the descent of the Holy Spirit upon the apostles and the Blessed Virgin, John and Peter preached in Jerusalem. At some point John moved to Ephesus, the greatest city of the Roman Empire in the east. There is a tradition that he brought the Blessed Virgin Mary with him to Ephesus. Pilgrims still visit a small stone house there that is said to have been Mary's home.

Among John's disciples was St. Ignatius of Antioch (died c.107). Ignatius' letters, written to the Christians of Asia Minor and Rome as he was being taken from Syria to Rome to be thrown to wild beasts in the arena, reveal his faith in the doctrines of the Trinity, the Incarnation, the perpetual virginity of Mary, and the Real Presence. All of these Ignatius, more than likely, learned from St. John.

Some of the earliest Fathers of the Church are our sources for other traditions concerning St. John. St. Justin Martyr (c.100-165) says John lived at Ephesus. St. Ireneaus (c.130-200), a disciple of St. Polycarp who was converted by John, says that the evangelist wrote his gospel in Ephesus. From the theologian Tertullian (c.160-220) we receive the story of John being miraculously preserved when Emperor Domitian had him lowered into a cauldron of boiling oil.

A tradition repeated by St. Jerome holds that when John was very old and too weak to walk, his disciples carried him to wherever Christians had assembled for the Eucharist. All he said to them was, "Little children, love one another." On one occasion someone in the congregation asked him why he always said the same thing. "Because these are the words of the Lord," John answered, "and if you do this, you do enough."

During the reign of Domitian, John was exiled to the island of Patmos in the Aegean Sea. A cave there is said to be the place where he received the apocalyptic visions which he subsequently recorded in the Book of Revelation.

St. John died peacefully in Ephesus in about the year 100. He was approximately 94 years old. He is the only apostle not to have died a martyr's death.

Many miracle stories have been told about St. John. One says that on the day he returned home to Ephesus from his exile on the island of Patmos, he encountered the funeral procession of a dear friend, an elderly woman named Drusiana. He approached the bier and in the name of Jesus Christ restored Drusiana to life.

Another story tells of a priest of the goddess Artemis who tried to poison John. John made the sign of the cross over the offered cup, and the poison emerged from the drink in the form of a serpent.

The eagle which is John's emblem in art symbolizes the soaring opening of his gospel, "In the beginning was the Word, and the Word was with God, and the Word was God."

Epilogue:
Queen of All Saints

The Magnificat

"My soul magnifies the Lord,
and my spirit rejoices in God my Savior,
for he has regarded the low estate of his handmaiden.
For behold, henceforth all generations will call me blessed;
for he who is mighty has done great things for me,
and holy is his name.
And his mercy is on those who fear him
from generation to generation.
He has shown strength with his arm,
he has scattered the proud in the imagination of their heart,
he has put down the mighty from their thrones,
and exalted those of low degree;
he has filled the hungry with good things,
and the rich he has sent empty away.
He has helped his servant Israel,
in remembrance of his mercy,
as he spoke to our father,
to Abraham and to his posterity forever."

Luke 1:46-55

In Every Necessity
The Blessed Virgin Mary

*"Every person carries in his heart," said Archbishop Fulton
Sheen, "a blueprint of the one he loves." The best-loved among the
saints is the Blessed Virgin Mary. Mary is the mirror of justice,
the seat of wisdom, the gate of Heaven. She is the health of the
sick, the refuge of sinners, the comforter of the afflicted, the cause
of our joy. We invoke her as Mother of Good Counsel, Mother of
Perpetual Help, Queen of Peace, and Help of Christians.*

When Gabriel declared Mary "full of grace" he laid the
foundation for devotion to the Mother of God. It is true that in
the first centuries of the Church the cult of the martyrs tem-
porarily overshadowed the cult of Mary, but Mary was never forgotten. About the year 100 as St. Ignatius of Antioch was being
dragged to Rome to be thrown to the lions he wrote a letter to
the Christians of Ephesus reminding them of the three great
mysteries of the faith: "the virginity of Mary, and her giving birth,
[and] the death of the Lord." It is interesting that two of Ignatius' three mysteries are Marian.

Both art and literature portray devotion to Mary in the
early Church. In Rome we find the earliest surviving image of
Our Lady; sometime between the years 150 and 200 an unknown
Christian painted on a wall in the Catacomb of St. Priscilla a picture of the Virgin and Child. Beginning about the year 150 a host
of apocryphal gospels such as the *Protoevangelium of James*
began to circulate among the churches, recounting stories of
Mary's birth, childhood and marriage to Joseph. By 275 we have

the earliest non-scriptural prayer to Mary. Known by its Latin title, *Sub Tuum Praesidium*, it reads: "We fly to thy patronage, O holy Mother of God; despise not our petitions in our necessities, but deliver us always from all dangers, O glorious and blessed Virgin. Amen."

When persecution of the early Church ended, devotion to Mary flourished. St. Ambrose (c.339-397) taught that Mary never committed a sin. The Council of Ephesus (431) asserted that she could rightly be called Mother of God. In Syria a poet named Jacob of Sarug (c.451-521) wrote hymns to Mary in which he praised her as the Mother of Mercy, the Virgin of Sorrows, the Mother of the Church—themes that have appeared again and again in Marian literature.

At the same time the Church increased the number of feast days it celebrated in Mary's honor; by the year 350 the Annunciation (March 25), by the year 500 Our Lady's Nativity, or birthday (September 8), by the year 600 her Assumption (August 15), and by the year 750 her Immaculate Conception (December 8). These holy days were a marked departure from earlier liturgical calendars that commemorated only the feast days of martyrs.

As love for Mary became more intense Christians looked for new ways to extol her. Around the year 800 a deacon named Paul composed the hymn *Ave Maris Stella*, invoking Mary for the first time as Star of the Sea. Between 1000 and 1100 *Salve Regina* and *Alma Redemptoris Mater* were written and the first rosaries appeared.

It is not an exaggeration to call the Middle Ages the age of Mary. Virtually every cathedral in France was dedicated to her, as were countless parish churches, monasteries, convents, and hospitals. Her image appeared everywhere—in sculptures, paintings, frescoes, and stained glass; on church vessels and private jewelry, on furniture and textiles, even on weapons. Dante and Chaucer sang her praises. Every nation had its shrine to Our

Lady: Walsingham in England, Chartres in France, Loreto in Italy, Montserrat in Spain, Mariazell in Austria, Einsiedeln in Switzerland, Czestochowa in Poland.

Devotion to Mary became so deeply rooted in the human heart that neither the iconoclasm of the Reformation, nor the skepticism of the Enlightenment, nor the materialism of the 19th and 20th centuries could displace her. If anything Mary's influence has been felt more strongly in the last 20 years than at any other time. Pope John Paul II sees Mary's hand in the collapse of the Soviet Empire and attributes to Mary his survival of an assassination attempt.

Today in the great shrines of Lourdes, Fatima, and Guadalupe, in parish churches around the world, or in some silent corner of the heart, millions cry out to Mary for help. She is, as Blessed Pope Pius IX said in 1851, "the best of Mothers, our safest confidant...the very motive of our hope."

Feast days:
January 1 (Solemnity of Mary)
February 11 (Our Lady of Lourdes)
March 25 (Annunciation)
May 13 (Our Lady of Fatima)
May 31 (Visitation)
August 15 (Assumption)
August 22 (Queenship of Mary)
September 8 (Birth of Mary)
September 15 (Our Lady of Sorrows)
October 7 (Our Lady of the Rosary)
November 21 (Presentation of the Blessed Virgin Mary)
December 8 (Immaculate Conception)
December 12 (Our Lady of Guadalupe)

Calendar of Saints' Feasts

January

1	Mary, Mother of God	21	St. Agnes
2	Ss. Basil the Great & Gregory Nazianzen	22	St. Vincent
		24	**St. Francis de Sales**
7	St. Raymond of Penyafort	25	Conversion of **St. Paul**
13	St. Hilary	26	Ss. Timothy & Titus
17	St. Anthony	27	St. Angela Merici
20	St. Fabian	28	**St. Thomas Aquinas**
	St. Sebastian	31	**St. John Bosco**

February

1	**St. Brigid***	11	Our Lady of Lourdes
2	Presentation of the Lord	14	Ss. Cyril & Methodius
3	**St. Blaise**		**St. Valentine***
	St. Ansgar	17	Seven Founders of the Order of Servites
5	**St. Agatha**	21	St. Peter Damian
6	Ss. Paul Miki & companions	22	Chair of **St. Peter**
8	St. Jerome Emiliani		**St. Margaret of Cortona***
9	**St. Apollonia***	23	St. Polycarp
10	**St. Scholastica**		

March

2	**St. Chad***	17	**St. Joseph of Arimathea***
4	St. Casimir	18	St. Cyril of Jerusalem
7	Ss. Perpetua & Felicity	19	**St. Joseph,** Husband of Mary
8	**St. John of God**	23	St. Turibius de Mongrovejo
9	St. Frances of Rome	25	Annunciation of the Lord
14	**St. Matilda***		**St. Dismas***
17	St. Patrick		

April

2	St. Francis of Paolo	23	**St. George**
4	**St. Isidore of Seville**	24	St. Fidelis of Sigmaringen
5	St. Vincent Ferrer	25	St. Mark
7	**St. John Baptist de la Salle**	27	**St. Zita***
11	St. Stanislaus	28	St. Peter Chanel
13	St. Martin I	29	St. Catherine of Siena
14	**St. Lydwina***	30	St. Pius V
16	**St. Benedict Joseph Labre***		**St. Adjutor***
21	St. Anselm		

May

1	St. Joseph the Worker
	St. Peregrine Laziosi*
2	St. Athanasius
3	Ss. Philip & James
4	St. Florian*
8	St. Acacius*
12	Ss. Nereus & Achilleus
	St. Pancras
14	St. Matthias
15	St. Isidore the Farmer*
	St. Dymphna*
16	St. Brendan*
18	St. John I
20	St. Bernardine of Siena
23	St. William of Rochester*
25	St. Bede the Venerable
	St. Gregory VII
	St. Mary Magdalene de Pazzi
26	St. Philip Neri
27	St. Augustine of Canterbury
28	St. Bernard of Menthon*
30	St. Joan of Arc*
31	Visitation of Mary

June

1	St. Justin
2	Ss. Marcellinus & Peter
	St. Erasmus*
3	Ss. Charles Lwanga & companions
5	St. Boniface of Mainz
6	St. Norbert
9	St. Ephrem
11	St. Barnabas
13	St. Anthony of Padua
15	St. Germaine Cousin*
19	St. Romuald
21	St. Aloysius Gonzaga
22	Ss. John Fisher & Thomas More
	St. Paulinus of Nola
24	Birth of St. John the Baptist
27	St. Cyril of Alexandria
28	St. Irenaeus
29	Ss. Peter & Paul
30	First Martyrs of the Church of Rome

July

2	St. Swithun*
3	St. Thomas the Apostle
4	St. Elizabeth of Portugal
	Bl. Pier Giorgio Frassati*
5	St. Anthony Zaccaria
6	St. Maria Goretti
11	St. Benedict
13	St. Henry
14	St. Camillus de Lellis
	Bl. Kateri Tekakwitha*
15	St. Bonaventure
16	Our Lady of Mount Carmel
21	St. Lawrence of Brindisi
22	St. Mary Magdalene
23	St. Bridget
24	St. Christina the Astonishing*
25	St. James the Greater
	St. Christopher*
26	Ss. Joachim & Anne
29	St. Martha
30	St. Peter Chrysologus
31	St. Ignatius Loyola

August

1	St. Alphonsus Liguori	16	St. Stephen of Hungary
2	St. Eusebius of Vercelli	18	St. Helen*
4	St. John Mary Vianney	19	St. John Eudes
5	Dedication of Basilica of Saint Mary Major	20	St. Bernard
	St. Emidius*	21	St. Pius X
6	Transfiguration	22	Queenship of Mary
7	Ss. Sixtus II & companions	23	St. Rose of Lima
	St. Cajetan	24	St. Bartholomew
8	St. Dominic	25	St. Louis
10	St. Lawrence		St. Joseph Calasanz
11	St. Clare of Assisi		St. Genesius*
13	Ss. Pontian & Hippolytus	27	St. Monica
	St. John Berchmans*	28	St. Augustine
14	St. Maximilian Mary Kolbe	29	Beheading of St. John the Baptist
15	Assumption of the Blessed Virgin Mary		
	St. Tarsicius*		

September

3	St. Gregory the Great	21	St. Matthew
8.	Birth of Mary	23	Bl. Padre Pio Forgione*
9	St. Peter Claver*	26	Ss. Cosmas & Damian
13	St. John Chrysostom	27	St. Vincent de Paul
14	Triumph of the Cross	28	St. Wenceslaus
15	Our Lady of Sorrows		Ss. Lawrence Ruiz & companions
16.	Ss. Cornelius & Cyprian	29	Ss. Michael, Gabriel & Raphael
17	St. Robert Bellarmine	30	St. Jerome
18	St. Joseph Cupertino*		
19	St. Januarius		
20	Ss. Andrew Kim Taegon & companions		

October

1	St. Therese of Lisieux	14	St. Callistus I
2	Guardian Angels	15	St. Teresa of Jesus
4	St. Francis of Assisi	16	St. Hedwig
5	St. Faustina Kowalska*		St. Margaret Mary Alacoque
6	St. Bruno		St. Gerard Majella*
7	Our Lady of the Rosary	17	St. Ignatius of Antioch
9	St. Denis & companions	18	St. Luke
	St. John Leonardi		

(continued from page 401)

19 Ss. Isaac Jogues &
    companions
    St. Paul of the Cross

23 St. John of Capistrano
24 St. Anthony Claret
28 Ss. Simon & **Jude**

November

1   All Saints
2   All Souls
3   **St. Martin de Porres**
    St. Hubert*
4   St. Charles Borromeo
6   **St. Leonard of Noblac***
9   Dedication of
    St. John Lateran
10 St. Leo the Great
11 **St. Martin of Tours**
12 St. Josaphat
13 **St. Francis Xavier Cabrini***
    (US only)
15 **St. Albert the Great**

16 St. Margaret of Scotland
    St. Gertrude the Great
17 **St. Elizabeth of Hungary**
18 Dedication of the Churches
    of Peter & Paul
21 Presentation of Mary
22 **St. Cecilia**
23 St. Clement I
    St. Columban
    Bl. Miguel Agustin Pro*
24 Ss. Andrew Dung-Lac &
    companions
30 St. Andrew

December

3   St. Francis Xavier
4   St. John Damascene
6   **St. Nicholas**
7   **St. Ambrose**
8   Immaculate Conception
11 St. Damasus I
12 St. Jane Frances de Chantal
    Our Lady of Guadalupe*
13 **St. Lucy**
14 St. John of the Cross

21. St. Peter Canisius
22 **St. Francis Xavier Cabrini***
23 St. John of Kanty
25 Christmas
26 **St. Stephen**
27 **St. John**
28 Holy Innocents
29 St. Thomas Becket
31 St. Sylvester I

This calendar lists the feast days of saints (in **bold** type) featured in *Saints for Every Occasion,* plus the feast days of other saints listed on the General Roman Calendar. The General Roman Calendar is the liturgical calendar of the entire Catholic Church.

It should be noted that the feast days of most canonized saints do not appear on the General Roman Calendar. Instead, the feasts are celebrated in local churches or in specific religious communities.

Saints who appear in *Saints for Every Occasion* but whose feasts do not appear on the General Roman Calendar are indicated here with an asterisk (*).

Sources

Ackroyd, Peter, *The Life of Thomas More* (Doubleday, 1998)

Acta Sanctorum, 64 volumes, (Antwerp, 1643-)

Armstrong, Regis J. and Ignatius C. Brady, *Francis and Clare: The Complete Works* (Paulist Press, 1982)

Armstrong, Regis J., J.A. Wayne Hellman, and William J. Short, *Francis of Assisi: Early Documents* (New City Press, 1999)

Augustine, *Confessions*, translated by Henry Chadwick (Oxford University Press, 1992)

Bede, *The Ecclesiastical History of the English Nation* (E.P. Dutton, 1910)

Berenbaum, Michael, editor, *A Mosaic of Victims: Non-Jews Persecuted and Murdered by the Nazis* (New York University Press, 1990)

The Book of Saints, sixth edition (Morehouse Publishing, 1989)

Brown, Peter, *Augustine of Hippo: A Biography* (University of California Press, 1969)

Budge, E.A.W., translator, "The Passion of St. George," *Bibliotheca Hagiographica Orientalis*, number 310, 1888

Buehrle, Marie Cecilia, *Kateri of the Mohawks* (Bruce Publishing Co., 1954)

Carr, John, "St. Gerard Majella," *A Treasury of Catholic Reading*, (Farrar, Straus & Cudahy, 1957)

Cavallini, Giuliana, translated by Caroline Holland, *Saint Martin de Porres: Apostle of Charity* (Tan Books, 1979)

Cepari, Virgilius, *The Life of St. Aloysius Gonzaga* (H. McGrath, 1884)

Chambers, R.W., *Thomas More* (University of Michigan Press, 1973)

Charbonneau-Lassay, Louis, *The Bestiary of Christ*, translated and abridged by D.M. Dooling (Parabola Books, 1991)

Davies, Oliver, with Thomas O'Loughlin, translators, *Celtic Spirituality* (Paulist Press, 1999)

de Cantimpré, Thomas, translated by Margot H. King assisted by David Wiljer, *The Life of Christina the Astonishing* (Peregrina Publishing Co., 2000)

de la Bedoyere, Michael, *Francis of Assisi: The Man Who Found Perfect Joy* (Sophia Institute Press, 1999)

de la Bedoyere, Michael, *Saintmaker: The Remarkable Life of Francis de Sales, Shepherd of Kings and Commoners, Sinners and Saints* (Sophia Institute Press, 1998)

de la Vega, Luis Lasso, *Huei Tlamahuitzoltica*, 1649

Delehaye, Hippolyte, *The Legends of the Saints: An Introduction to Hagiography* (University of Notre Dame Press, 1961)

Saints for Every Occasion

D'Evelyn, Charlotte and Mill, Anna J., editors, *The South English Legendary*, 3 volumes (Oxford University Press, 1967)

de Silva, Alvaro, editor, *The Last Letters of Thomas More* (William B. Eerdmans Publishing Company, 2000)

de Voragine, Jacobus, *The Golden Legend*, 2 volumes (Princeton University Press, 1993)

Donaldson, Christopher, *Martin of Tours: Parish Priest, Mystic and Exorcist* (Routledge & Kegan Paul, 1980)

Duffy, Eamon, *Saints & Sinners: A History of the Popes* (Yale University Press, 1997)

Duffy, Eamon, *The Stripping of the Altars: Traditional Religion in England 1400-1580* (Yale University Press, 1992)

Dunney, Joseph A., *Church History in the Light of the Saints*

Eddius Stephanus, *The Life of Bishop Wilfrid*, trans. Bertram Colgrave (Harvard University Press, 1927)

Englebert, Omer, *The Lives of the Saints* (David McKay Co., 1951)

Eusebius Pamphilius of Caesarea, "The Life of the Blessed Emperor Constantine", translated by Ernest Cushing Richardson, *Nicene and Post-Nicene Fathers*, Volume I Wm. B. Eerdmans, 1955)

Falasca, Stefania Falasca, "The Humble Splendor of the First Witnesses: The Catacombs of Saint Callixtus in Rome," *30 Days*, No. 4, 1996

Farmer, David Hugh, general consultant editor, *Butler's Lives of the Saints: New Full Edition*, 12 volumes (The Liturgical Press, 1995-2000)

Fitzgerald, Allan D., general editor, *Augustine through the Ages: An Encyclopedia* (William B. Eerdmans Publishing Company, 1999)

Foley, Leonard, "Who Is St. Anthony?," St. Anthony Messenger Press, 2001

Fortescue, Adrian, *Latin Hymns* (Roman Catholic Books)

Furlong, Monica, *Therese of Lisieux* (Random House, 1987)

Gallagher, Jim, *Padre Pio: The Pierced Priest* (HarperCollins, 1995)

Gheon, Henri, *Secrets of the Saints*, Sheed & Ward, 1944

Goodier, Alban, *Saints for Sinners*, (Image Books, 1959)

Graham, Edward P., translator, *Acts of the Hieromartyr Januarius, Bishop of Benevento*, 1909

Grant, Michael, *Constantine the Great: The Man and His Times* (Charles Scribner's Sons, 1993)

Hamman, A., editor, translated by Walter Mitchell, *Early Christian Prayers* (Longmans, Green & Co., Ltd., 1961)

Haskins, Susan, *Mary Magdalen: Myth and Metaphor* (HarperCollins, 1993)

Huysmans, J.K., translated by Agnes Hastings, *Saint Lydwina of Schiedam* (Kegan Paul, Trench, Trubner & Co. Ltd., 1923)

Jones, C.A., *The Life of St. Elizabeth of Hungary, Duchess of Thuringia* (Swift & Co., 1877)

Jones, Charles W., *Saint Nicholas of Myra, Bari, and Manhattan: Biography of Legend* (University of Chicago Press, 1978)

Jones, Frederick M., *Alphonsus de Liguori: Saint of Bourbon Naples* (Liguori Publications, 1992)

Jungmann, Joseph A., *The Mass of the Roman Rite: Its Origin and Development*, 2 volumes, translated by Francis A. Brunner, C.SS.R. (Christian Classics, 1986)

Kalvelage, Francis M., *Kolbe: Saint of the Immaculate* (Franciscans of the Immaculate, 2001)

Kowalska, Maria Faustina, *Diary: Divine Mercy in My Soul* (Marians of the Immaculate Conception, 2001)

Lapomarda, Vincent A., *The Jesuits and the Third Reich* (The Edwin Mellen Press, 1989)

Lecompte, Edward, translated by Florence Ralston Werum, *Glory of the Mohawks: The Life of the Venerable Catherine Tekakwitha* (Bruce Publishing Co., 1944)

Lightfoot, J.B. and J.R. Harmer, translators, *The Apostolic Fathers, Second Edition* (Baker Book House, 1989)

The Little Flowers of St. Francis (The Daughters of St. Paul, 1976)

MacDonald, Iain, *Saint Brendan* (Floris Books, 1992)

Madrid, Patrick, *Any Friend of God's Is a Friend of Mine: A Biblical and Historical Explanation of the Catholic Doctrine of the Communion of Saints* (Basilica Press, 1998)

Maier, Paul L., translator, *Eusebius: The Church History* (Kregel Publications, 1999)

Martindale, C. C., *The Vocation of Aloysius Gonzaga* (B. Herder Book Co., 1927)

Martindale, C. C., *What Are Saints: Fifteen Chapters in Sanctity* (Benzinger Brothers, 1932)

Mauriac, Francois, *St. Margaret of Cortona*, translated by Bernard Frechtman (Philosophical Library, 1948)

MacDonald, Iain, editor, Saint Bride (Floris Books, 1992)

McCaffrey, John, *Blessed Padre Pio: The Friar of San Giovanni* (Roman Catholic Books)

McGinley, J., and H. Mursurillo, translators, *The Translation of Saint Nicholas*, (Bolletino di S. Nicola, Number 10, Studi e testi, October 1980)

McLynn, Neil B., *Ambrose of Milan: Church and Court in a Christian Capital* (University of California Press, 1994)

McNabb, Vincent J., *St. Elizabeth of Portugal* (Sheed & Ward, 1938)

Meissner, W.W., *Ignatius of Loyola: The Psychology of a Saint* (Yale

University Press, 1992)

Michalenko, Sophia, *The Life of Faustina Kowalska: The Authorized Biography* (Charis Books, 1999)

Molinari, Paolo, translated by José María Fuentes, S.J., "Blessed Miguel Augustin Pro, Martyr for the Faith," *La Civiltà Cattolica*, 1988

Monda, Andrea, "A Troublesome Saint," *Inside the Vatican*, April 1999

Murphy, Francis X., *A Monument to St. Jerome: Essays on Some Aspects of His Life, Works and Influence* (Sheed & Ward, 1952)

Murphy-O'Connor, Jerome, *The Holy Land* (Oxford University Press, 1998)

Musurillo, Herbert, *Acts of the Christian Martyrs* (Oxford University Press, 1972)

New Advent, Inc., The Fathers of the Church, Electronic version, 1997

O'Grady, Desmond, *Caesar, Christ, & Constantine: A History of the Early Church in Rome* (Our Sunday Visitor Publishing Division, 1991)

Pastrovicchi, Angelo, *Saint Joseph of Copertino* (B. Herder Book Co., 1918)

Pernoud, Regine, *Joan of Arc: By Herself and Her Witnesses*, translated by Edward Hyams (Scarborough House, 1994)

Ricciotti, Giuseppe, *The Age of Martyrs* (TAN Books and Publishers,1999)

Riches, Samantha, *St. George: Hero, Martyr and Myth* (Sutton Publishing, 2000)

Roberts, Alexander Roberts, and James Donaldson, editors, "History of Joseph the Carpenter," *Ante-Nicene Fathers, Volume VIII*, (Hendrickson Publishers, 1994)

Roberts, Alexander Roberts, and James Donaldson, editors, "The Passing of Mary," *Ante-Nicene Fathers, Volume VIII* (Hendrickson Publishers, 1994)

Roberts, Alexander Roberts, and James Donaldson, editors, "The Protoevangelium of James," *Ante-Nicene Fathers, Volume VIII* (Hendrickson Publishers, 1994)

Roper, William, *A Man of Singular Virtue being a Life of Sir Thomas More* (The Folio Society Ltd 1980)

Rutler, George William, *The Curé of Ars Today: St. John Vianney* (Ignatius Press, 1988)

Sackville-West, Vita, *Saint Joan of Arc* (Immage Books, 1991)

Schwertner, Thomas M., *St. Albert the Great* (Bruce Publishing Co., 1932)

Schmucki, Octavian, translated by Canisius F. Connors, *The Stigmata of St. Francis of Assisi: A Critical Investigation in the Light of Thirteenth-century Sources* (The Franciscan Institute, 1999)

Sellner, Edward C., *Wisdom of the Celtic Saints* (Ave Maria Press,1996)

Sheen, Fulton J., *The World's First Love* (Image Books, 1952)

Stinehart, Anne C., "'Renowned Queen Mother Mathilda:' Ideals and Realities of Ottonian Queenship in the Vitae Mathildis Reginae (Mathilda of Saxony, 895?-968)," *Essays in History, Vol. 40* (Corcoran Department of History at the University of Virginia, 1998)

Sulpitius Severus, *The Life of St. Martin*, Translation and Notes by Alexander Roberts, A Select Library of Nicene and Post-Nicene Fathers of the Christian Church, Second Series, Volume 11, 1894

Thiede, Carsten Peter, and Matthew D'Ancona, *The Jesus Papyrus* (Bantam Books, 2000)

Trotta, Liz, *Jude: A Pilgrimage to the Saint of Last Resort* (HarperCollins, 1998)

von Weinrich, Franz Johannes, *St. Elizabeth of Hungary*, translated by I.J. Collins (Burns Oates & Washbourne Ltd, 1933)

Walsh, John Evangelist, *The Bones of St. Peter*, (Sinag-Tala, 1982)

Webb, J. F. and D.H. Farmer, translators, *The Age of Bede* (Penguin Books, 1985)

Weisheipl, James A., *Friar Thomas D'Aquino: His Life, Thought, and Works* (The Catholic University of America Press, 1983)

Wintz, Jack, "Why St. Anthony Holds the Child Jesus," *St. Anthony Messenger*, June 2000

Woods, David, translator, "The Passion of St. Christopher," *Bibliotheca Hagiographica Latina Antiquae et Mediae Aetatis*, number 1764, 1999

Woods, David, translator, "The Passion of St. Florian," *Bibliotheca Hagiographica Latina Antiquae et Mediae Aetatis*, number 3054, 1999

Zimmermann, Odo J. and Avery, Benedict R., translators, *Life and Miracles of St. Benedict*, by St. Gregory the Great (The Liturgical Press)

For Further Reading

The Age of Martyrs, by Giuseppe Ricciotti (TAN Books and
    Publishers,1999)

Alphonsus de Liguori: Saint of Bourbon Naples, by Frederick M.
    Jones, (Liguori Publications, 1992)

*Any Friend of God's Is a Friend of Mine: A Biblical and Historical
    Explanation of the Catholic Doctrine of the Communion of
    Saints*, by Patrick Madrid, (Basilica Press, 1998)

Augustine of Hippo: A Biography, by Peter Brown, (University of
    California Press, 1969)

Blessed Padre Pio: The Friar of San Giovanni, by John McCaffrey
    (Roman Catholic Books)

The Bones of St. Peter, by John Evangelist Walsh (Sinag-Tala, 1982)

The Curé of Ars Today: St. John Vianney, by George William Rutler,
    (Ignatius Press, 1988)

Francis of Assisi: The Man Who Found Perfect Joy, by Michael de la
    Bedoyere (Sophia Institute Press, 1999)

Ignatius of Loyola: The Psychology of a Saint, by W.W. Meissner, S.J.
    (Yale University Press, 1992)

Jude: A Pilgrimage to the Saint of Last Resort, by Liz Trotta
    (HarperCollins, 1998)

The Last Letters of Thomas More, edited by Alvaro de Silva (William
    B. Eerdmans Publishing Company, 2000)

The Life of Faustina Kowalska: The Authorized Biography, by Sister
    Sophia Michalenko, C.M.G.T. (Charis Books, 1999)

The Life of Thomas More, by Peter Ackroyd (Doubleday, 1998)

The Little Flowers of St. Francis (The Daughters of St. Paul, 1976)

Mary Magdalen: Myth and Metaphor, by Susan Haskins
    (HarperCollins, 1993)

St. George: Hero, Martyr and Myth, by Samantha Riches (Sutton
    Publishing, 2000)

Saint Joan of Arc, Vita Sackville-West (Image Books, 1991)

Saint Martin de Porres: Apostle of Charity, by Giuliana Cavallini,
    translated by Caroline Holland, (Tan Books, 1979)

*Saintmaker: The Remarkable Life of Francis de Sales, Shepherd of
    Kings and Commoners, Sinners and Saints*, by Michael de la
    Bedoyere (Sophia Institute Press, 1998)

Salvation: Scenes from the Life of St. Francis, by Valerie Martin
    (Knopf, 2001)

Therese of Lisieux, by Monica Furlong (Random House, 1987)

The World's First Love, by Fulton J. Sheen (Image Books, 1952)

Subject Index

Abortion 242
Acacius, Saint 269
Accused 347
Actors 192
Adjutor, Saint 217
Adopted Children 364
Advertisers 131
Agatha, Saint 282
AIDS 284
Albert the Great, Saint 51
Aloysius Gonzaga, Saint 284
Alphonsus de Liguori, Saint 60
Altar Servers 81
Ambrose, Saint 44
Anne, Saint 337
Anthony of Padua, Saint 375
Apollonia, Saint 270
Aquinas, Saint Thomas 308
Arc, Saint Joan of 114
Archers 189
Arimathea, Saint Joseph of 153
Armed Services 133
Arthritis 275
Assisi, Saint Clare of 380
Assisi, Saint Francis of 233
Astronauts 135

Baptist, Saint John the 157
Benedict Joseph Labre, Saint 227
Benedict, Saint 326
Berchmans, Saint John 81
Bernard of Menthon, Saint 206
Bernardine of Siena, Saint 131
Bible 55
Blaise, Saint 273
Blessed Virgin Mary 395
Booksellers 137
Bosco, Saint John 366
Breast Cancer 282

Brendan, Saint 239
Brigid, Saint 41

Cabrini, Saint Francis Xavier 229
Camillus de Lellis, Saint 166
Cancer 280
Cecilia, Saint 208
Chad, Saint 262
Chefs 140
Child Abuse 247
Children 361
Children, Disappointing 27
Christian Living 90
Christina the Astonishing, Saint 176
Christopher, Saint 299
Church, When Hurt by 114
Clare of Assisi, Saint 380
Claver, Saint Peter 251
Confession 75
Cortona, Saint Margaret of 10
Cosmas, Saint 170
Cousin, Saint Germaine 247
Cupertino, Saint Joseph 135

Damian, Saint 170
De la Salle, Saint John Baptist 178
De Porres, Saint Martin 344
De Sales, Saint Francis 181
Deacons 102
Discrimination 344
Dismas, Saint 303
Divine Mercy 341
Divorce 22
Drama Students 192
Drought 305
Dying 355
Dymphna, Saint 293

Earthquakes 314

Elizabeth of Hungary, Saint	15	Housework	31
Elizabeth of Portugal, Saint	19	Hubert, Saint	204
Emidius, Saint	314	Hunters	204
Entertaining	34		
Environment	233	Ignatius Loyola, Saint	84
Erasmus, Saint	272	Immigrants	229
Expectant mothers	5	Impossible Cases	353
Eye Trouble	278	Infertile	337
		In-law Problems	15
Falsely accused	347	Isidore of Seville, Saint	386
Family Rifts	19	Isidore the Farmer, Saint	142
Farmers	142		
Faustina Kowalska, Saint	341	James the Greater, Saint	275
Financial Professionals	144	Januarius, Saint	315
Firefighters	145	Jerome, Saint	55
First Communicants	73	Joan of Arc, Saint	114
Fishermen	193	John Baptist de la Salle, Saint	178
Florian, Saint	145	John Berchmans, Saint	81
Florists	147	John Bosco, Saint	366
Forgione, Blessed Padre Pio	75	John Mary Vianney, Saint	107
Frances Xavier Cabrini, Saint	229	John of God, Saint	137
Francis de Sales, Saint	181	John the Baptist, Saint	157
Francis of Assisi, Saint	233	John the Evangelist, Saint	389
Frassati, Blessed Pier Giorgio	219	Joseph Cupertino, Saint	135
Friendship	389	Joseph of Arimathea, Saint	153
Funeral Directors	153	Joseph, Saint	355
		Jude, Saint	353
Gabriel the Archangel, Saint	175		
Genesius, Saint	192	Kateri Tekakwitha, Blessed	90
George, Saint	133	Kolbe, Saint Maximilian Maria	256
Gerard Majella, Saint	5	Kowalska, Saint Faustina	341
Germaine Cousin, Saint	247		
Gonzaga, Saint Aloysius	284	Labre, Saint Benedict Joseph	227
Goretti, Saint Maria	249	Lapsed Catholics	94
Guadalupe, Our Lady of	242	Lawrence, Saint	140
		Lawyers	160
Hairdressers	155	Laziosi, Saint Peregrine	280
Headaches	269	Learning	44
Helen, Saint	22	Leonard of Noblac, Saint	351
Highway Construction Workers	157	Lightning	308
Homeless	227	Liguori, Saint Alphonsus de	60
Horseback Riders	198	Lisieux, Saint Therese of	147

Lost Objects	375	Police	172
Lovelorn	335	Political Prisoners	256
Loyola, Saint Ignatius	84	Postal Workers	175
Lucy, Saint	278	Pregnancy	337
Luke, Saint	212	Priests	107
Lydwina, Saint	214	Prisoners	351
		Pro, Blessed Miguel Agustin	347
Majella, Saint Gerard	5	Psychiatrists	176
Margaret of Cortona, Saint	10		
Maria Goretti, Saint	249	Racial Justice	251
Martha, Saint	34	Raphael the Archangel, Saint	372
Martin de Porres, Saint	344	Religious Doubts	339
Martin of Tours, Saint	198	Retreats	84
Mary, Blessed Virgin	395	Rheumatism	275
Mary Magdalene, Saint	155	Rock Climbers	206
Matilda, Saint	27		
Matthew, Saint	144	Scholastica, Saint	105
Maximilian Maria Kolbe, Saint	256	Science	51
Mentally Ill	293	Sebastian, Saint	189
Menthon, Saint Bernard of	206	Seville, Saint Isidore of	386
Michael the Archangel, Saint	172	Sexual Abuse	249
Miguel Agustin Pro, Blessed	347	Siena, Saint Bernardine of	131
Monica, Saint	94	Singers	208
More, Saint Thomas	160	Single Mothers	10
Mountain Climbers	206	Skaters	214
Musicians	208	Snakebite	317
		Sports	219
Nicholas, Saint	361	Stephen, Saint	102
Nightmares	372	Stomach Ailments	272
Noblac, Saint Leonard of	351	Students	41
Nuns	105	Swimmers	217
Nurses	166	Swithun, Saint	305
Padre Pio Forgione, Blessed	75	Tarsicius, Saint	73
Padua, Saint Anthony of	375	Teachers	178
Painters	212	Tekakwitha, Blessed Kateri	90
Paul, Saint	317	Television	380
Peregrine Laziosi, Saint	280	Temptations	326
Peter Claver, Saint	251	Therese of Lisieux, Saint	147
Peter, Saint	193	Thieves	303
Physicians	170	Thomas Aquinas, Saint	308
Pier Giorgio Frassati, Blessed	219	Thomas More, Saint	160

Thomas the Apostle, Saint   339
Throat Ailments   273
Time management   60
Toothaches   270
Tours, Saint Martin of   198
Travel   299

Valentine, Saint   335
Vianney, Saint John Mary   107
Volcanic Eruptions   315

Web Surfing   386
Whales   239
William of Rochester, Saint 364
Writers   181

Youth   366

Zita, Saint   31

About Stampley

Stampley is the imprint of C.D. Stampley Enterprises, Inc., publisher of deluxe heirloom Bibles, religious and educational titles. Founded in 1940, Stampley is best known for its "World's Most Beautiful Bibles," a broad line of elegant Family Bibles especially designed for reverent display in the home. Stampley's Family Bibles include comprehensive commentaries, scholarly resources, family record sections on Parchtex paper, scores of Old Master paintings in full color, scenes from historic lands of the Bible and many additional features.

Stampley Bibles are manufactured using high-quality Bible paper. Page edges are gilded and covers, made of handsome durable materials, are stamped using gold foil.

Stampley's "World's Most Beautiful Bibles" are available in English, Spanish, French and Portuguese. A recent Bible features the Catholic edition Revised Standard Version translation (RSV-CE)—a translation praised both for its beauty and for its fidelity to original biblical texts. All Scripture quotes in *Saints for Every Occasion* are taken from the RSV-CE.

Stampley Family Bibles are available at many fine dealers nationwide. For information about a Stampley dealer near you, or to inquire about Stampley Bibles for your own marketing channel or school or parish fundraising program, contact us at:

C.D. Stampley Enterprises
P.O. Box 33172
Charlotte, N.C. 28233

Toll-free 1-800-280-6631
Fax: (704) 336-6932
Email: info@stampley.com

Wanted: Your Favorite Saint Story

Stampley Enterprises is preparing a sequel to *Saints for Every Occasion*—and we're looking for saints to include.

Do you have a favorite patron whom you would like included in a future saints book? Or has a special saint answered your prayers in some miraculous way? If so, we would love to hear from you.

To recommend a new patron or to report your saint story, write to us at:

Saints for Every Occasion
c/o Stampley Enterprises
P.O. Box 33172
Charlotte, N.C. 28233

Or, email us at:
saints@stampley.com

If you would like your suggestion to be acknowledged, please include a self-addressed stamped envelope when you write to us. Thank you in advance for your help.

The Editors
Stampley Enterprises